Denise Brown
New Hampshire
Artist

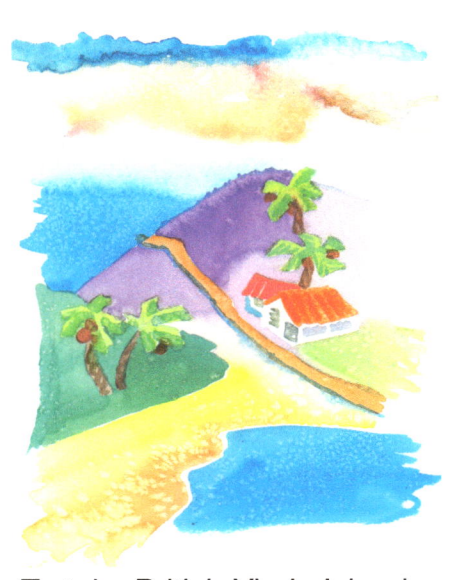

Tortola, British Virgin Islands

Artwork, Comments

and Artist Tips

by

Denise F. Brown

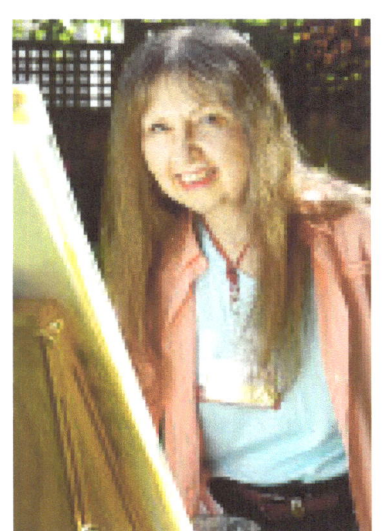

"Denise Brown, New Hampshire Artist"
ISBN: 978-0-9977485-2-9

Front Cover Painting:
Old Man of the Mountains

www.raccoonstudios.com
Published by Raccoon Studios
692 Sagamore Avenue, Portsmouth, NH 03801

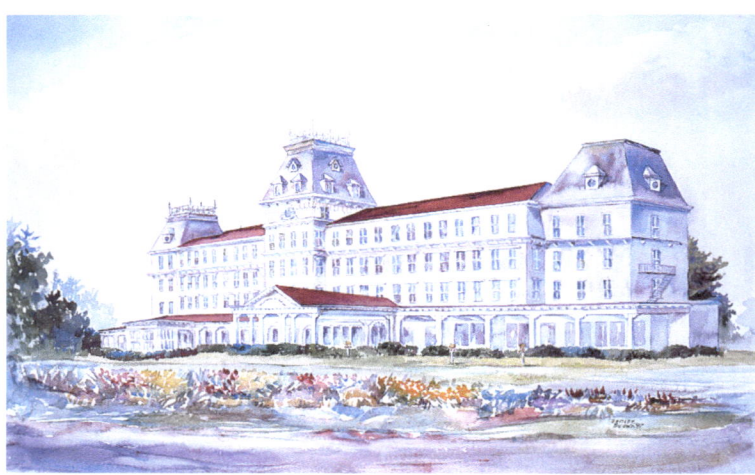

Wentworth by the Sea, New Castle

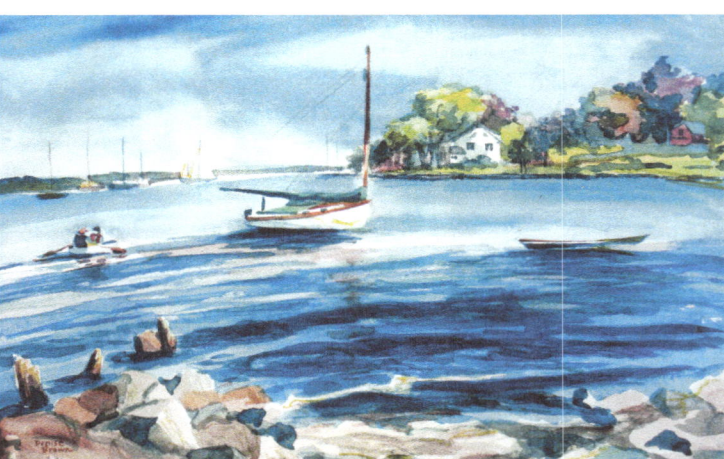

New Castle Inlet

Tip #1:

To have a career and a lifetime immersed in artwork, you must be persistent and hard-shelled enough to blank out the noise and focus on your art.

I've met many talented people in the art world. Some are professional artists and others are hobbyists that just love to be creative. Each one has a unique perspective, style, and talent. A few of these people have influenced my life and passion.

I hope you enjoy my art book and some tips for this obsession called art.

— *Denise F. Brown*

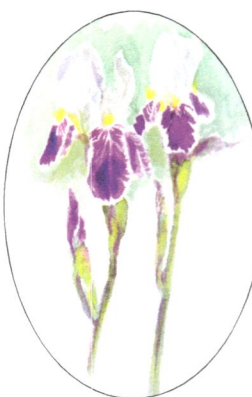

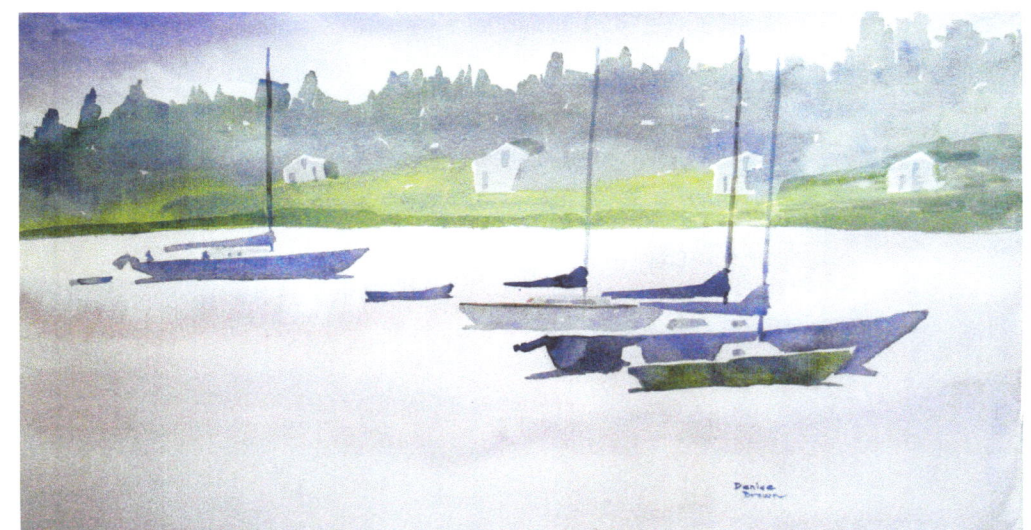

Port
Clyde,
Maine

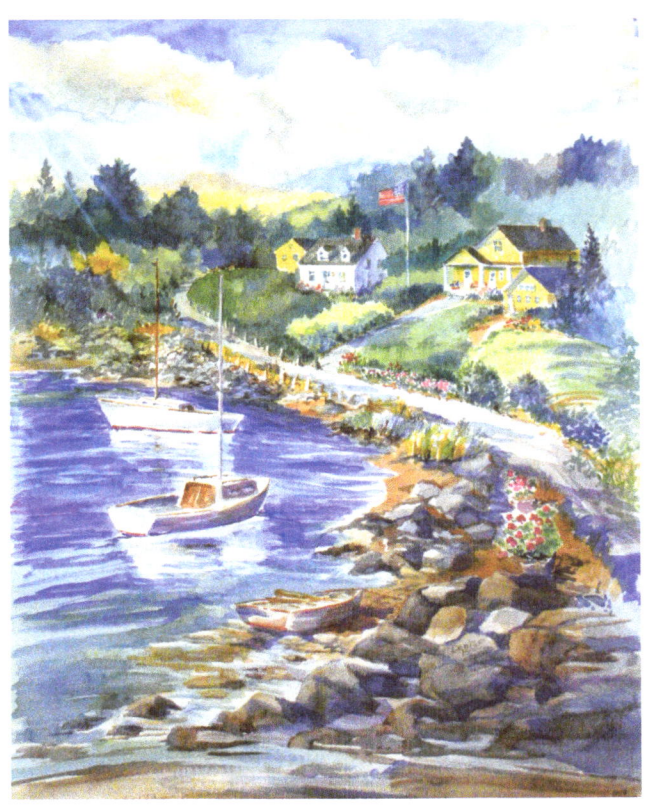

New
Castle
Inlet

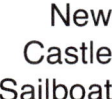

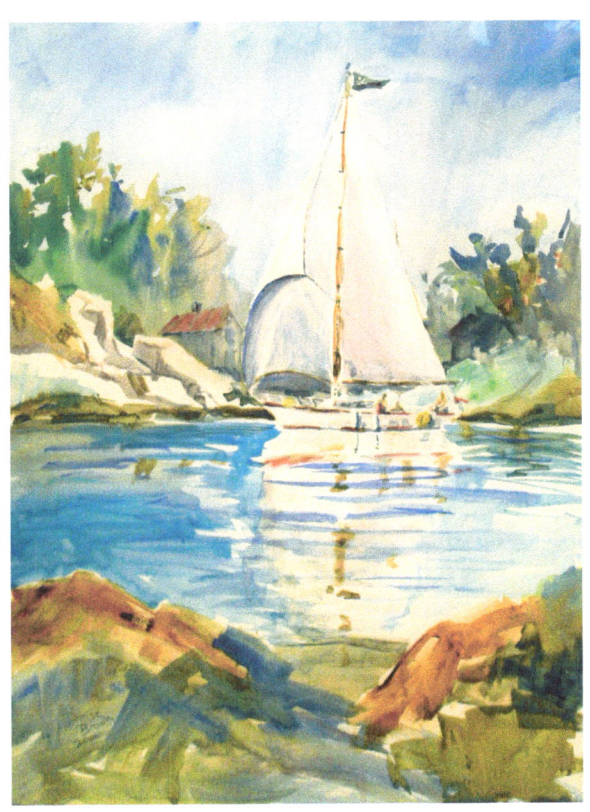

New
Castle
Sailboat

The book is dedicated to Professor John W. Hatch,
my advisor at UNH, favorite professor, favorite artist, and friend.

3

Early Work, Rye and Portsmouth

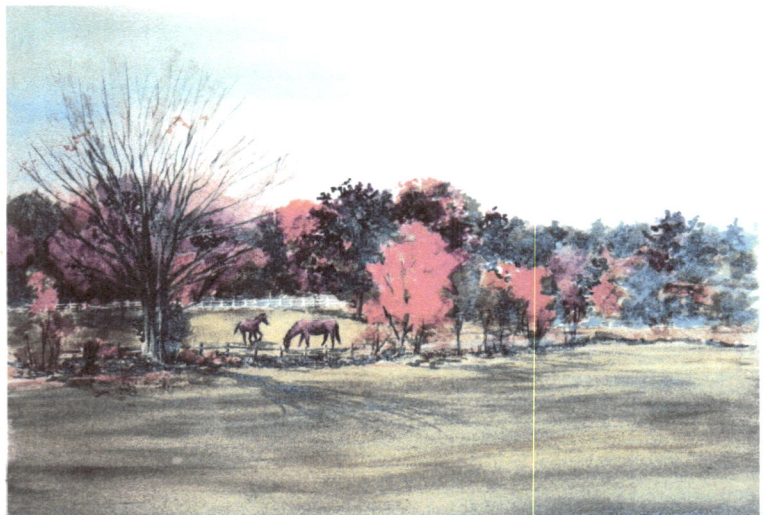

Dad's Field

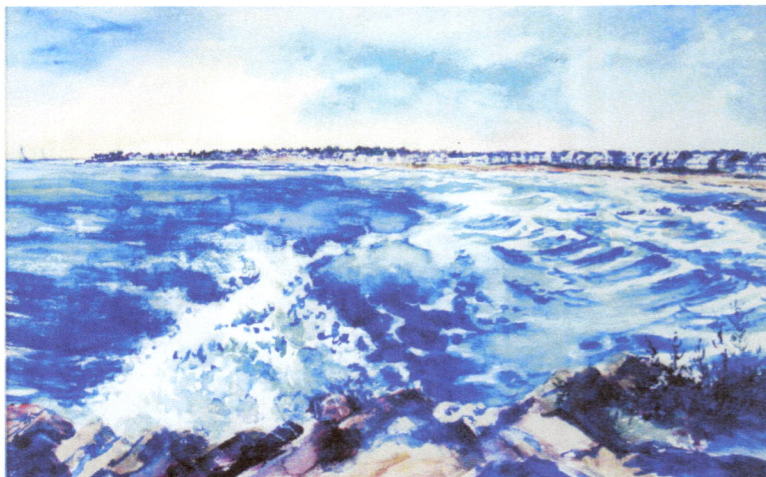

Rye Beach

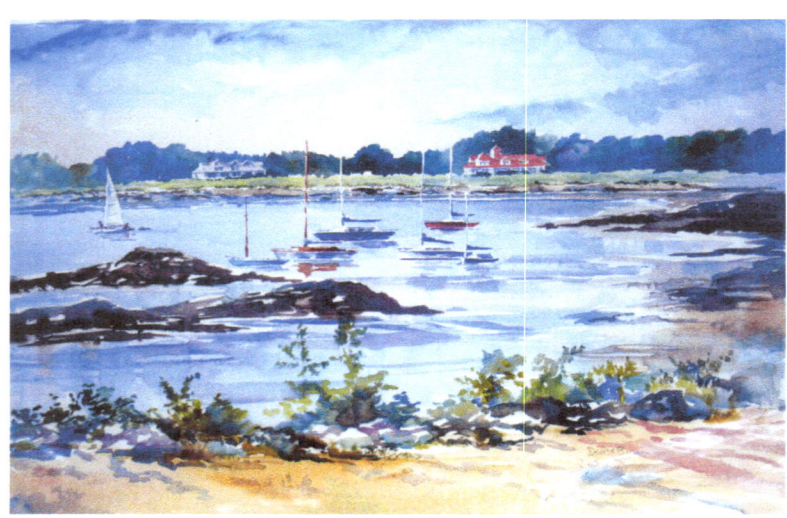

Wentworth Golf Club Homes

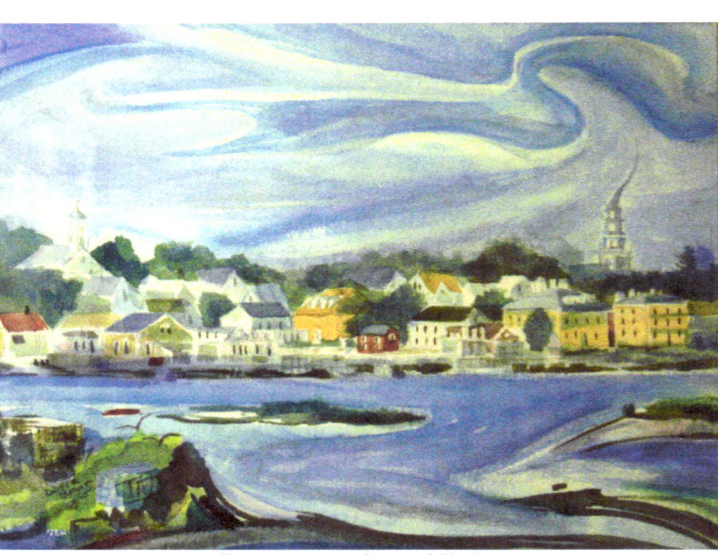

Portsmouth at Night

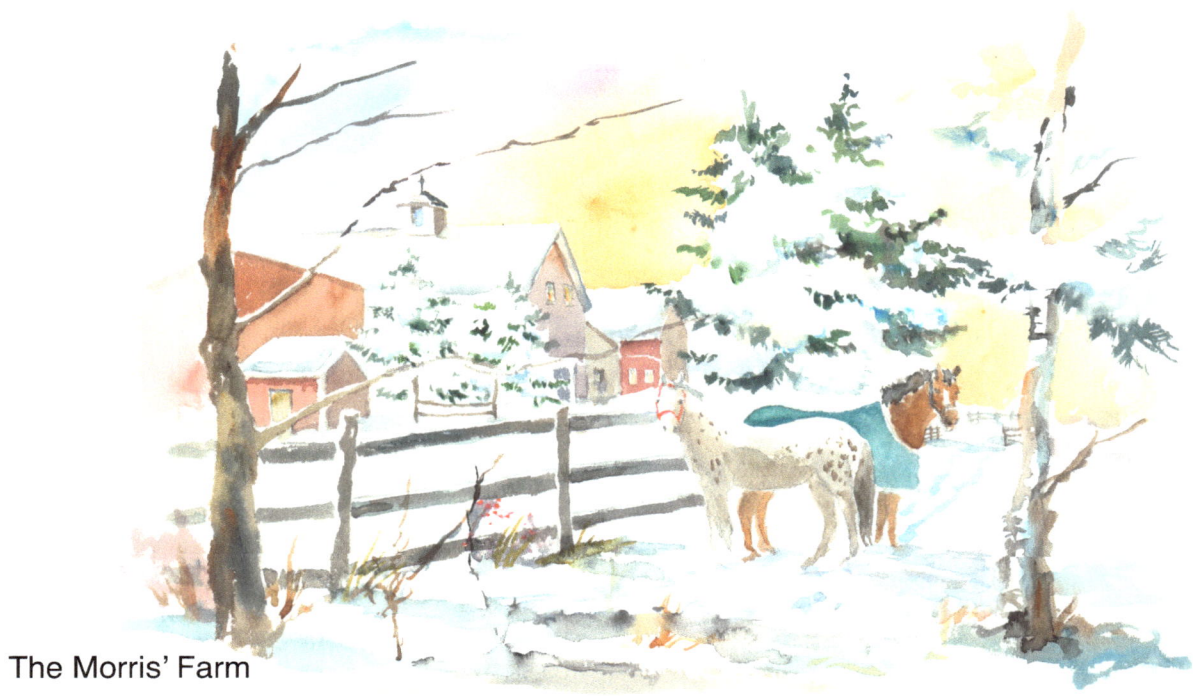

The Morris' Farm

A Horse Crazy Kid:

I grew up next to four horse farms in Rye, New Hampshire. That's where my love of horses and animals began...

Sitting in the sunlit fields and pastures behind my parents' house was where I spent summers sketching outdoors. You'd find me watching and drawing the neighbors' horses, a gray donkey named Henry, two small herds of Black Angus cows and brown and white Jersey cows, a bull, chipmunks, woodchucks, my cats, and multitudes of orange and black Monarch butterflies. These animal and butterfly friends of mine filled up my early sketchbooks.

At Rye elementary school, my art teacher was Miss Suzanne Perfect. She had a beehive hairdo and wore hot pink dresses and high heels. Miss Perfect was a wildly fun art teacher, but not an easy "A" — you had to earn it. She hoped I would take art in high school, but I signed up for academic courses like geometry, algebra, science, and French, so I had very little time for art.

My passion for drawing
and painting horses has
never waned...

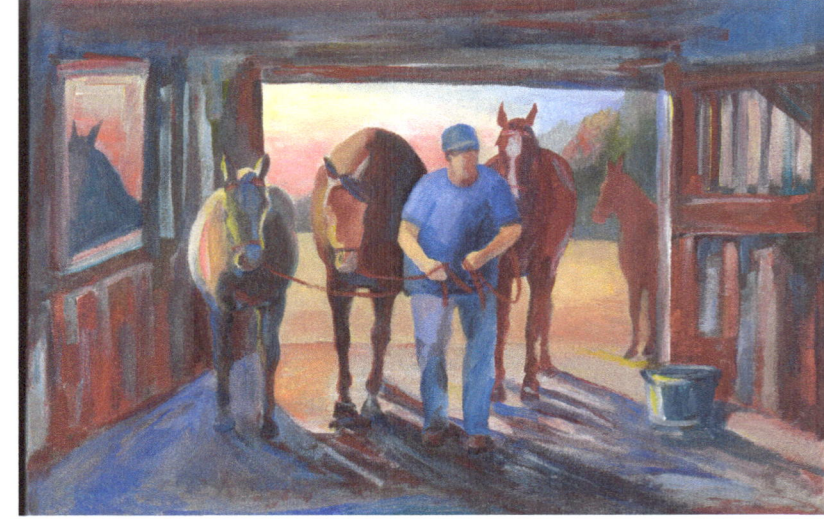

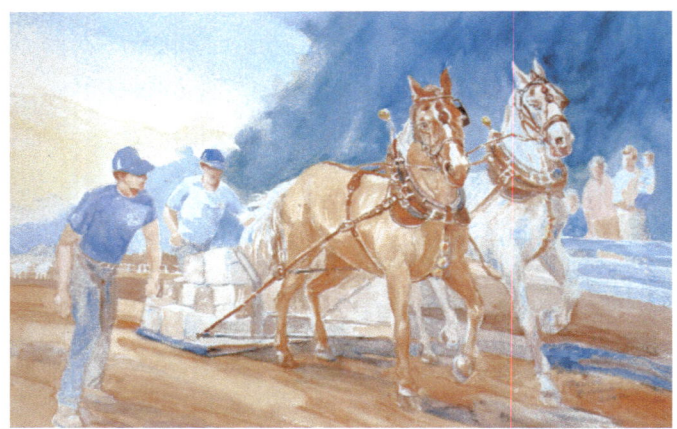

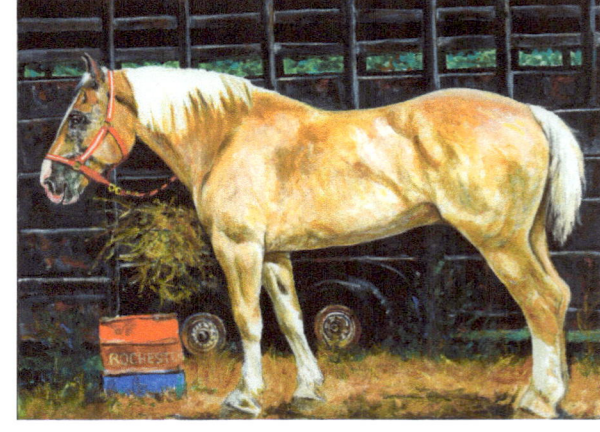

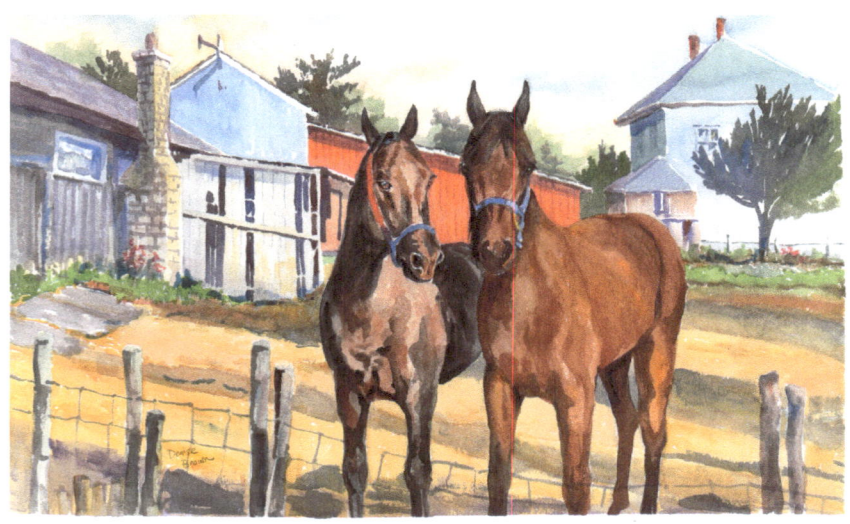

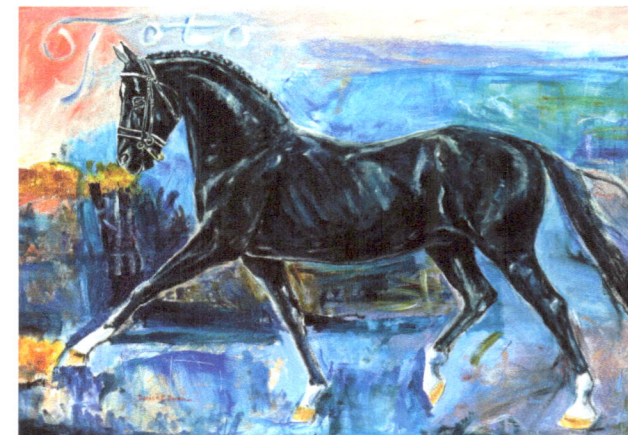

Horse Power

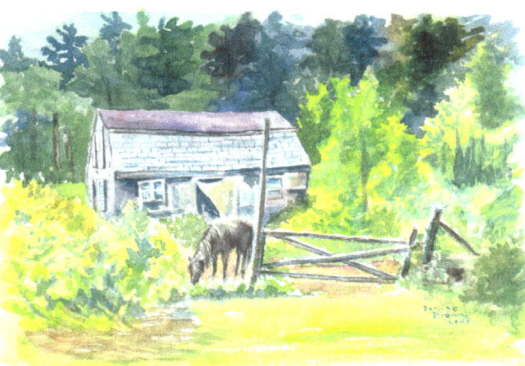

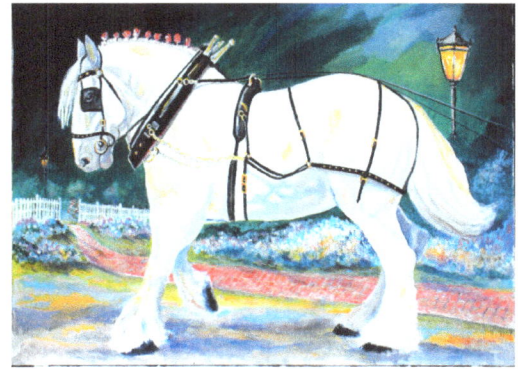

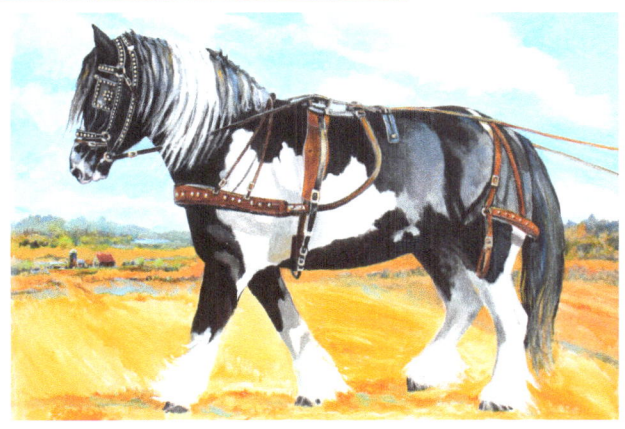

Every horse is different and has unique features.

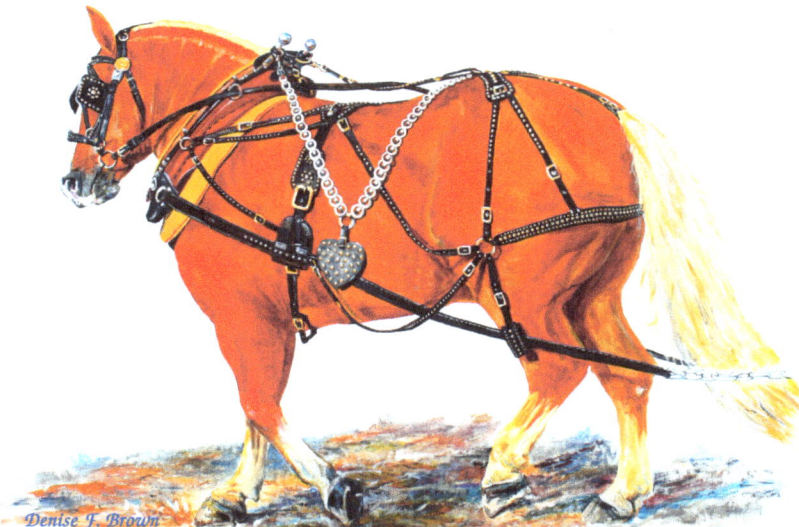

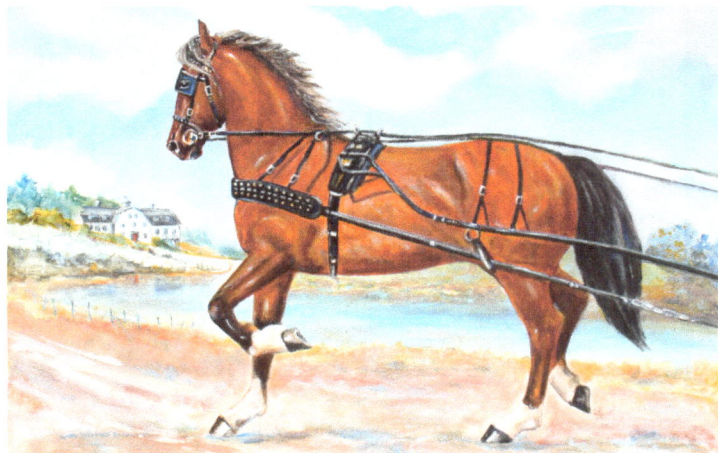

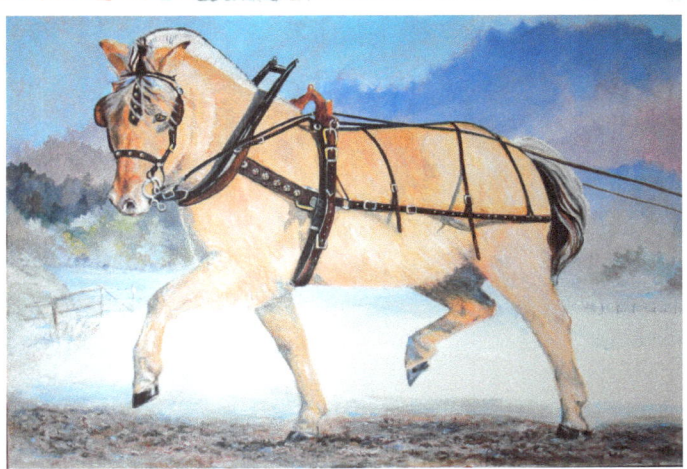

Besides horse anatomy, you need to study the leather harness and driving equipment.

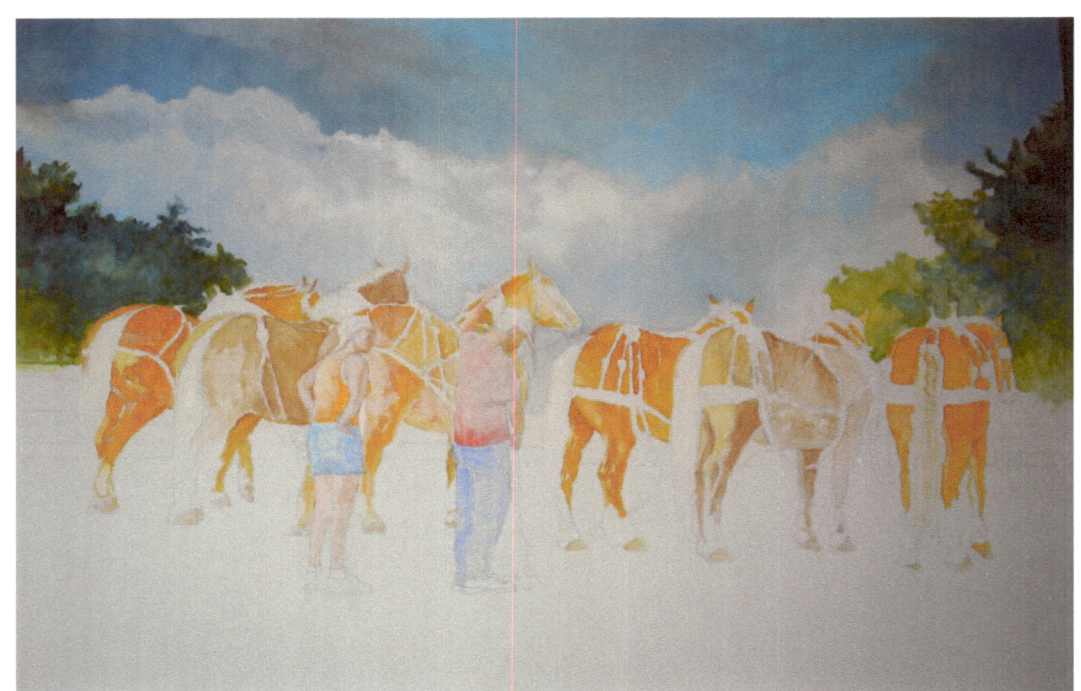

"Behind the Scenes at the Fair"

Left:
roughing out the painting

Below:
the finished painting

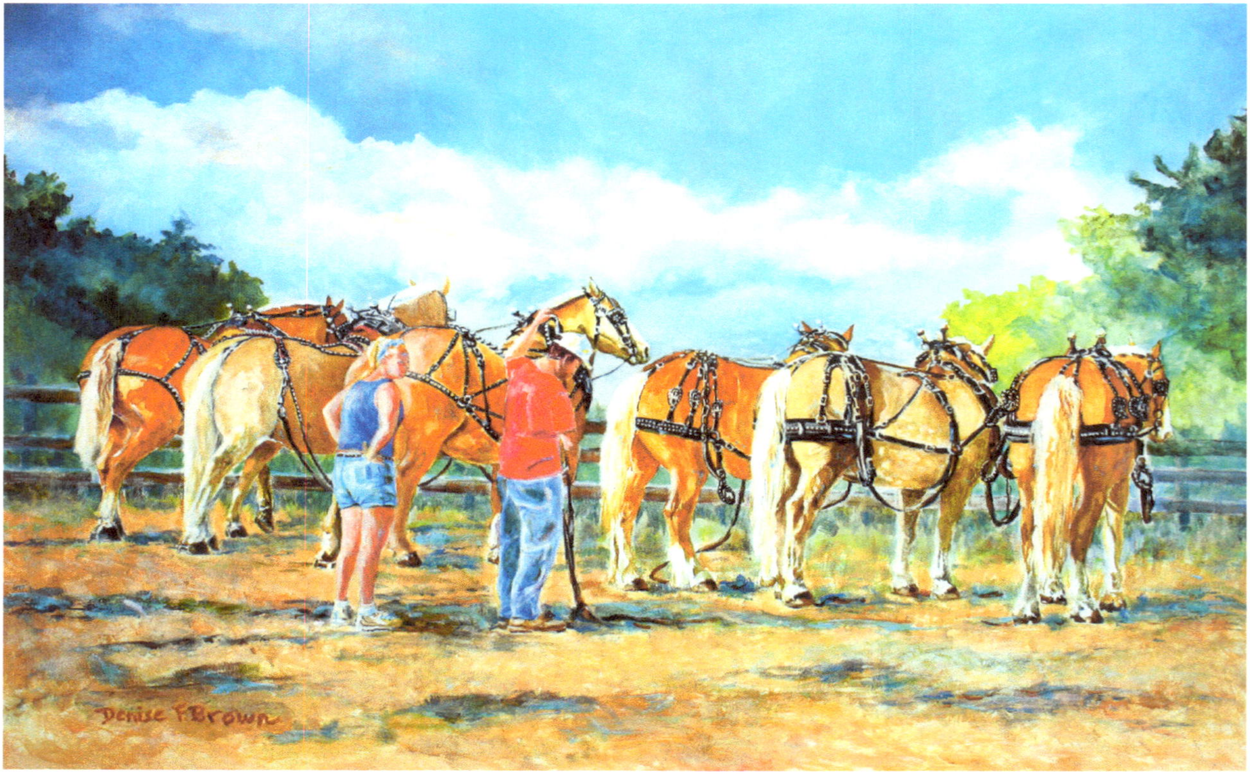

Denise F.Brown

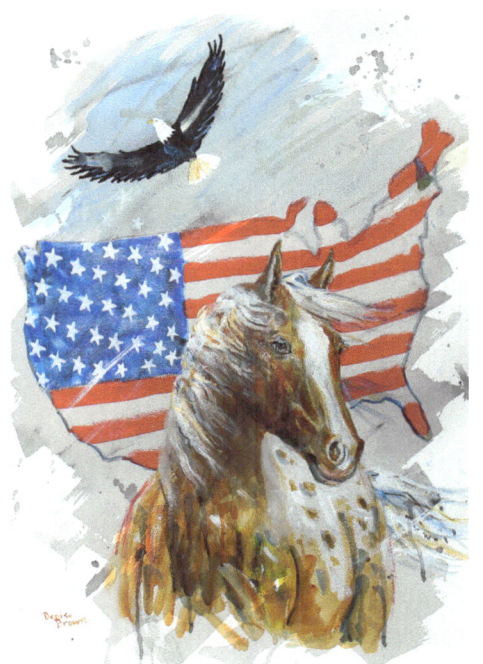

America's Icons
Plight of Wild Horses

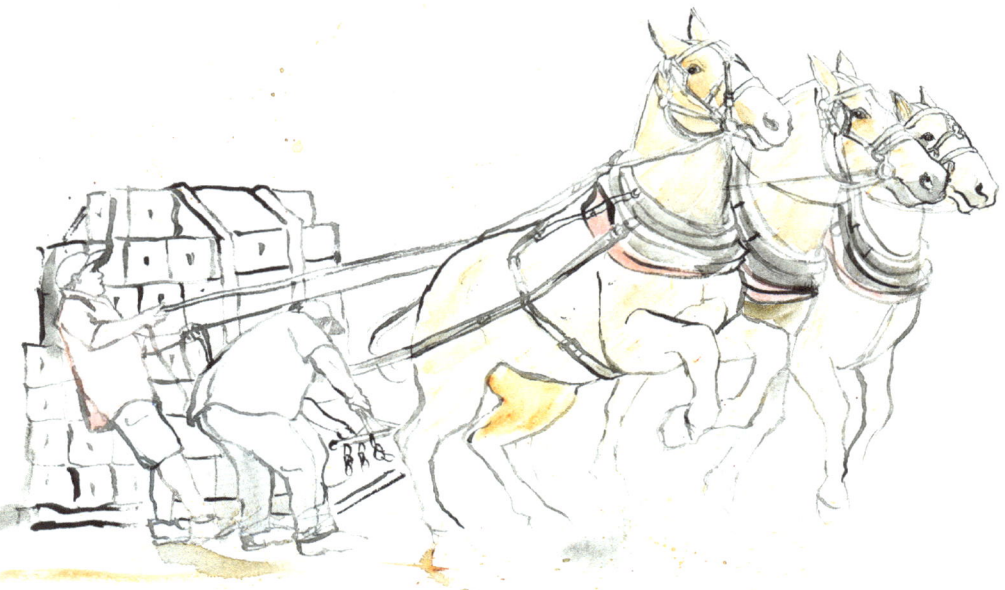

"Locomotives"

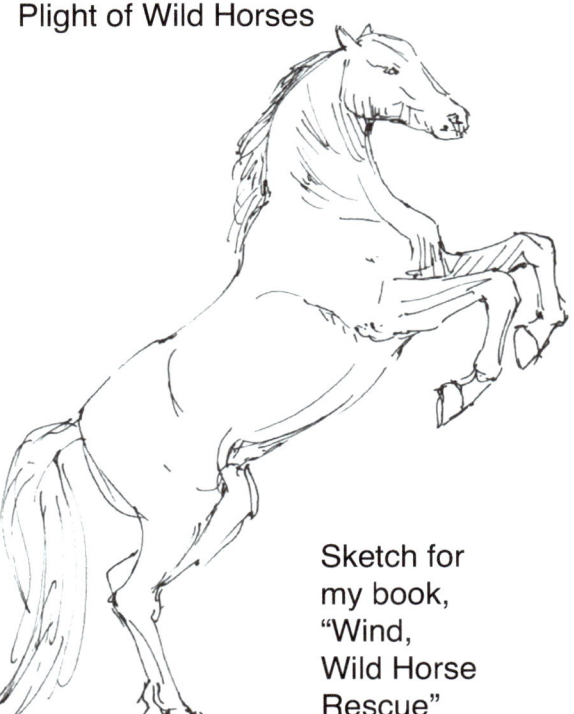

Sketch for
my book,
"Wind,
Wild Horse
Rescue"

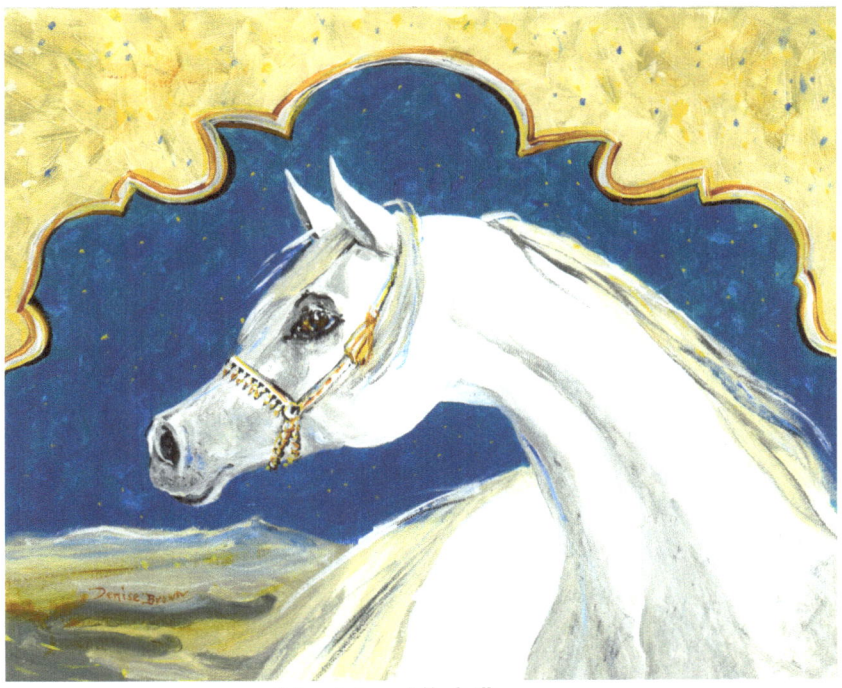

"Arabian Night"

9

Finding Me...

College Sparked the 'Art' Side of My Brain.

As a freshmen at UNH, I signed up for a drawing class with Professor John Woodsum Hatch.

Wow, everything changed that year when I took Drawing with Professor Hatch, who was also my advisor. I realized I found something I loved to do. Hatch liked my work and encouraged me to pursue more art classes. It all sounded great, but, I wanted to make a living, and not just draw pictures.

I thought about going into advertising and using my artwork in a career. Determined to be a successful artist and business person, I self-designed my own major combining Fine Arts, Commercial Art, Advertising, and Business.

There were no computers or any courses for graphics yet at the University of New Hampshire, so, I signed up for all the fine arts courses (drawing, painting, and sculpture), photography, architectural rendering, mechanical drafting, advertising, marketing, economics and business classes. I got a work-study job as a graphic assistant at Goodhue and Gunther Advertising in North Hampton, New Hampshire for two years, where I earned eight credits and got paid, too. I also drew political cartoons for the campus newspaper.

I never changed my mind about my career and have stayed on track working in art and business throughout my life.

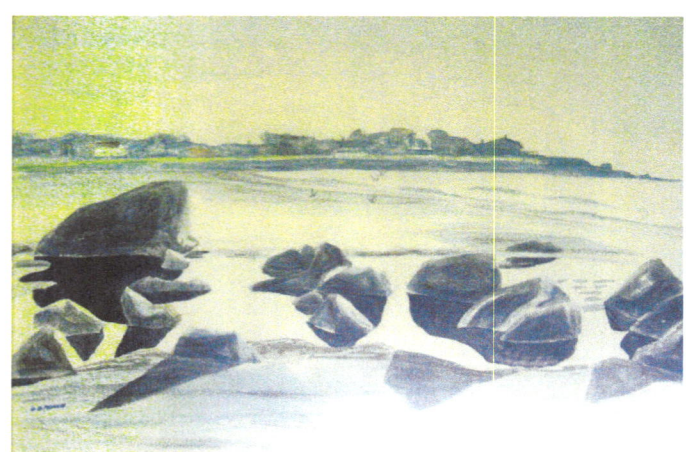 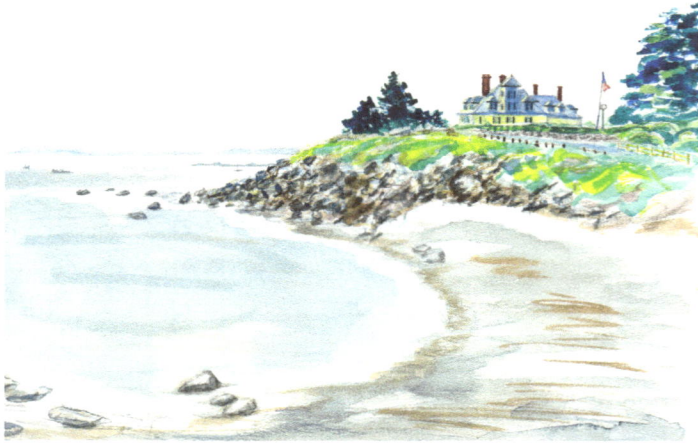

Early Work, Rye's Jenness Beach and North Hampton Curve

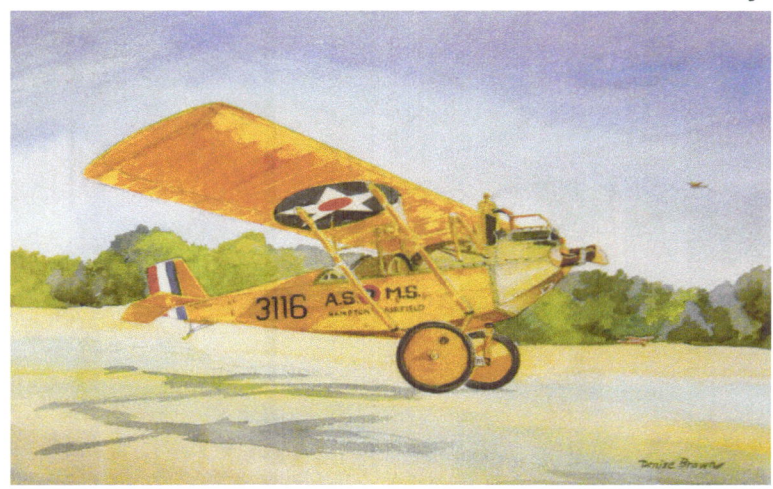

Hampton Airfield

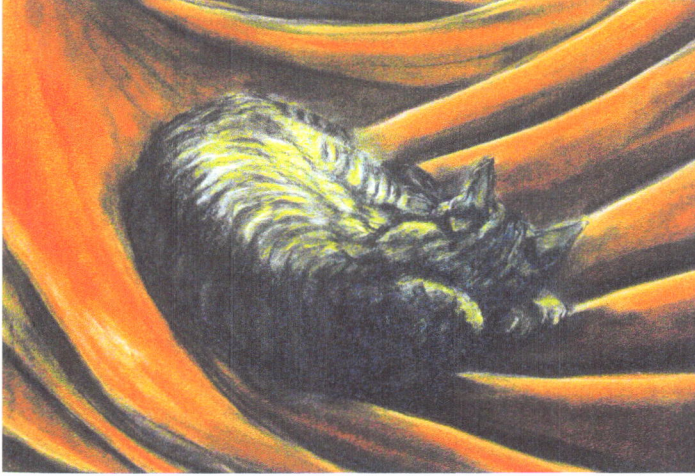

My first cat, Tiggy

Tip #2:

Gravitate towards people who encourage your passion.
Seize the courage to follow your muse.

Professor John Hatch has always been my favorite artist and teacher. He painted wonderful watercolors that captured a sense of place and color. Hatch's art influenced me as a watercolor painter. In 1997, he received New Hampshire's Living Treasure Award.

After John Hatch passed away in 1998, I bought a few pieces of his artwork at an auction that his wife Marianna set up in Durham, New Hampshire. Some of his sketches that I bought were from a Caribbean sailing vacation I went on with John Hatch, Marianna, and twenty other local people. I will always treasure the pieces of his artwork that I own, and the vacation memories of seeing what Hatch painted each day.

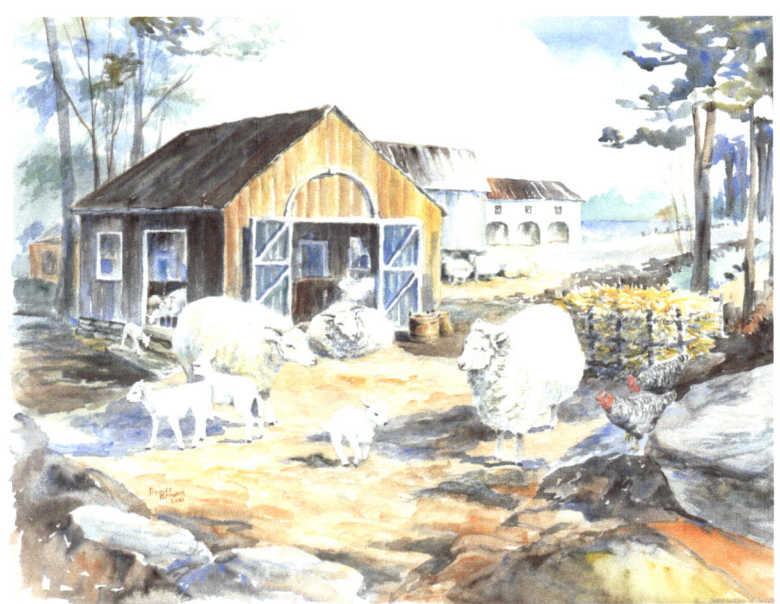

Springtime at the Sheep Barn

11

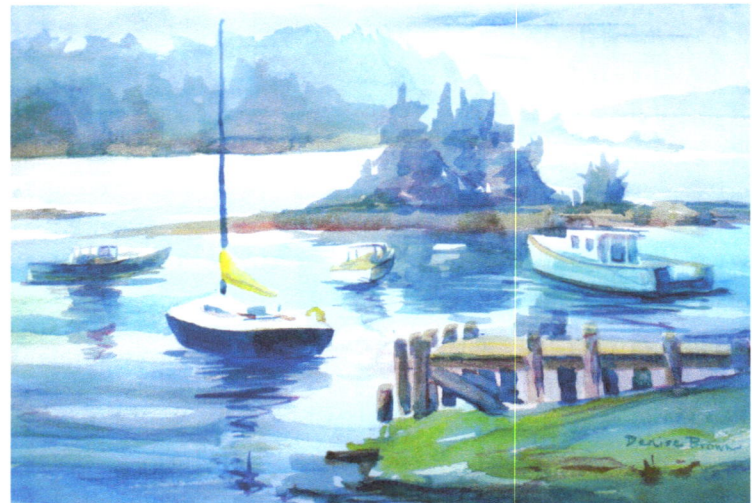

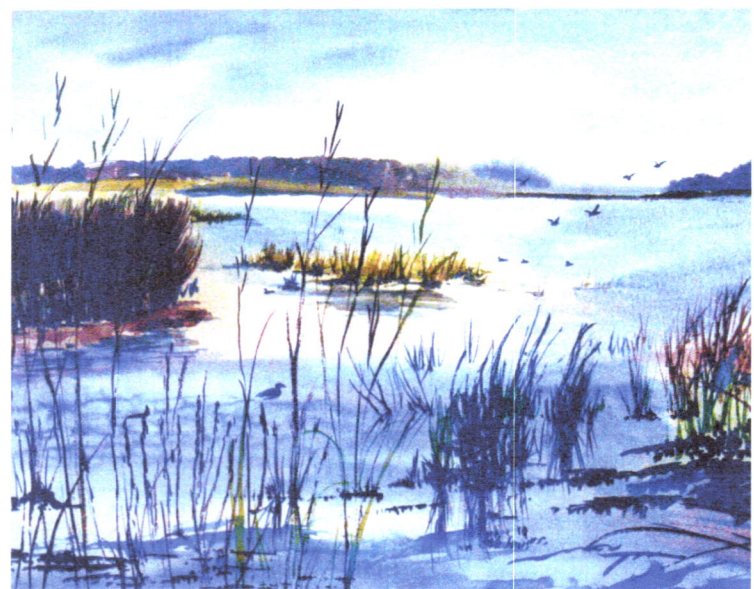

Favorite professors at UNH:

John W. Hatch
drawing, watercolor

Sigmund Abeles
drawing — his drawings of horses
and his family are excellent

Richard Merritt
black/white and color photography

Arthur Balderacchi
drawing, sculpture

Conley Harris
Conley took us outside to paint
watercolors every chance he could.
Though he never had much to say —
except to mumble a few words as
he walked by you — his spectacular
watercolors are unforgettable
magical colors and designs
like no other artist I know.

Favorite watercolor workshop teachers after college:
*Robert Steedman, Robert Chase, Eli Boynton,
Christopher "Toff" Schink, Doris Rice, Dustin Knight*

I attended two annual '*Watermedia Week*' Workshops
in Houston, Texas with famous instructors: *Catherine
Anderson, Timothy Clark, Judy Morris, Paul Jackson,
Betsy Dillard Stroud, Steven Quiller, and Zoltan Szabo*

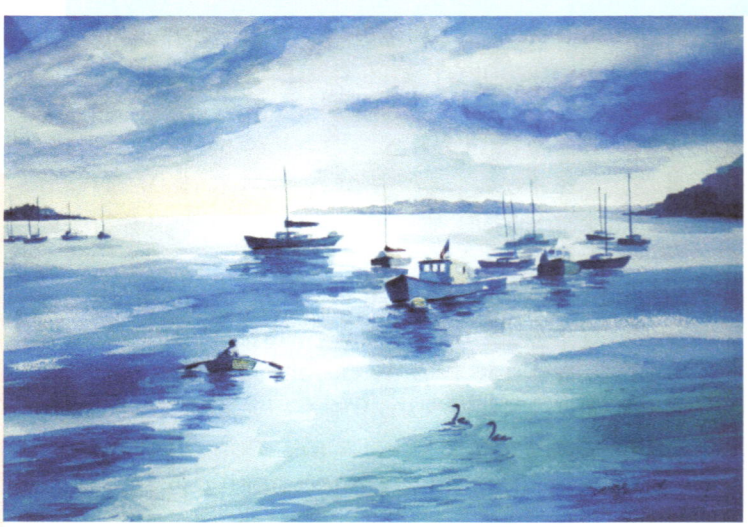

Seacoast New Hampshire

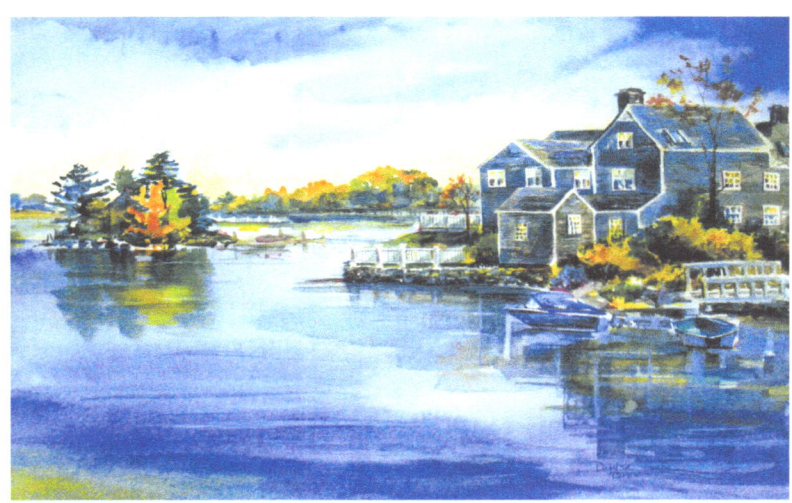

Portsmouth

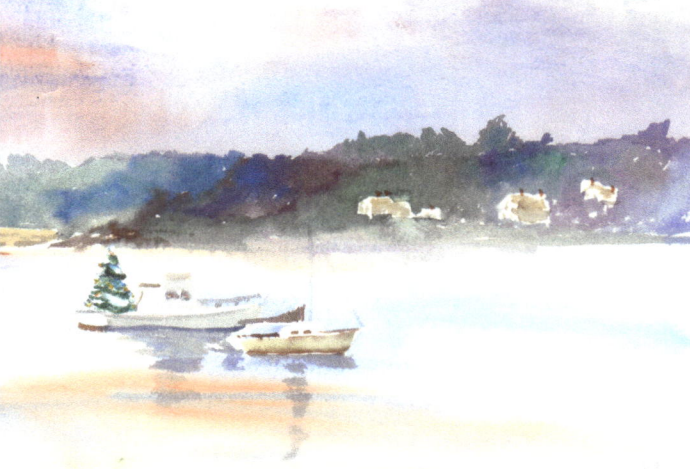

New Castle

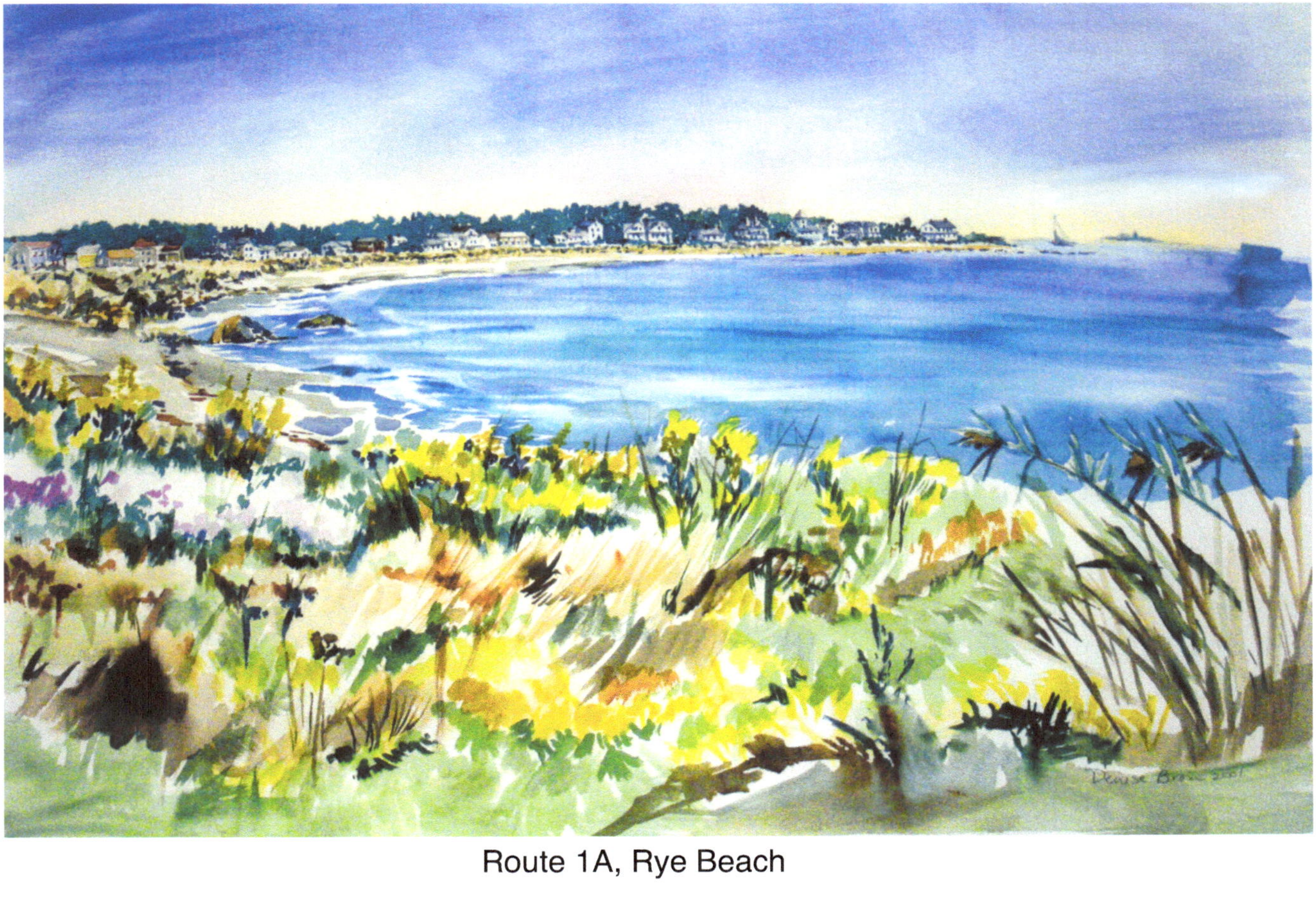

Route 1A, Rye Beach

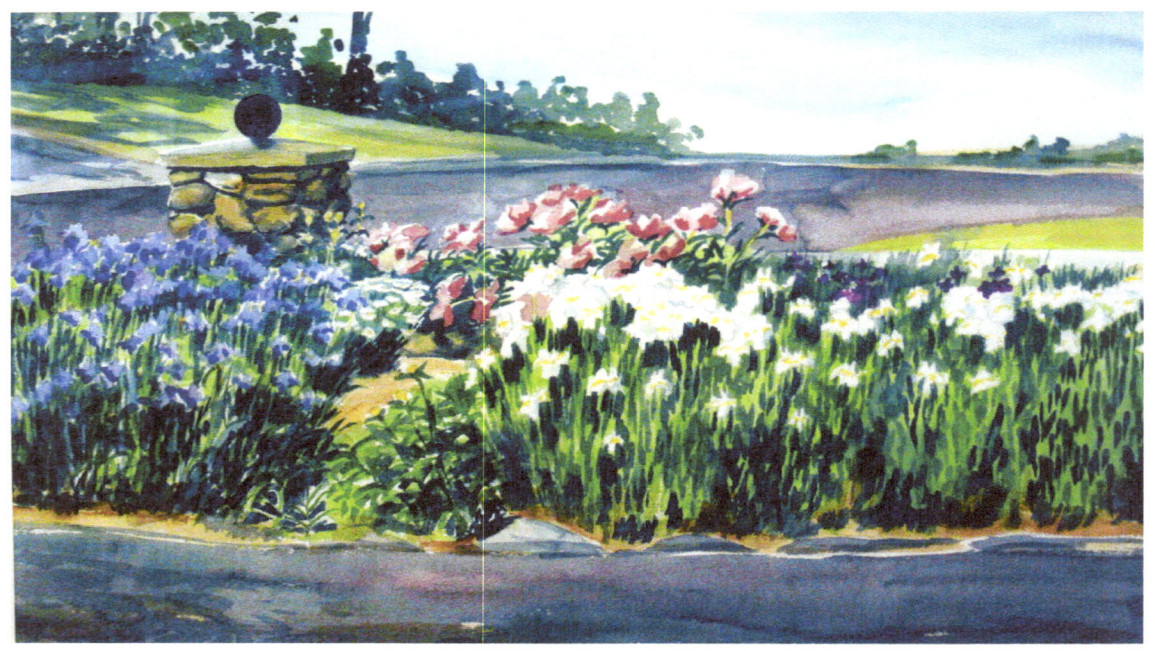

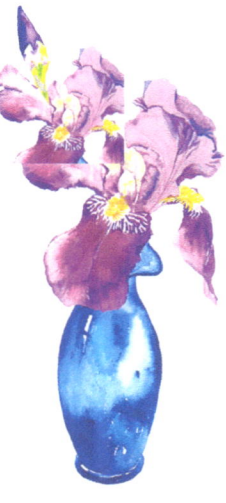

Purple Iris

Great Aunt Jen's Garden, (now Denise's garden)

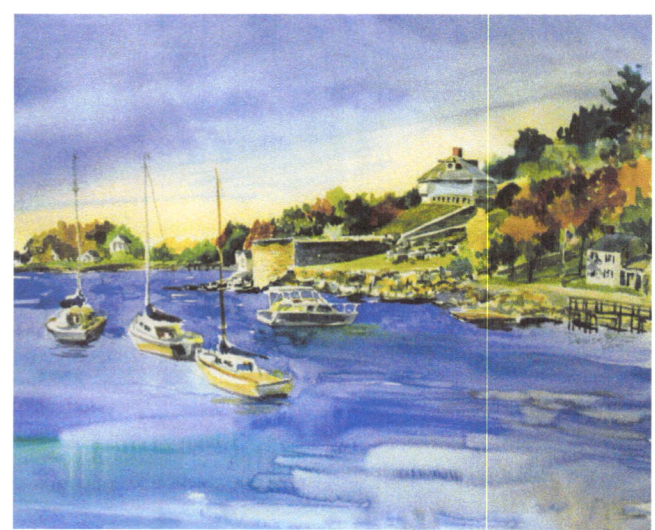

Fort McClary, Kittery, Maine

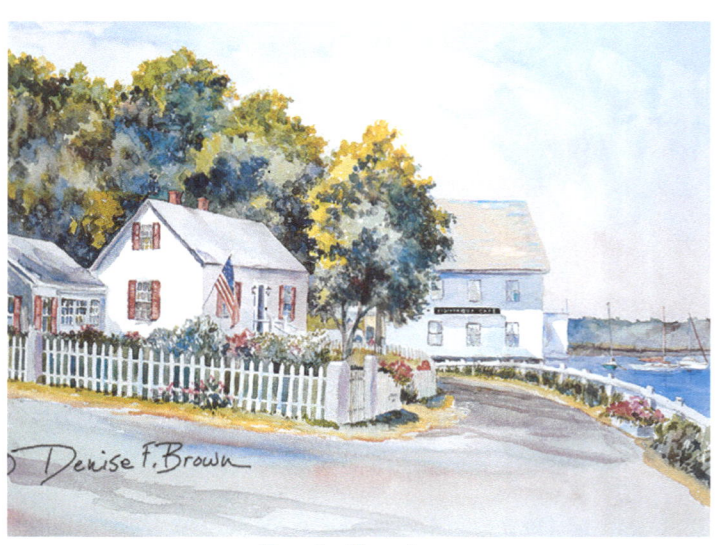

Sue's Garden

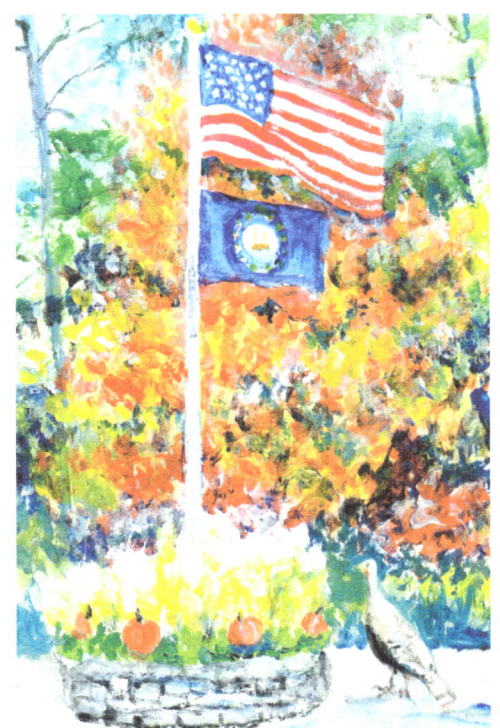

Edgewood Centre's
Flags and Turkey

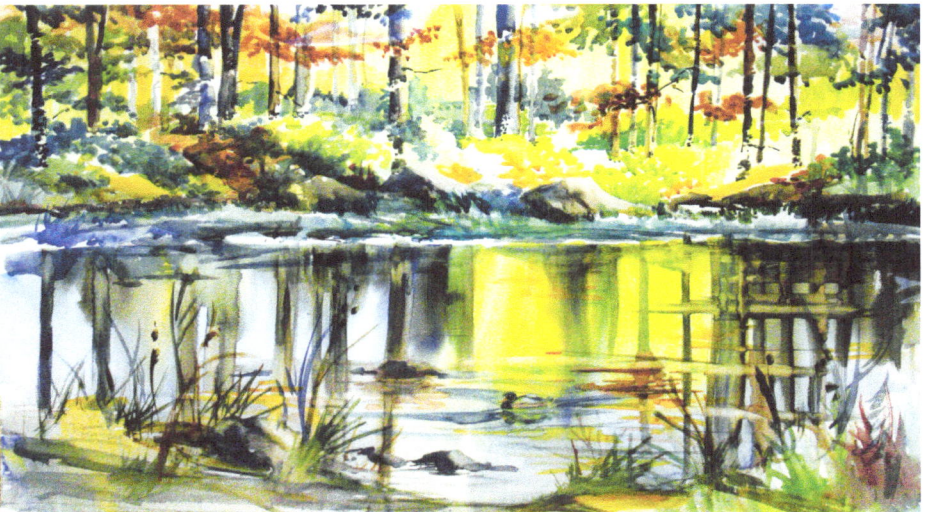

Sagamore Creek

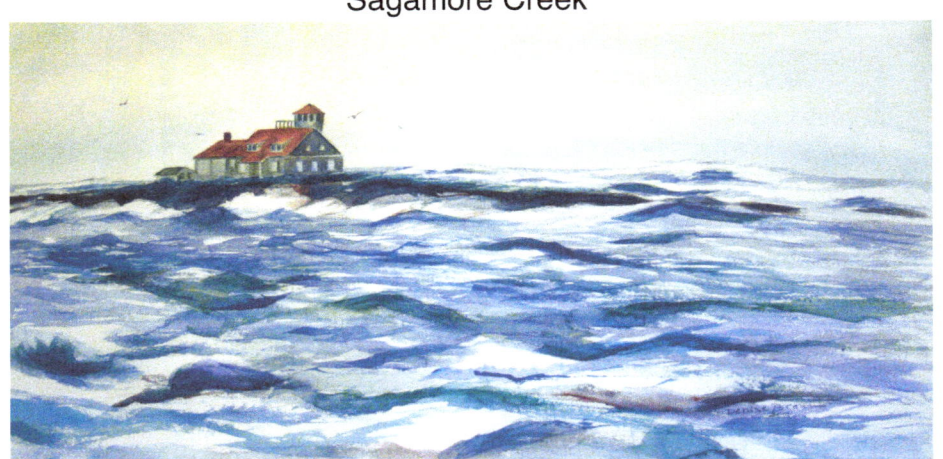

Whaleback Lighthouse Station

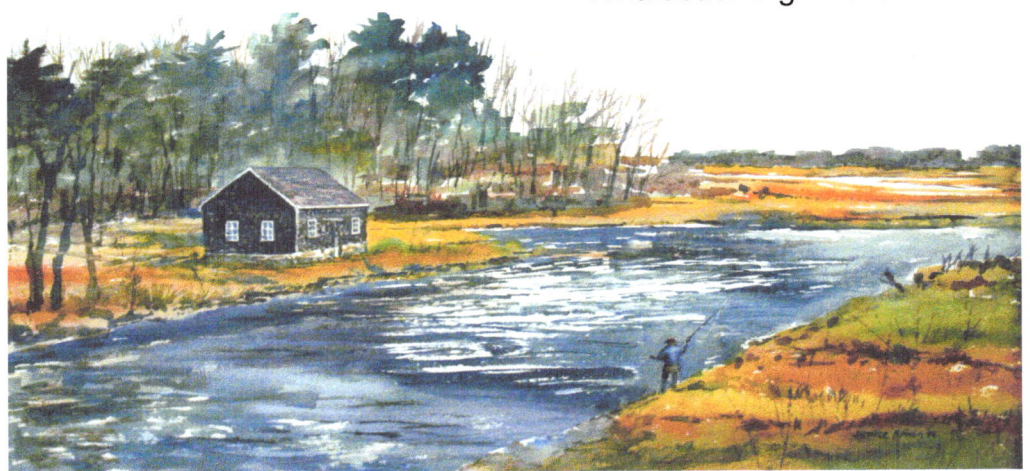

Rye Creek

15

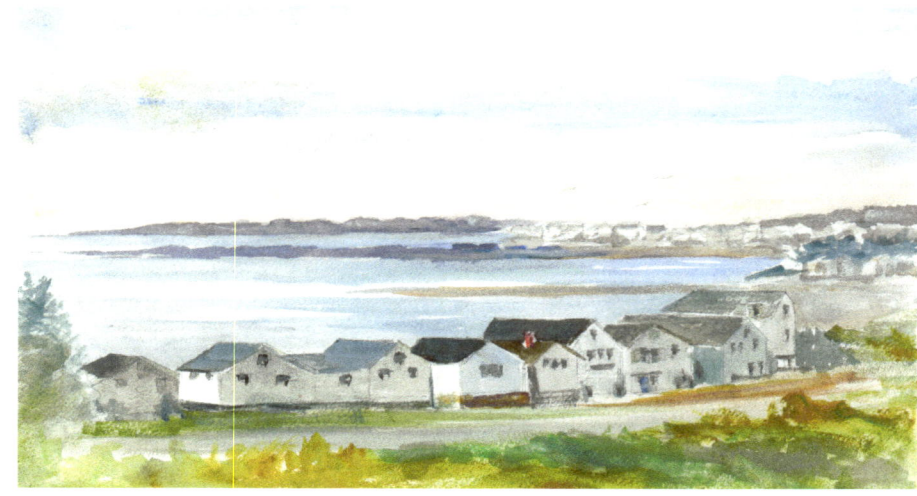

North Beach
Fish Shacks

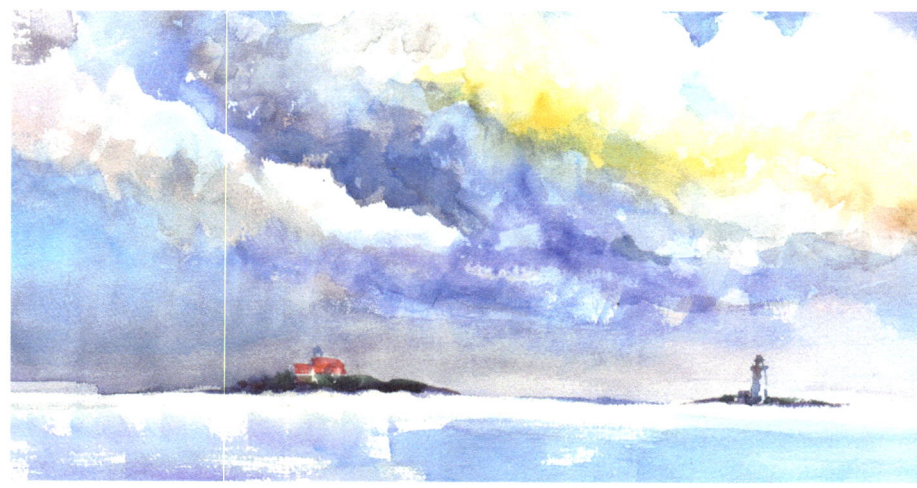

Whaleback
and
Ram Island
Lighthouses

Meigs'
Ocean
View at
Straw's
Point

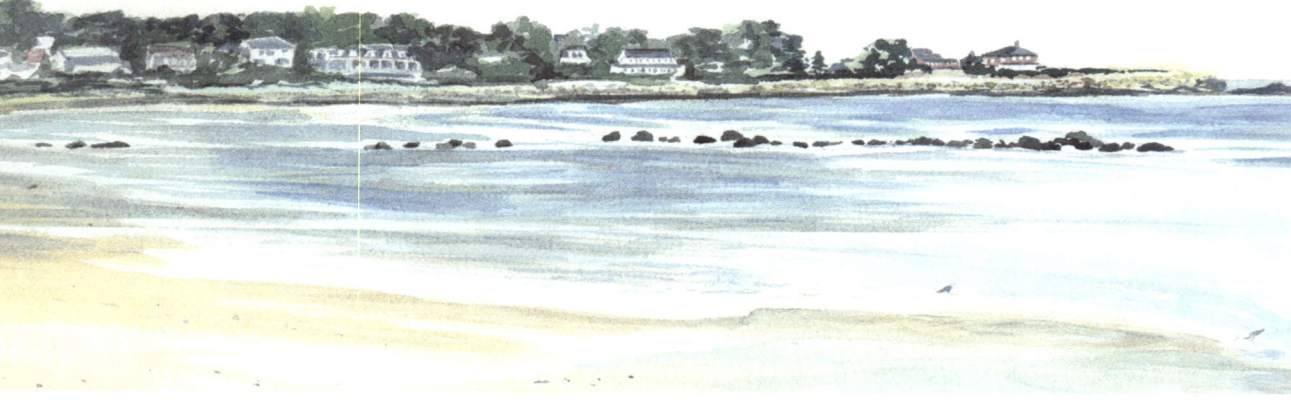

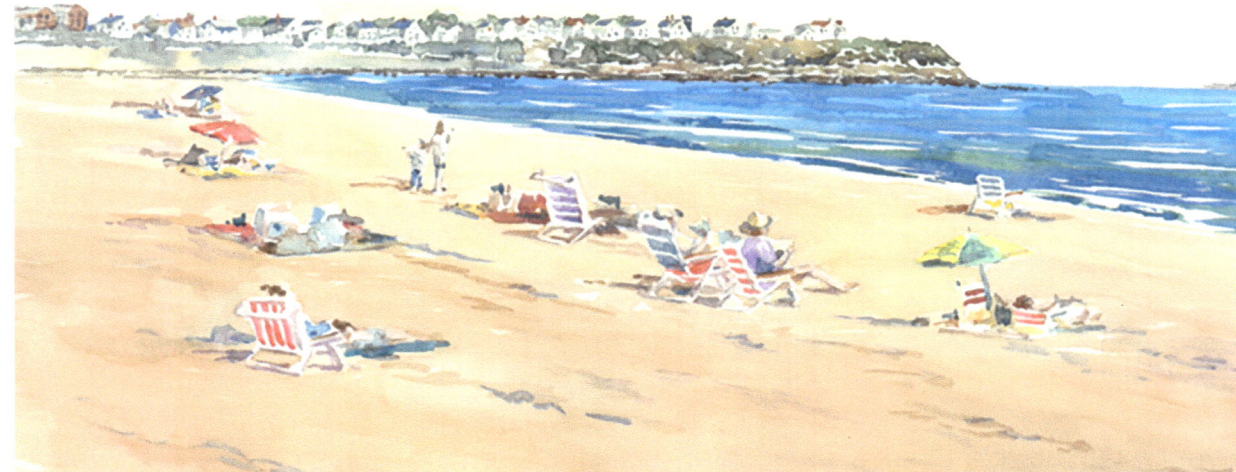

Hampton
Beach

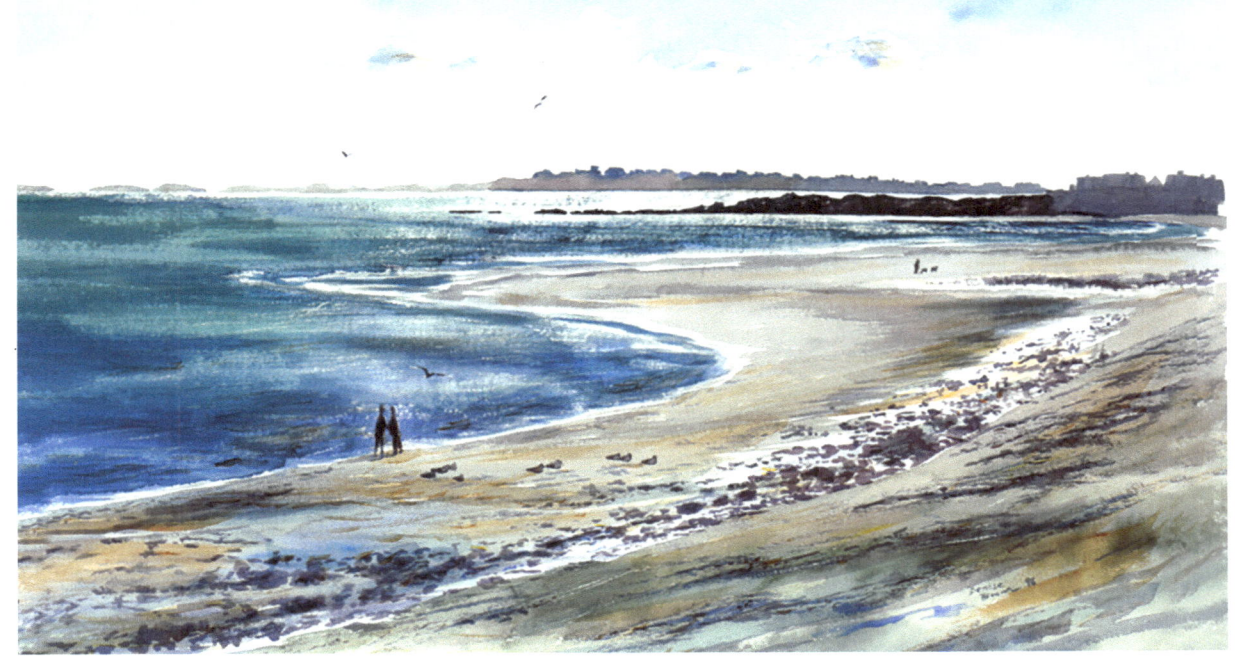

North
Beach

New Horizons...

Tip #3:

Even if you start small... Think BIG!

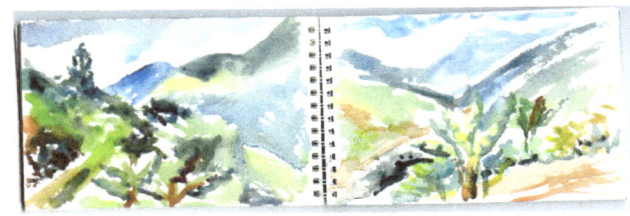

AFTER COLLEGE —
I got a job as an ad rep at the *Times-Record Newspaper* in Brunswick, Maine. My territory was Bath (a working port with a Naval shipyard), and the scenic towns Damariscotta, Boothbay, Wiscasset, and Camden, Maine.

I learned how to sell ads, and at the end of the day, I mocked up at least a dozen ads for the next day's paper. The ad department was a rowdy bunch of stressed out jokesters, always laughing and kidding at work.

I didn't have much time for artwork, but the job was fun, the seaside communities were charming, and I could observe the dark green Atlantic ocean any day.

After a year as an ad rep, I took a vacation to visit a friend on St. Thomas in the U.S. Virgin Islands. I was mesmerized by the tropical paradise with cerulean blue water and orange sherbet sunsets. One week of snorkeling among schools of neon colored fish was not enough for me. I called my parents and my boss and told them I had taken a job on a sailboat as the cook and the crew.
I didn't know how to cook or sail, but I said, "I can do this."

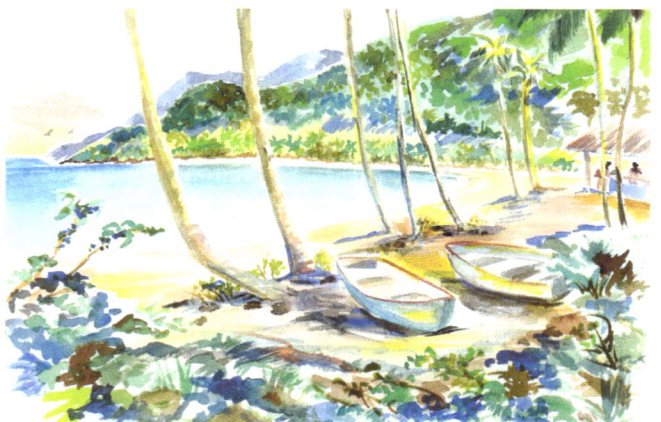

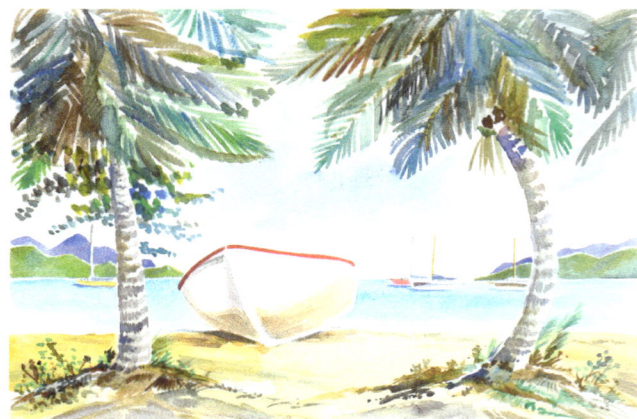

U.S and British Virgin Islands

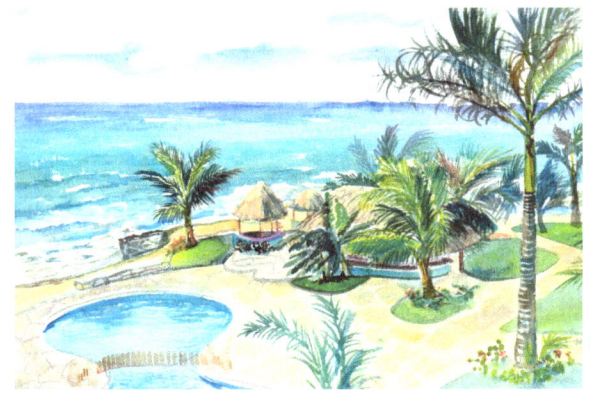

Caribbean Watercolor
Paintings

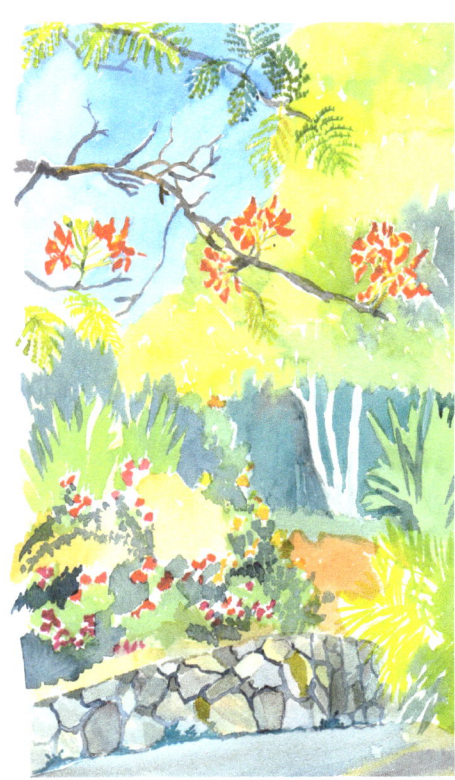

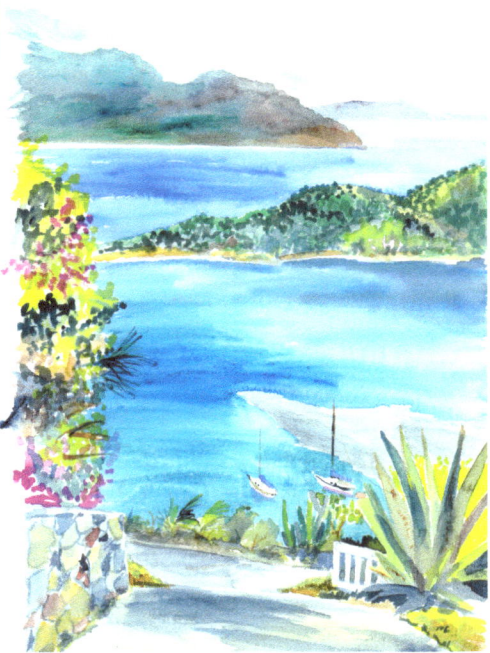

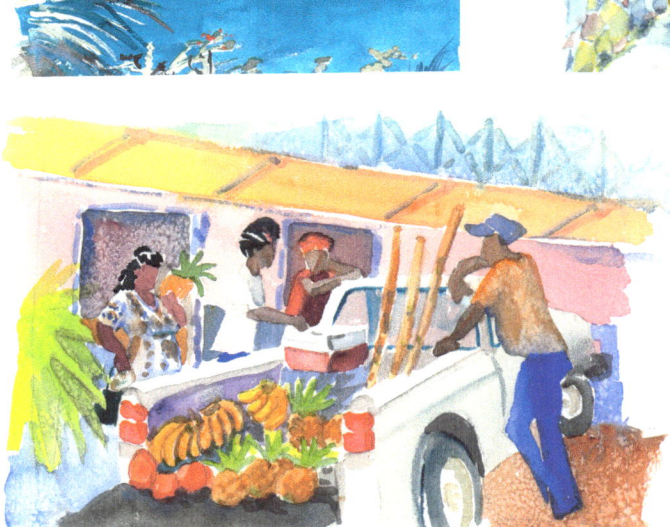

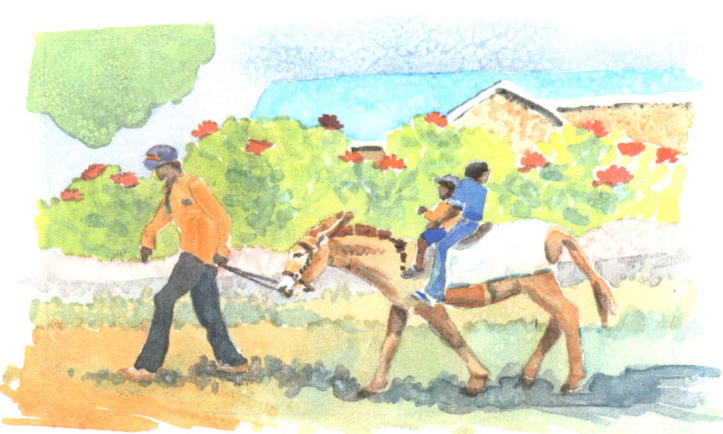

19

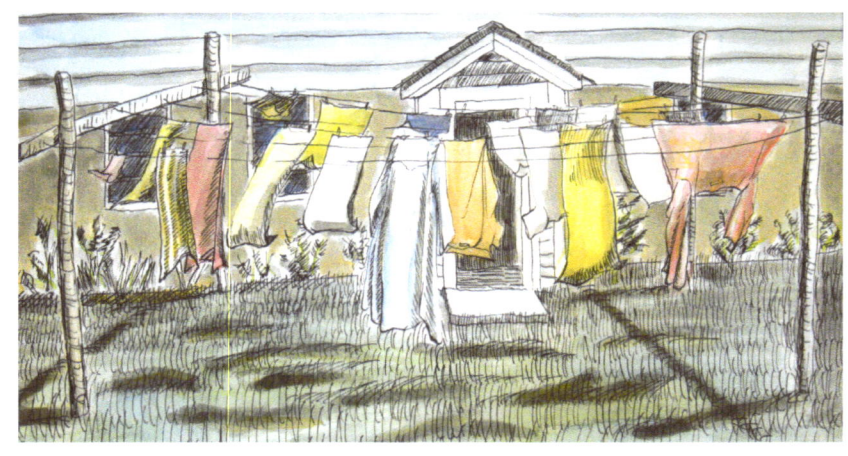

Mom's
Clothes Line

After three months of reggae music and sailing around the U.S. and British Virgin Islands, I flew back to the States. First, I stopped at Disney World in Florida to spend my meager earnings from being the cook and crew. Then I took a motorcycle ride with a friend; he hit the soft shoulder off the road and dumped the big bike on my ankle, which got cut to the bone. An ambulance took me to the ER to get it wrapped up and I immediately flew home. I had a tan as brown as a nut and bright white bandages on my foot. My parents, who were glad I made it back alive, picked me up at Boston's Logan Airport, and helped me recuperate my ankle for three months. I spent most of that summer sitting in the backyard, again sketching my cat, Tiggy, the horses next door, and watching the clothes dry in the sun.

My ankle finally healed and I got a job at UNH as graphic artist for Student Activities. I had my own office, which was the big dusty Crafts Room, and worked on publicity, brochures, posters and ads for events on campus. It was fun to be back at UNH, but after a year, I wanted a real advertising job.

My next job was paste-up artist for McAllister & Company, a typesetting firm in Portsmouth. They designed books, brochures, and anything printable. I learned all about proofreading, fonts, kerning and picas. I cut red rubylith overlays with an X-acto knife. I did color separation overlays and inked crop marks by hand with a T-square and triangles, and prepared files for printing, then mounted the layouts on matte board with a colored paper overlay for presentations. There were no computers yet, so everything was created on the drawing board and light table.

After a year, I wanted to work at a local ad agency, and landed a graphic designer job at Fickett and Walsh Advertising in Portsmouth. We worked on ad campaigns, logos and identity packages (lots of presstype). There were only five ad agencies in Portsmouth then, so I was running out of options for bigger career moves.

Moving Up...

Tip #4:

Always be willing to learn new things and keep up with new technology. An artist needs to try the latest tools.

I became one of the fastest paste-up artists north of Boston, and started to get freelance artwork jobs. I decided to open my own business and named it Ad-cetera Graphics, eventually hiring six employees. My husband, John, joined the business, did my accounting, and set up our typesetting department. We bought an $80,000 Compugraphic typesetter machine that ran out sheets of type. I ran it through the waxer and pasted it up onto boards for printing. There were no computers yet.

Next came fax machines, computers and scanners that were rapidly taking over the world. No one knew how to use this new equipment. There was no training, no computer classes, no books that made any sense. It was sink or swim, so we jumped in 100% and learned everything from scratch. We had to learn immediately how to use them to do our work.

The learning curve got easier, the computers got smarter, and the scanners got better. Adobe Illustrator, Photoshop and Quark were now the new tools to produce artwork. It was an exciting time as we learned amazing new technologies that increased the speed of work. Computers forced deadlines to "I need it now." rather than allowing two or three weeks to finish a job.

My world changes constantly in order to keep up with it all. Lots of stress and big jobs, and faster deadlines are now the norm. The days of presstype and rubylith are long over.

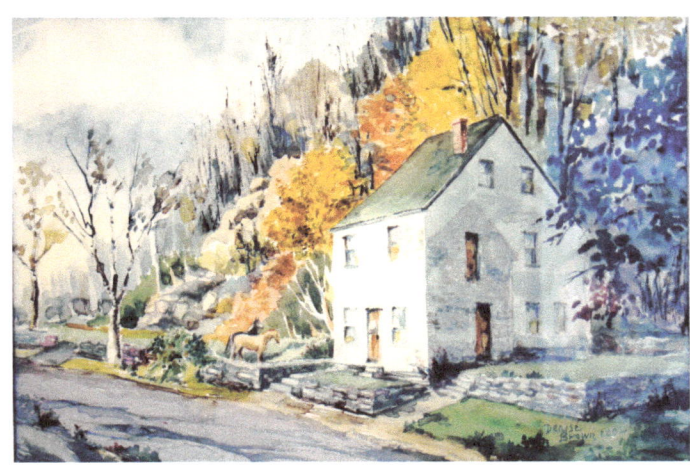

Harper's Ferry Civil War House

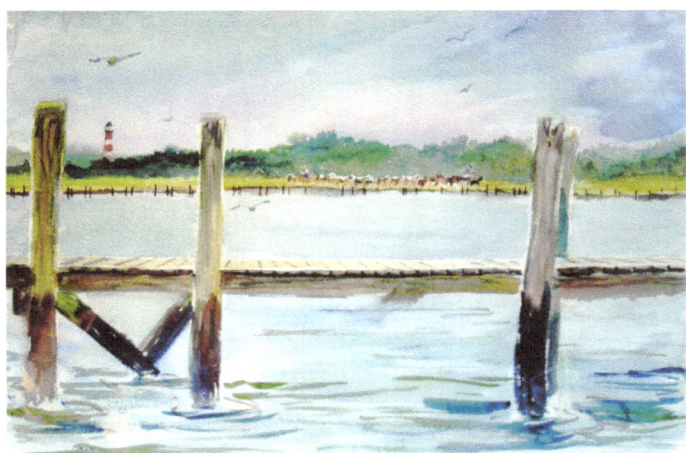

Chincoteague Island Ponies

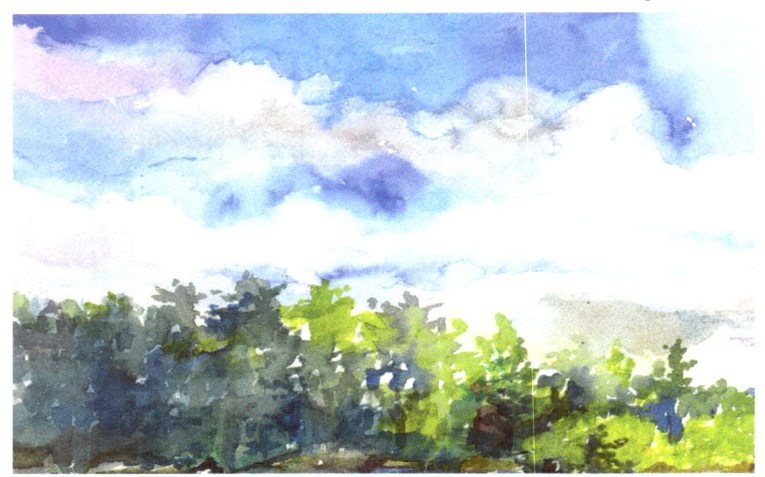

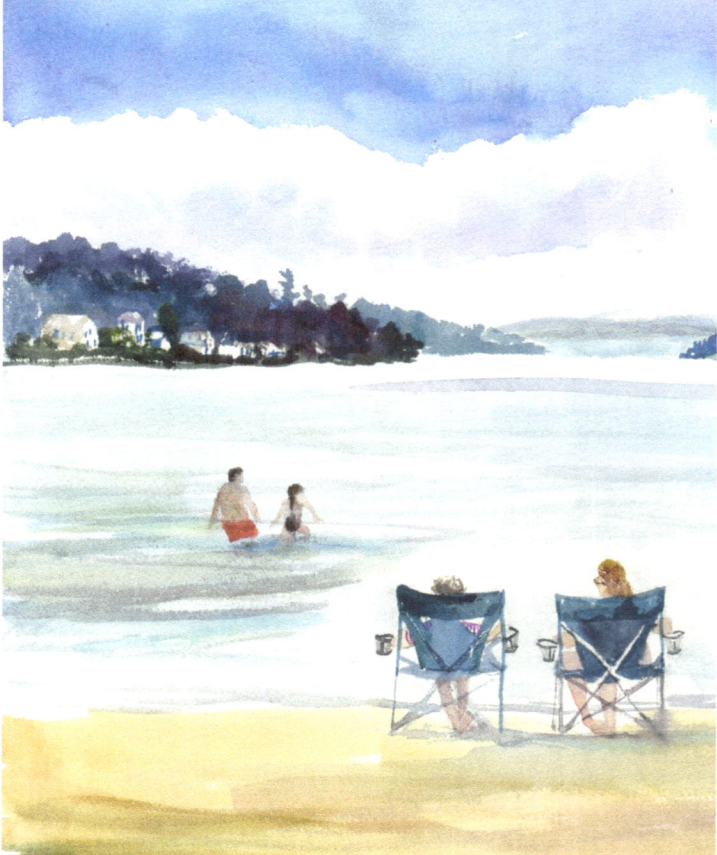

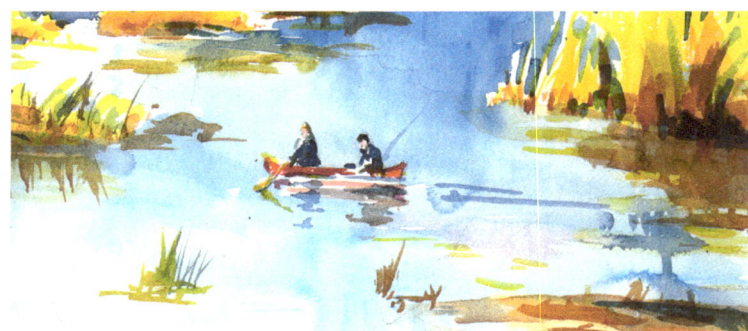

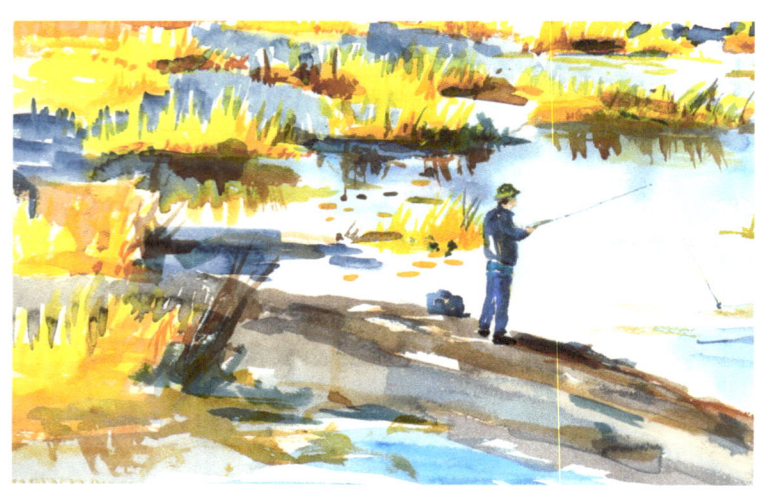

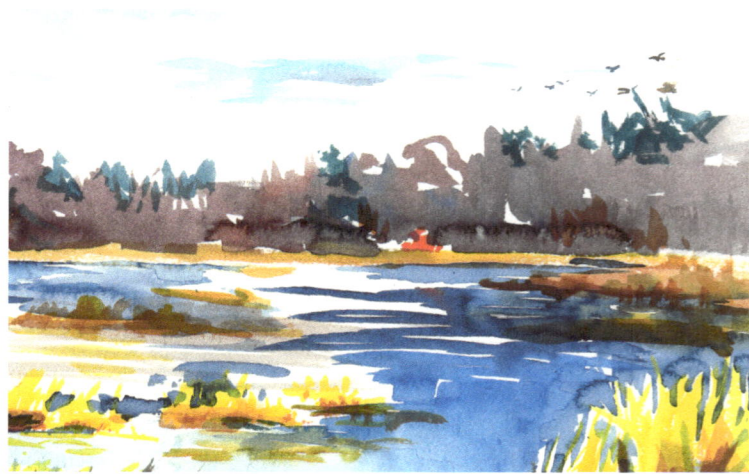

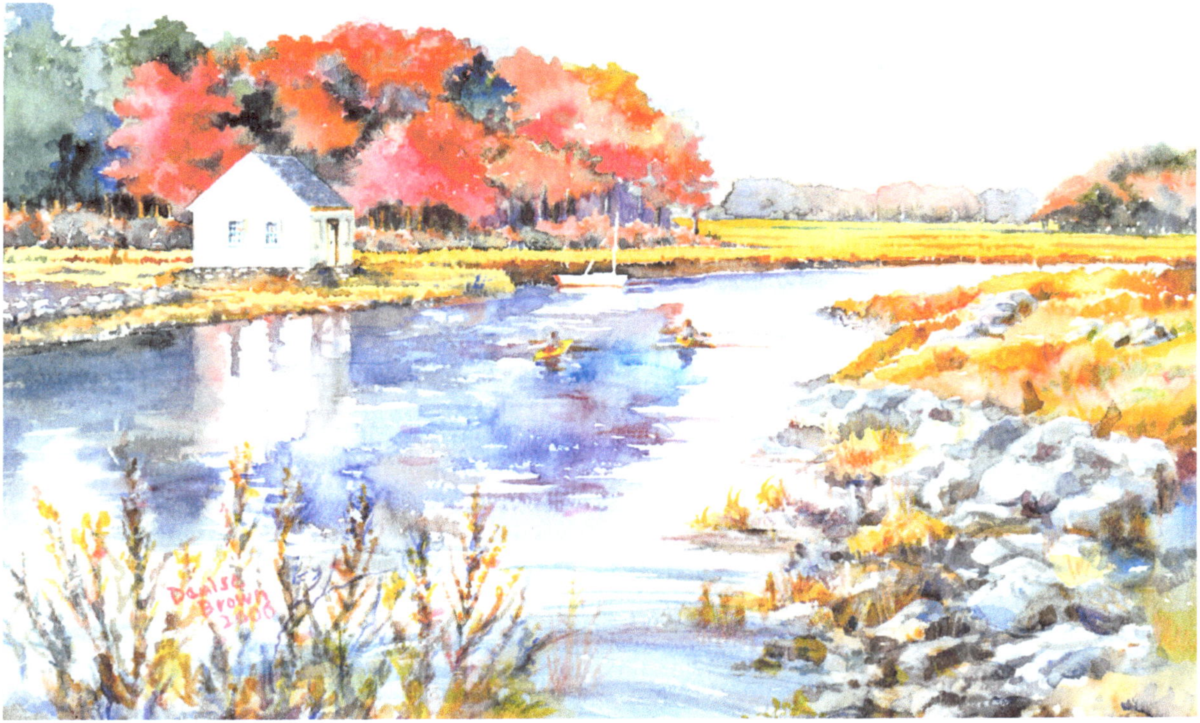

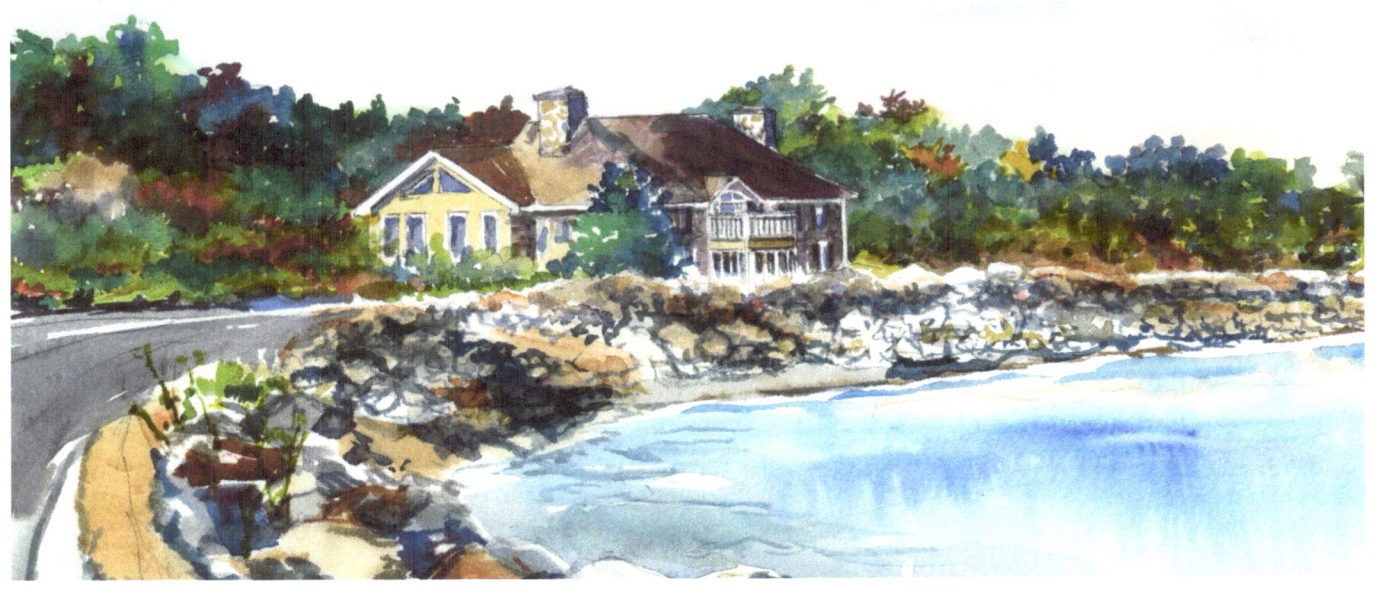

Rye Creek

North Hampton Curve on Route 1A

Maine Favorites

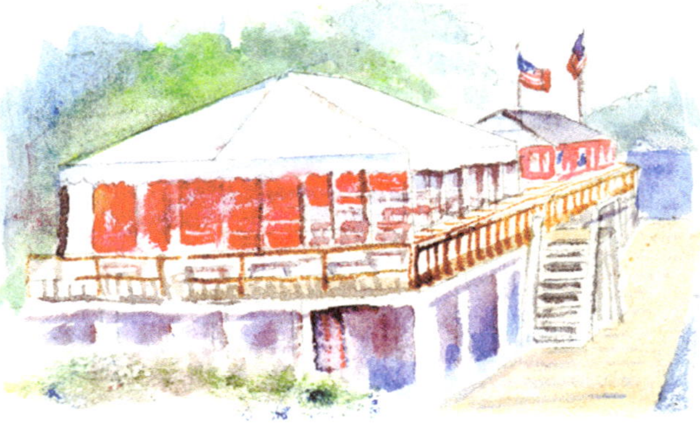

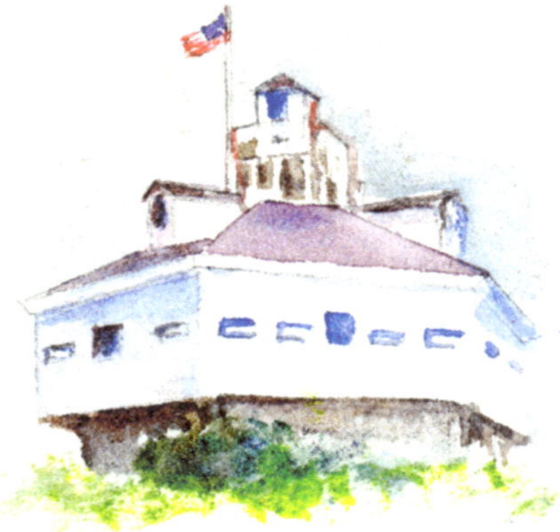

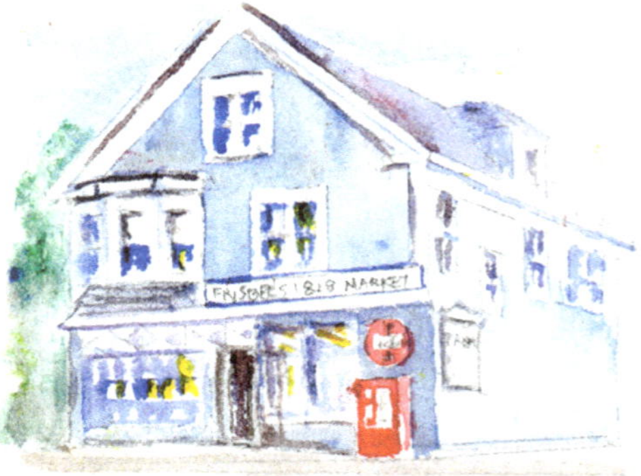

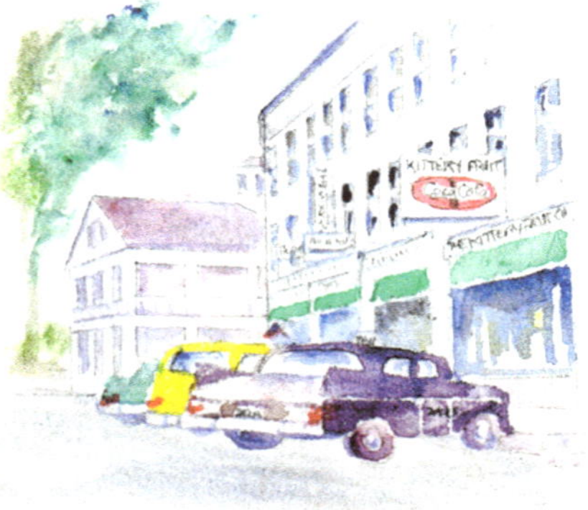

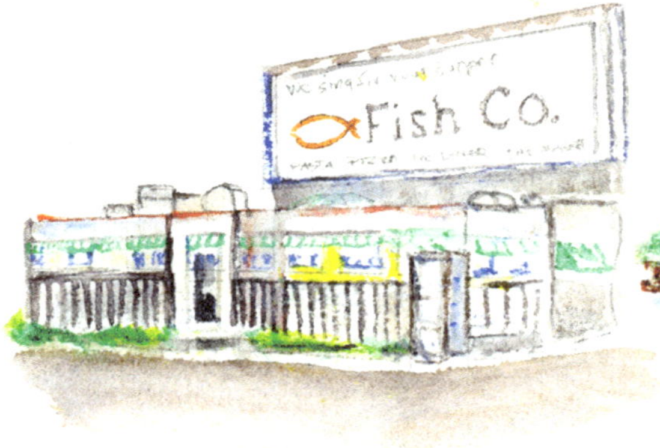

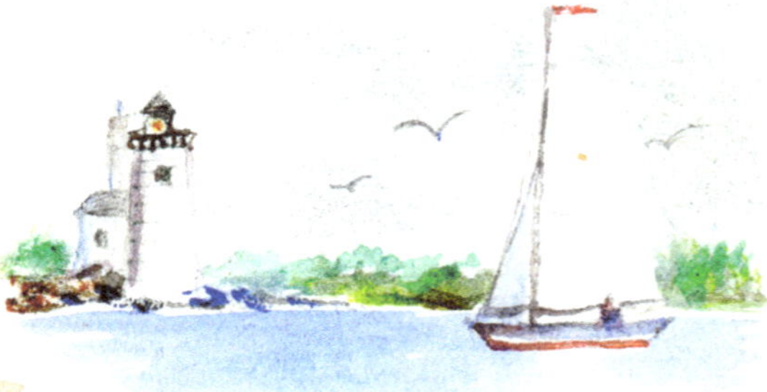

The Chauncey Creek
Lobster Pier,
Fort Foster,
Frisbee's Market,
Kittery Foreside's
Main Street,
Sea Gull Diner,
Whaleback Light
and Lifeboat Station

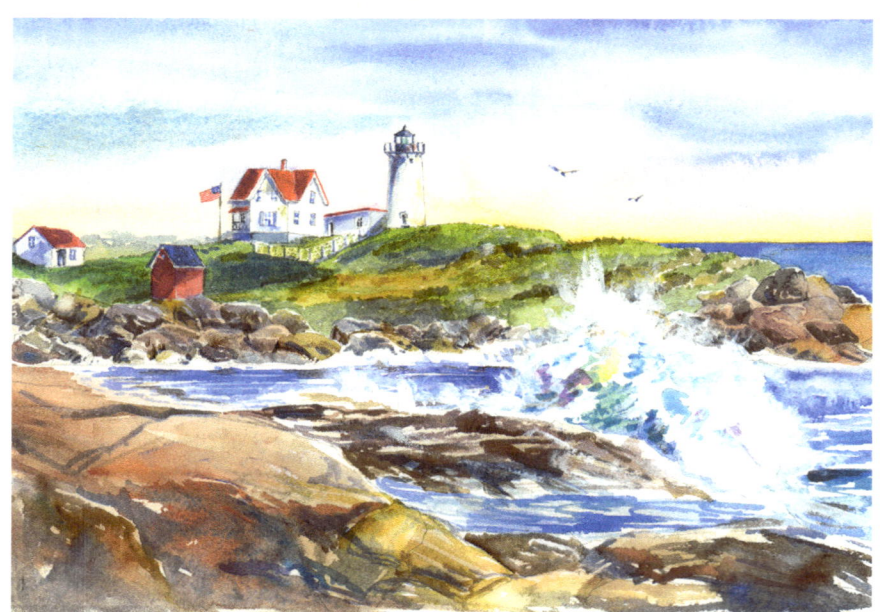

Nubble
Light

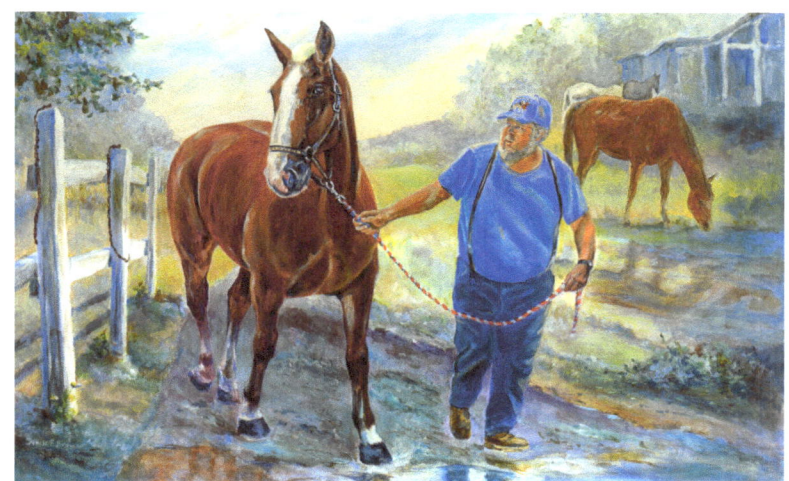

Man Walking Horse

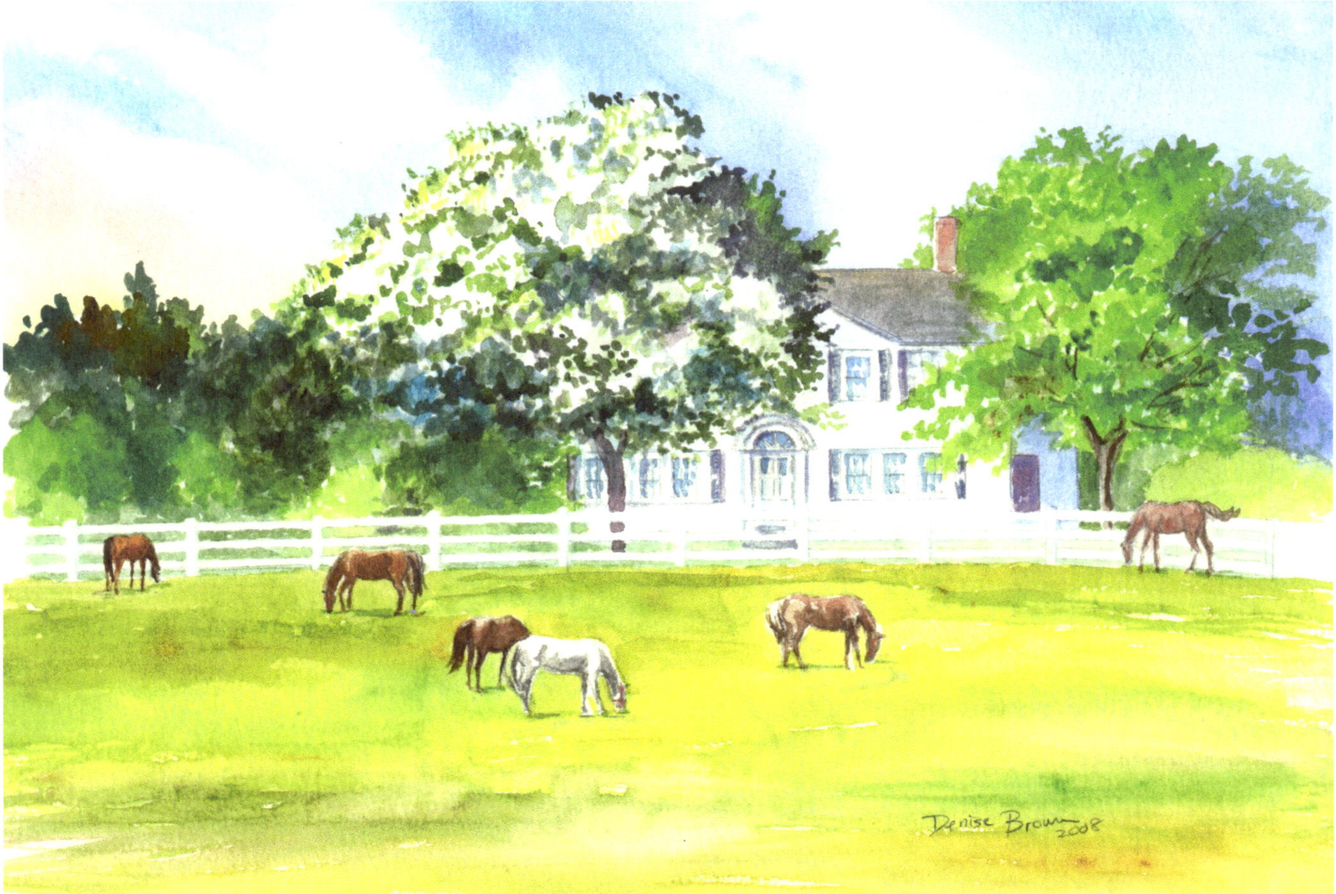

Hett Farm in Portsmouth

Always Art...
Tip #5:
If you love your work, it's not really work... even on vacation you can draw and paint.

A sailing vacation to the U.S. and British Virgin Islands with 26 Seacoast New Hampshire mates was the experience of a lifetime. The boat was a 110 foot triple-masted wooden Brigantine that looked like an old pirate ship with billowing white sails. I found out that Professor John Hatch and his wife were part of the group. Hatch painted and sketched all week — which was fantastic to watch. He was also quite a jokester and kept everyone laughing. One day, he climbed the crow's nest, and his wife Marianna quickly reprimanded him, saying, "John, you come down from there right now." He did! It was a week of snorkeling, reggae dancing, and belly-busting laughs, even amongst the endless cockroaches all over the galley and bunks. We opted to sleep on deck and woke to orange sunrises, sparkling blue water, and hungry pelicans diving for fish.

Sailing vacations in the Caribbean, and beach vacations in Jamaica, Nevis, and Mexico, meant painting more watercolors under a shady palm tree.

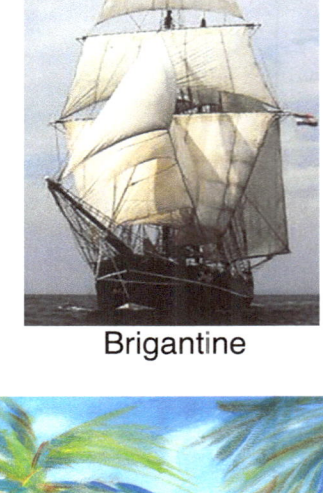

Brigantine

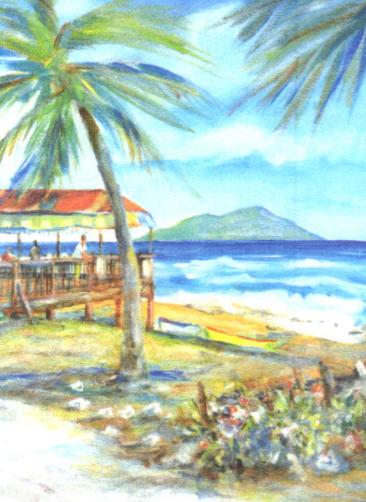

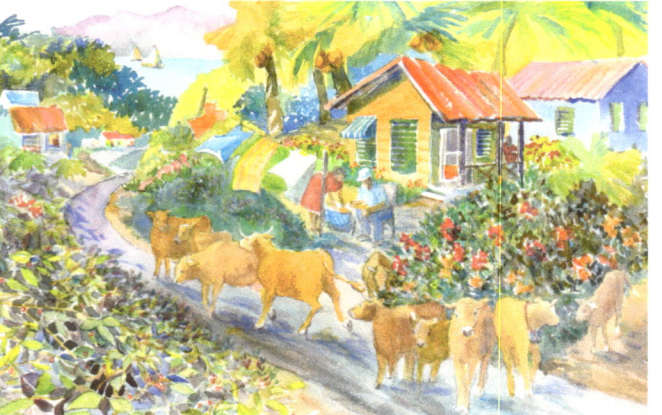

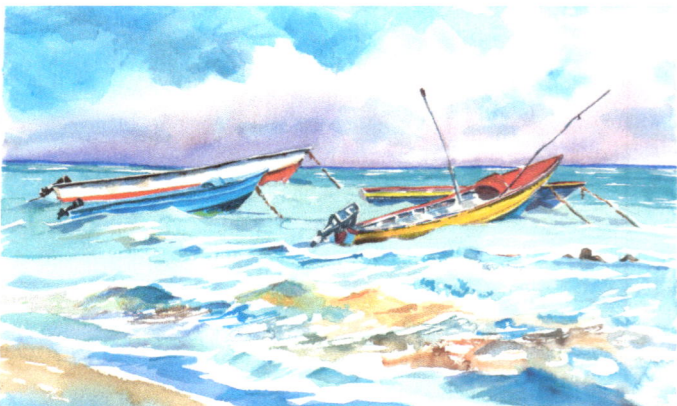

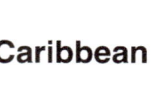

Caribbean

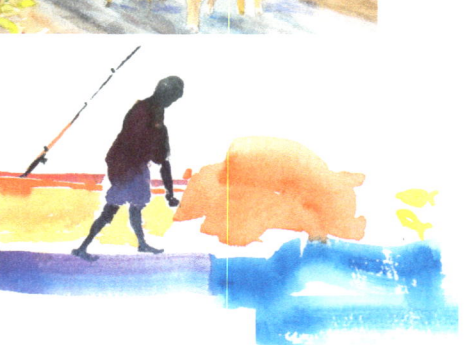

26

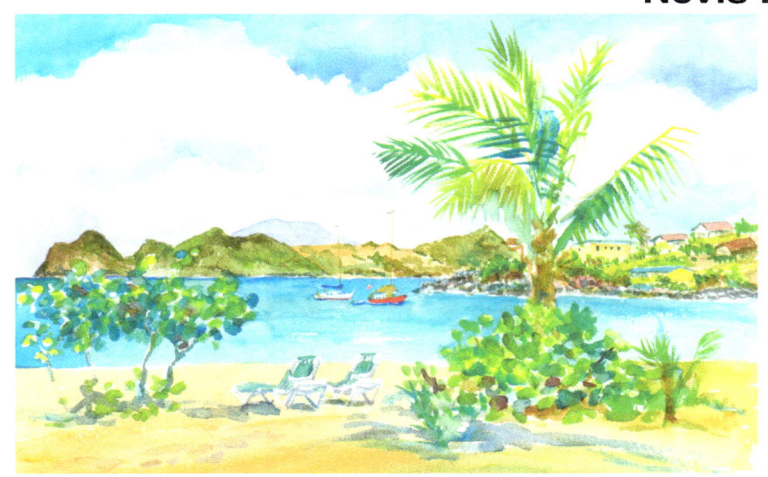

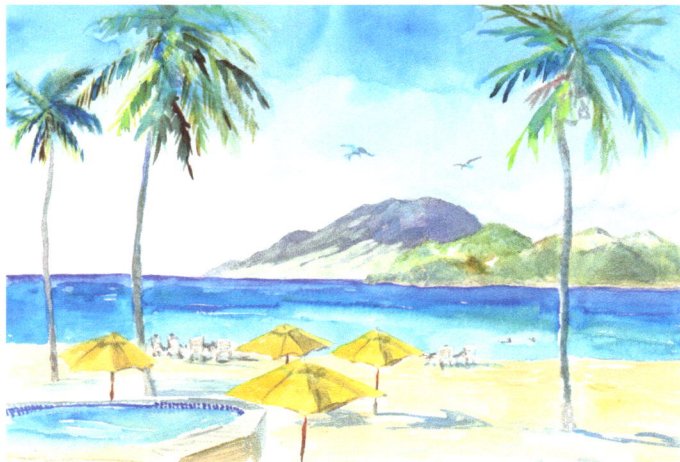

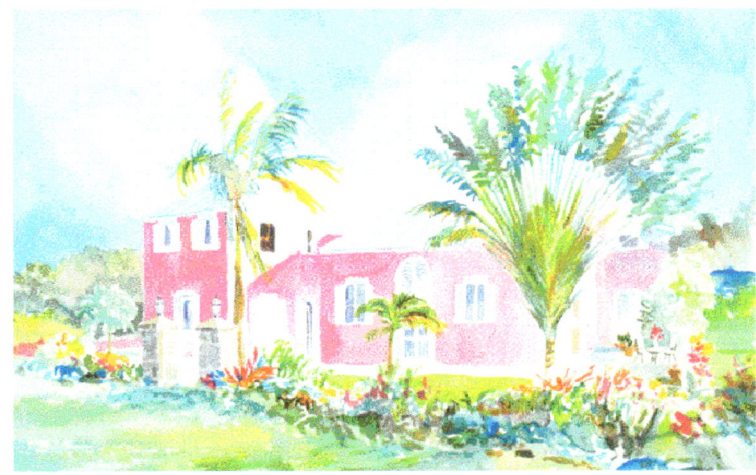

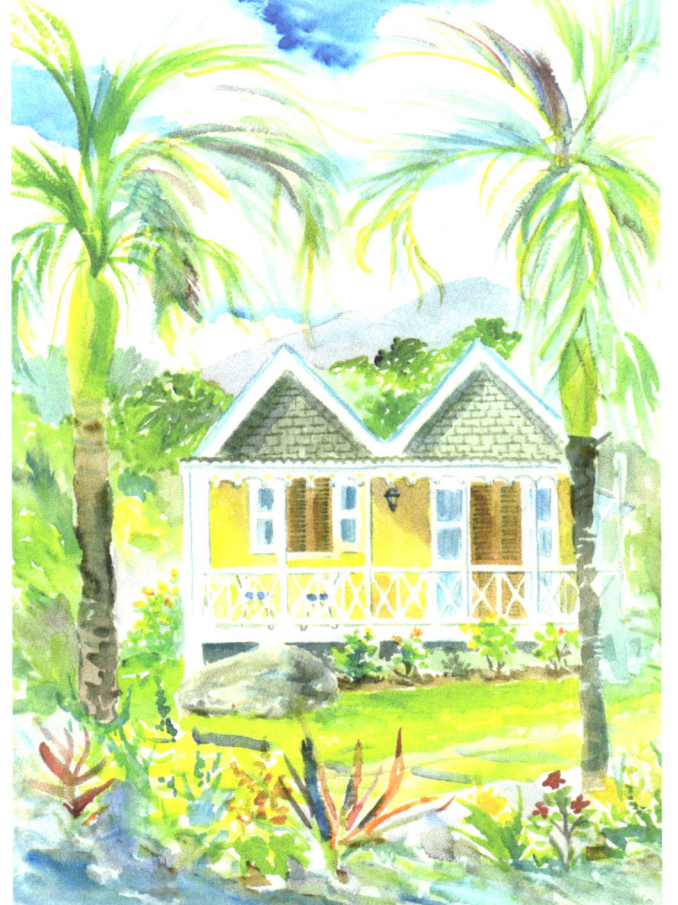

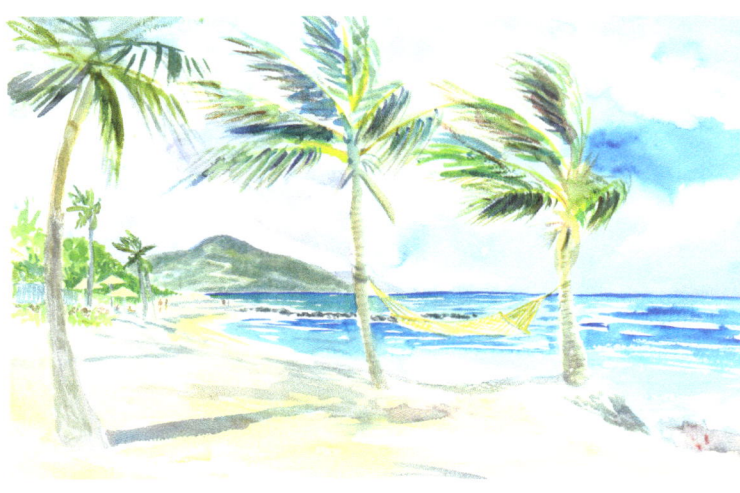

Tip #6:

Take workshops and classes to try something new, hone your skills, and renew your passion.

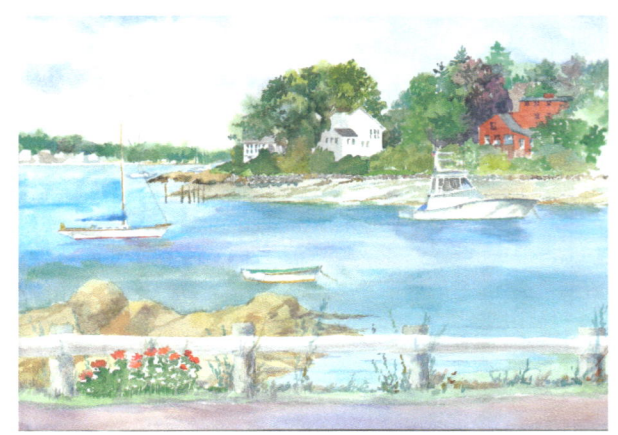

New Castle Inlet

Two of my favorite workshops were 'Watermedia Weeks' in Houston, Texas that I attended two years in a row in the 1980's. Stunning artist exhibits were set up in bank lobbies, restaurants, hotels, and businesses all over the city. Daily demos and art classes, packed with artists and teachers from around the world, and an expo of art vendors when you could 'try and buy' the latest products, paints and papers, was like Christmas for artists. It was total art emersion.

The guest motivational speaker was Eric Rhoads, artist and publisher of "PleinAir" and "Fine Art Connoisseur" magazines. After the workshops, my head was exploding with new ideas. My bags were packed with new tools, paints and watercolor papers, and my heart pounded with excitement to get back home and attack my watercolor paintings with renewed courage and energy.

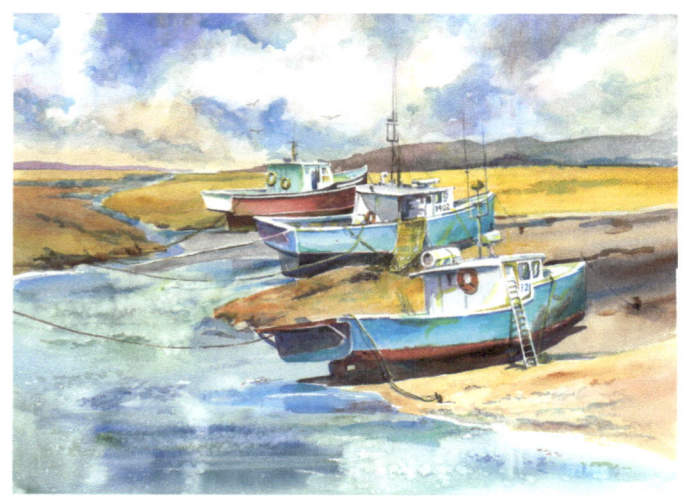

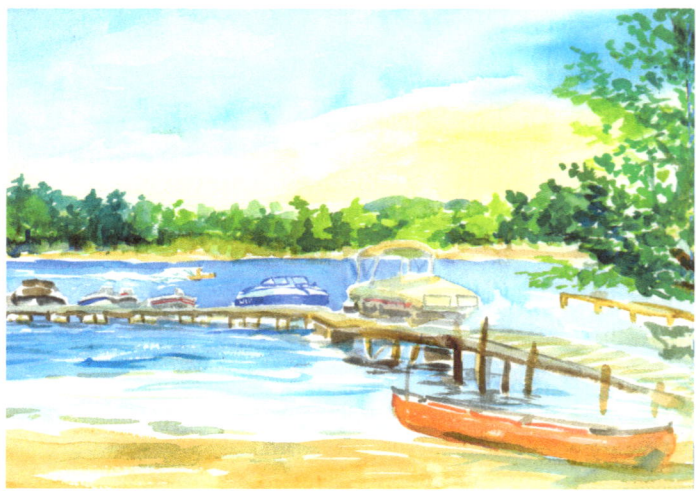

Nova Scotia Boats   New Hampshire Lake Dock

New Castle

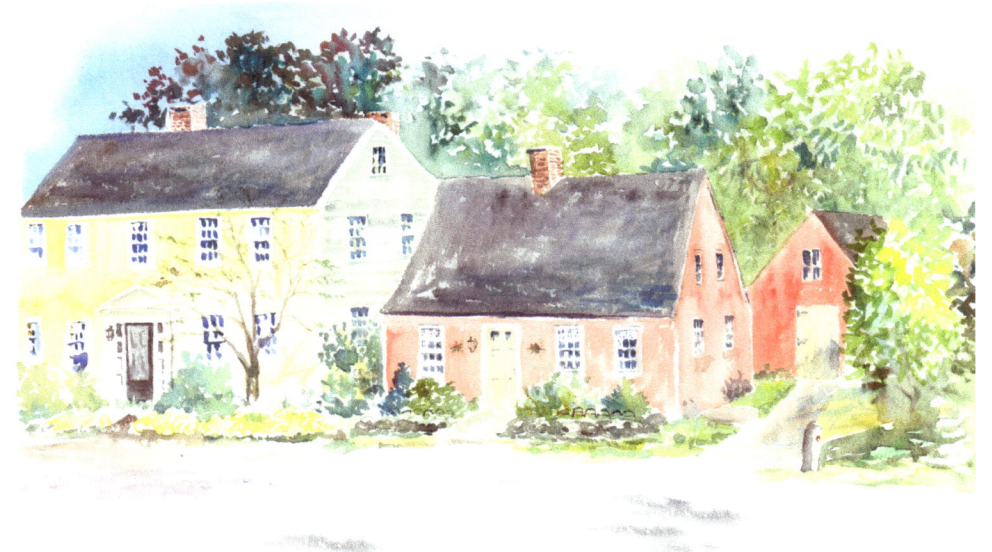

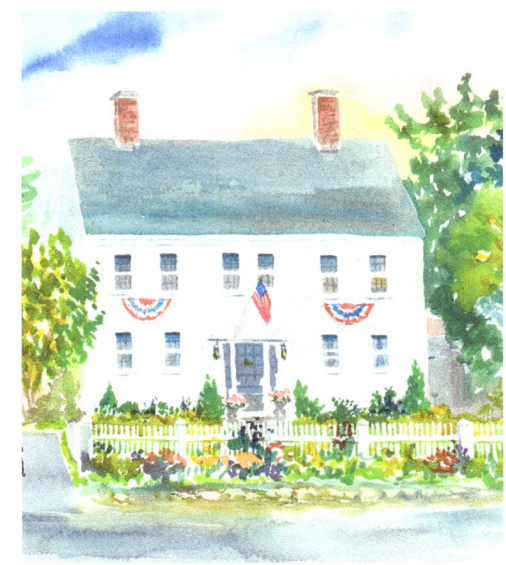

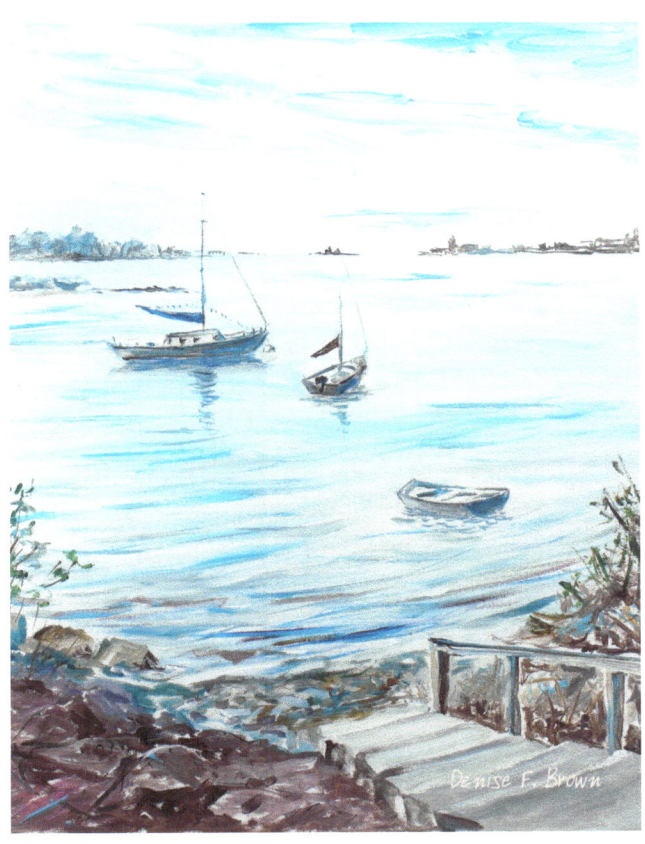

Denise F. Brown

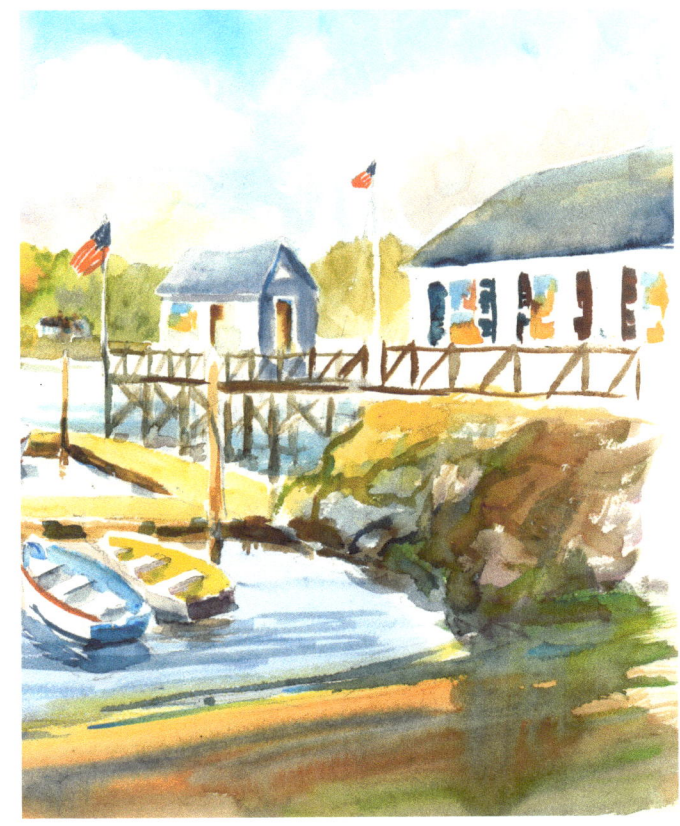

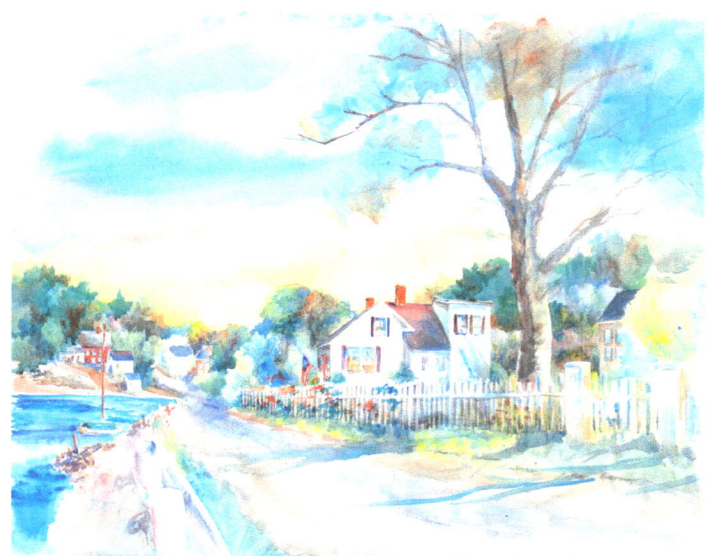

Watercolor Painting with Bob Steedman at Sue's

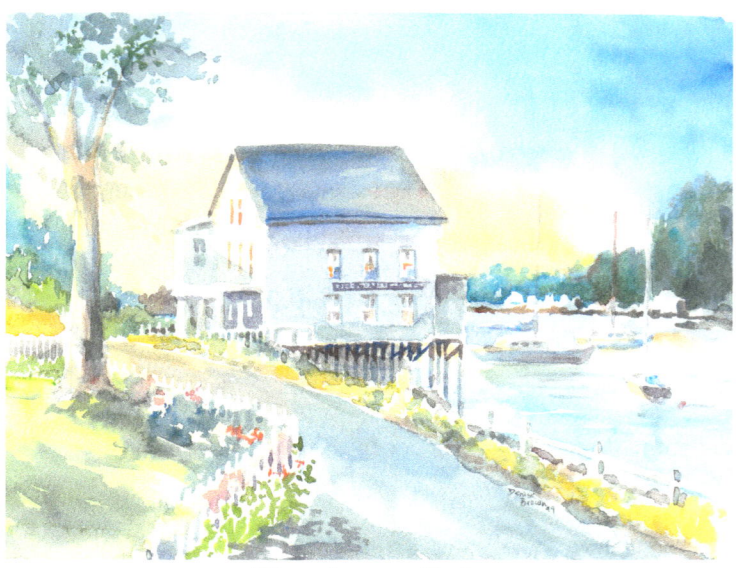

Piscataqua Cafe

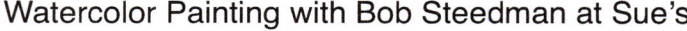

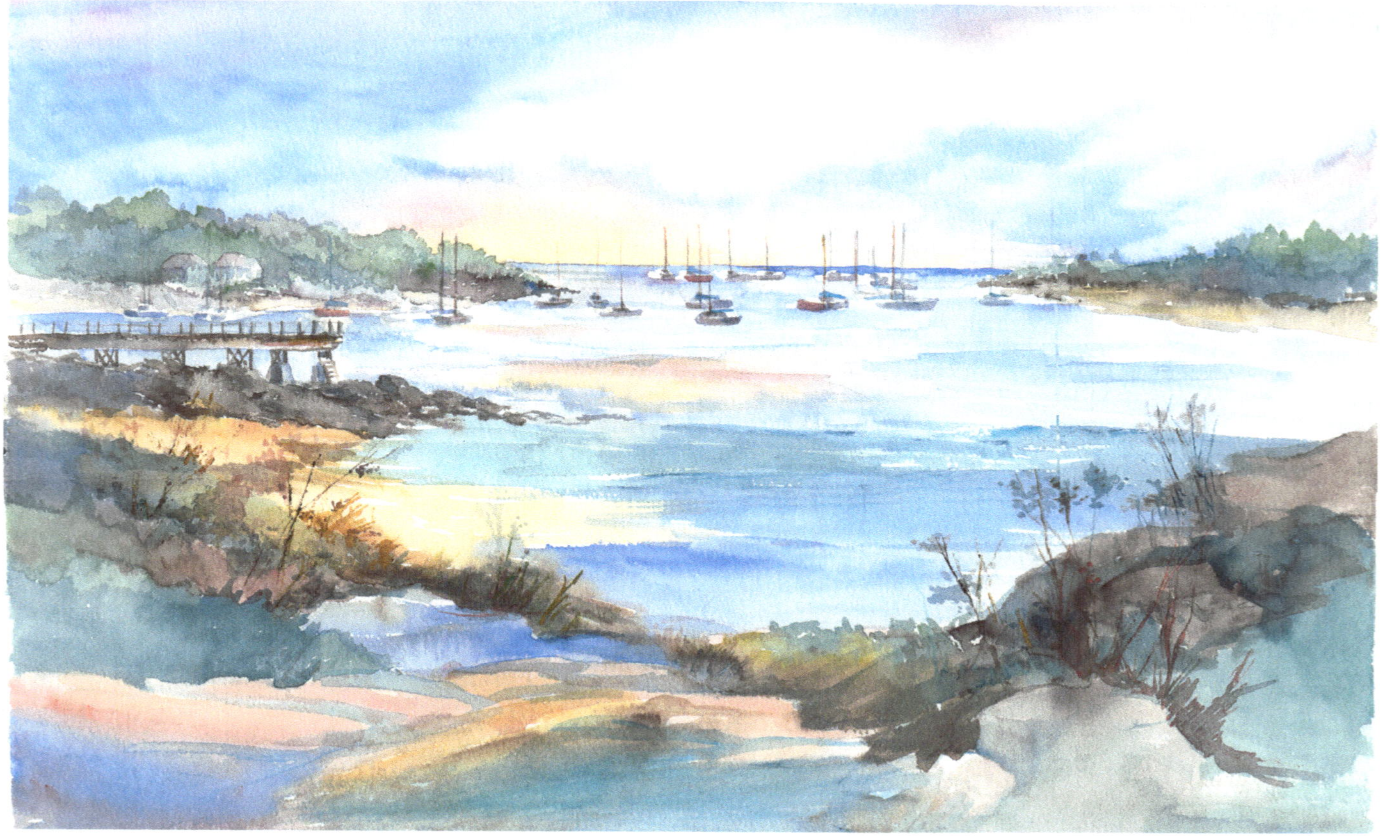

New Castle Harbor

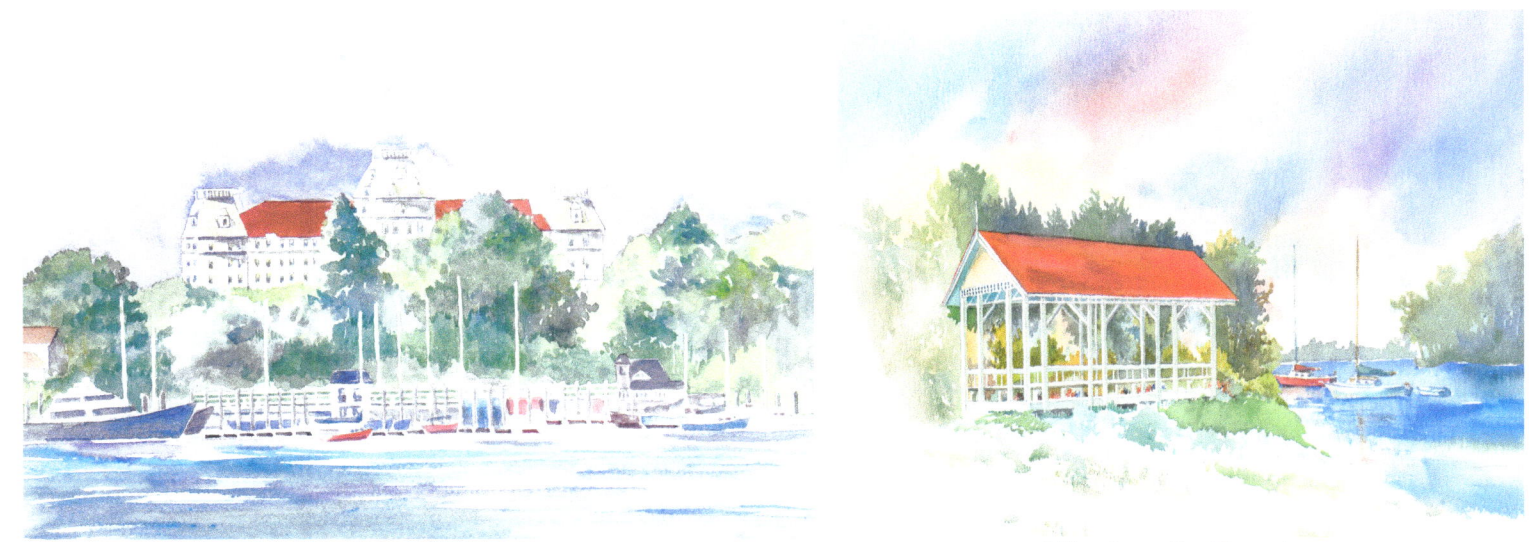

Wentworth Marina

Wentworth Gazebo

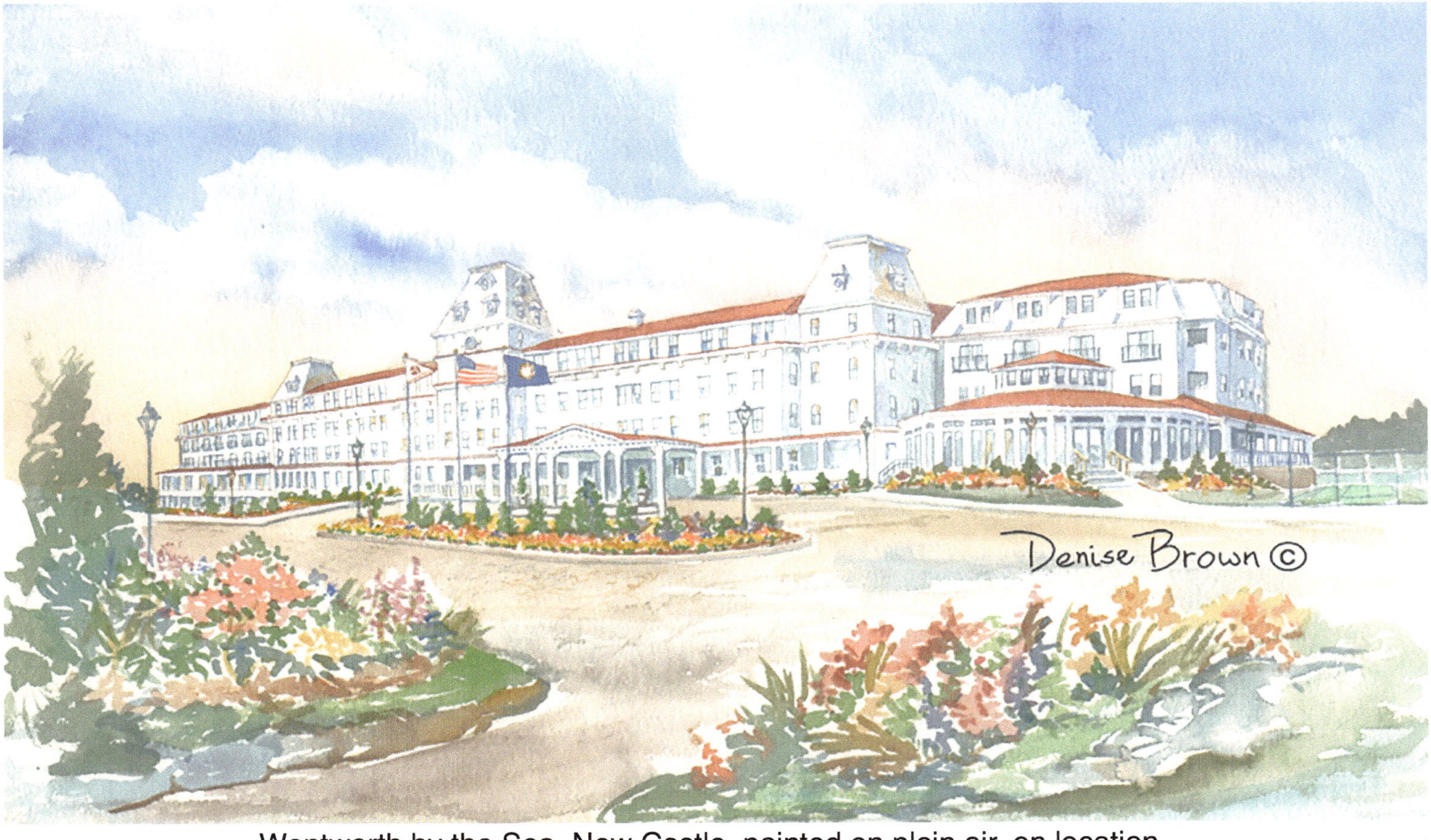

Denise Brown ©

Wentworth by the Sea, New Castle, painted en plein air, on location

31

Quick Study

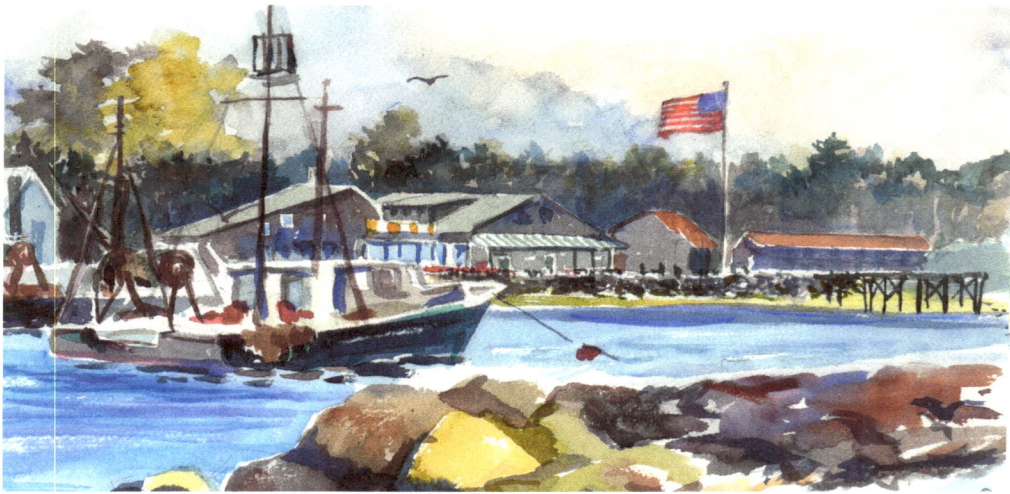

Saunders
at Rye
Harbor

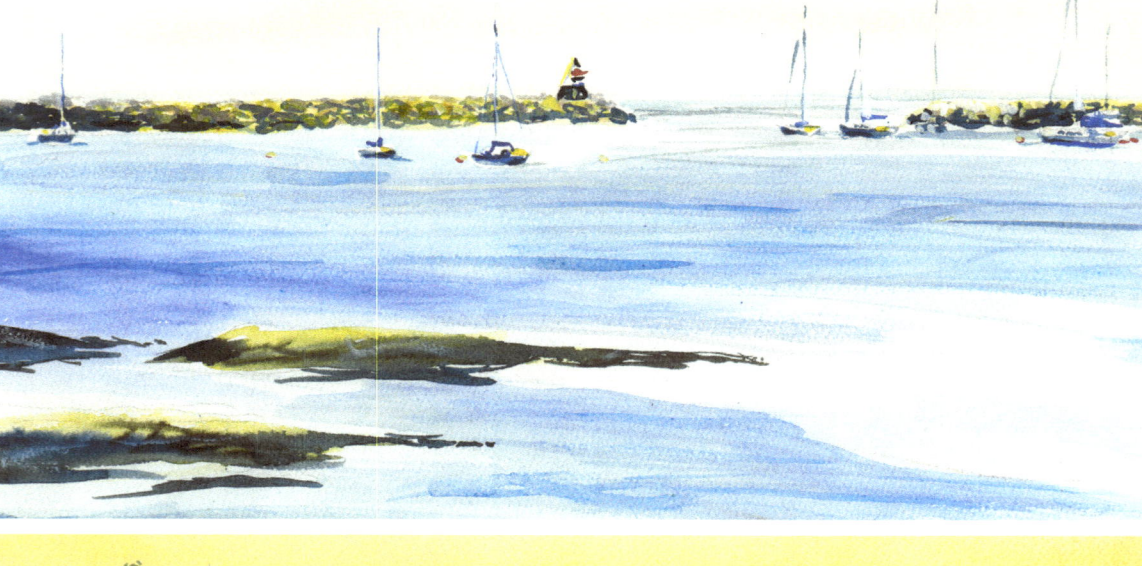
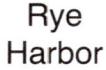

Rye
Harbor

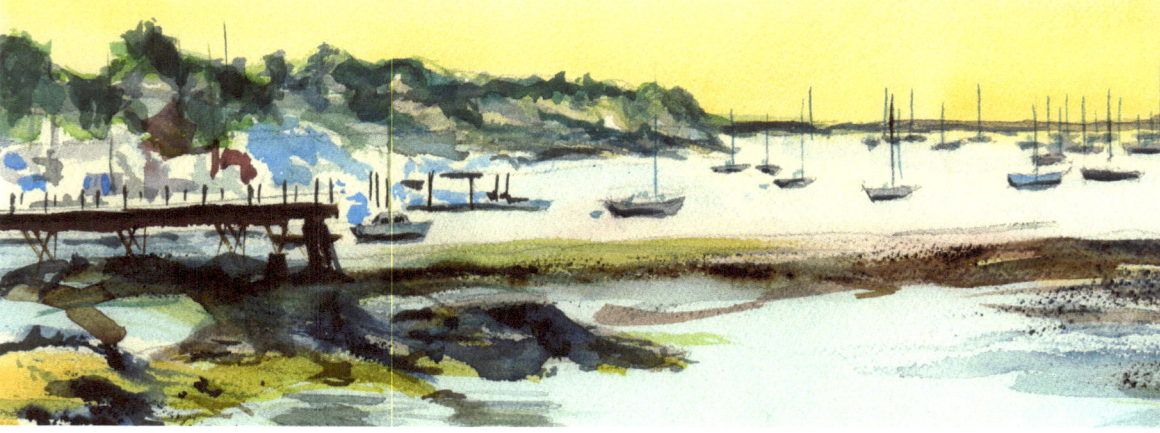

New
Castle
Marina

An Artist Emerges...

Tip #7:
Step outside of the box.

Strolling at the beach

After years of learning and working on art, I finally realized that I was a real artist, both a fine art painter, and a graphic designer. You need to use both sides of the brain for art and business. I recommend reading the book, "Drawing on The Right Side of the Brain" for artists, by Betty Edwards.

My house gradually filled up with art work and paintings. It was time to have my own art show. The art needed framing, cataloging, and pricing. I had to learn how to sell art, which is not always easy for artists to do. Since my art is part of me, it wasn't easy to exhibit it for everyone to examine and critique.

In August 2011, I was invited to hang a two month show at the Discover Portsmouth Center in Portsmouth, New Hampshire. I titled it "An Exhibit of a Lifetime" with 100 pieces of my artwork. Sales went well during the month of August. All was good in the world, but suddenly 911 struck and four passenger planes were hijacked and flown directly into the sides of both Twin Towers in New York City, into the Pentagon, and into a field in Pennsylvania. That tragedy threw everyone into a depressed funk. The days of innocence and possible world peace changed to fear, terrorism, and worries of traveling in a dangerous world. My art sales seemed to stop that September. It took a long time for the country to recover from this attack on American soil. However, the world eventually got back to business as normal and people began to purchase art again.

Since then, I have participated in many fairs and art shows, and have painted and done demos at events. My fans like to see what my latest project is and ask me, "How long did it take to paint that?" I paint fast, so I usually confess, "It took me a couple of hours," or, "Come back in an hour and I will be almost finished with the painting." They usually return and sometimes buy my paintings unframed.

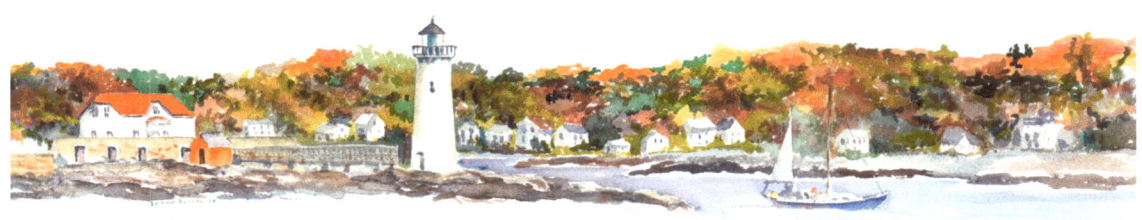

New Hampshire Seacoast

Two Girls at the Beach

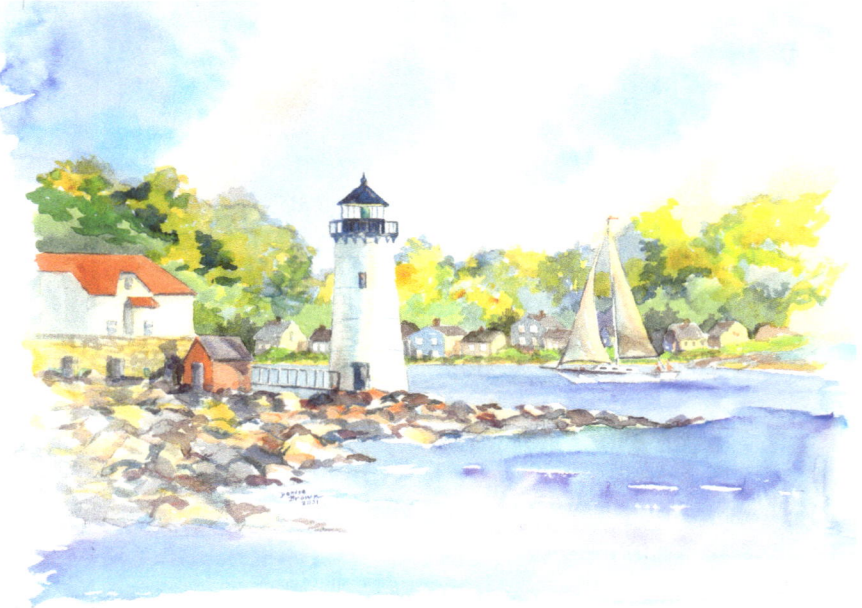

Sailing by the U.S. Coast Guard Light

Fuller's Runnymede Mansion, study from an historic photograph

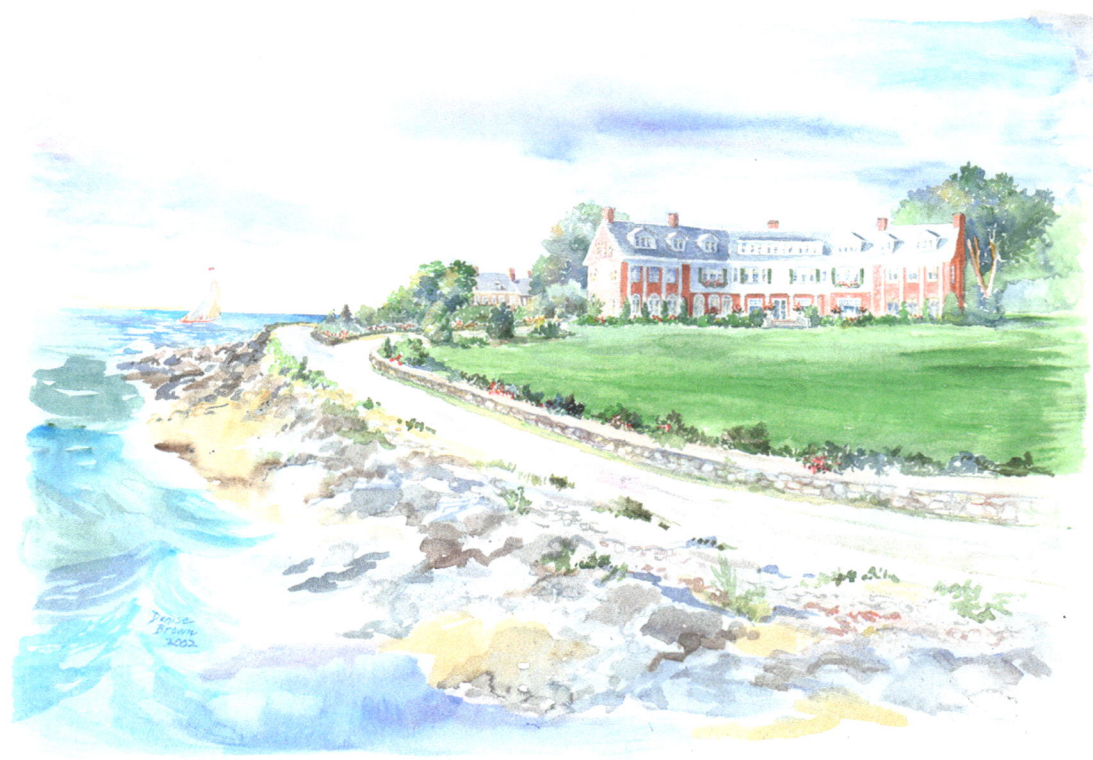

Into the Light...

Tip #8:

Get outdoors and meet your admirers. 'Plein-air painting' is great exposure, plus you get to paint outside and observe light.

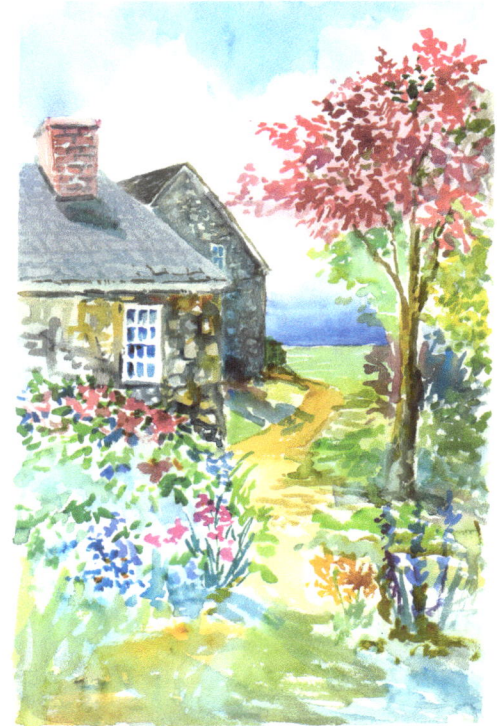

Isles of Shoals Path

My commissioned work requires more detail and concentration, so I paint them indoors in my studio, often using reference photos from clients. However, my favorite painting time is outdoors "en plein-air." This French term means "in the open air." Artists use it to describe outdoor painting, capturing landscapes in natural light, which is the best light to paint in.

Quickly changing sunlight and shadows, bugs and mosquitos, crowds of people, interruptions, and changing weather can chase you back to your vehicle. When that happens, I have to finish the painting in my studio, remembering what caught my eye on location. Painting outside makes you work faster and looser. Bring water, bug spray, sunscreen, snacks, binoculars, and business cards.

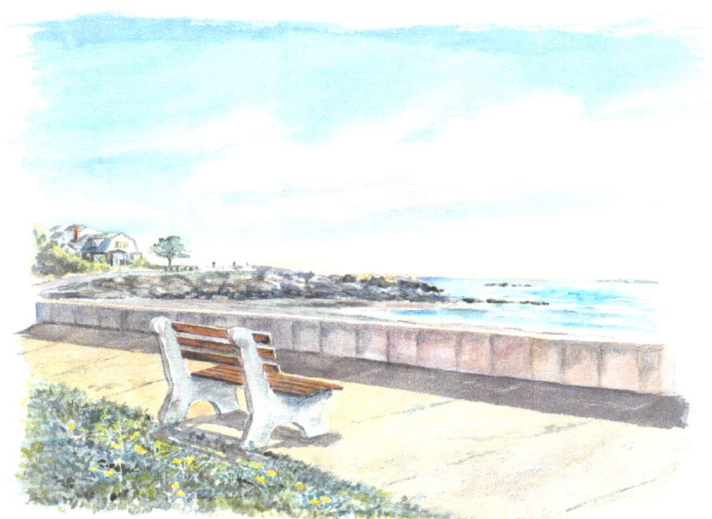

Wallis Sands Rye Beach

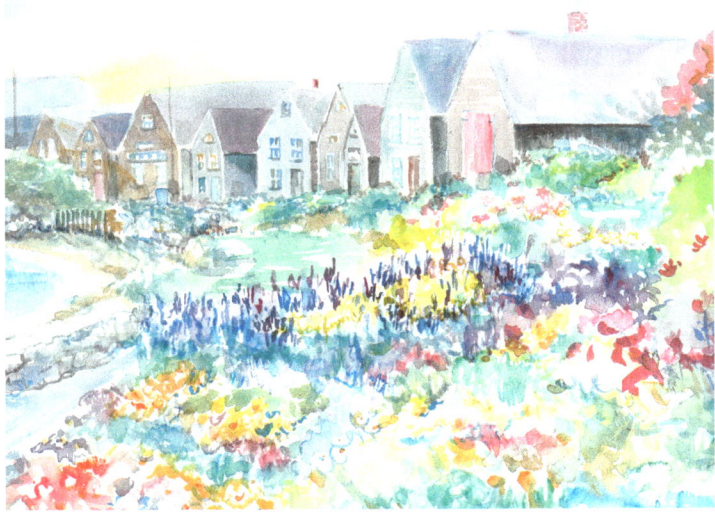

North Hampton Fish Shacks

35

Churches and Town Halls

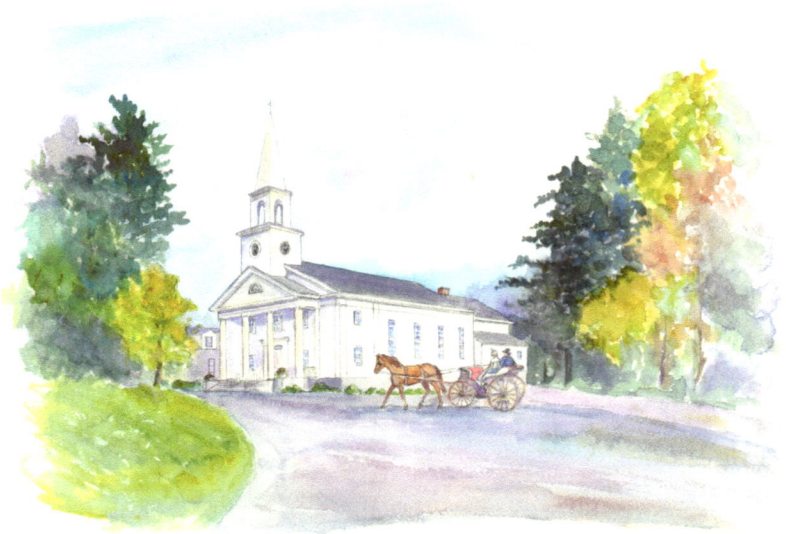

Rye Congregational Church

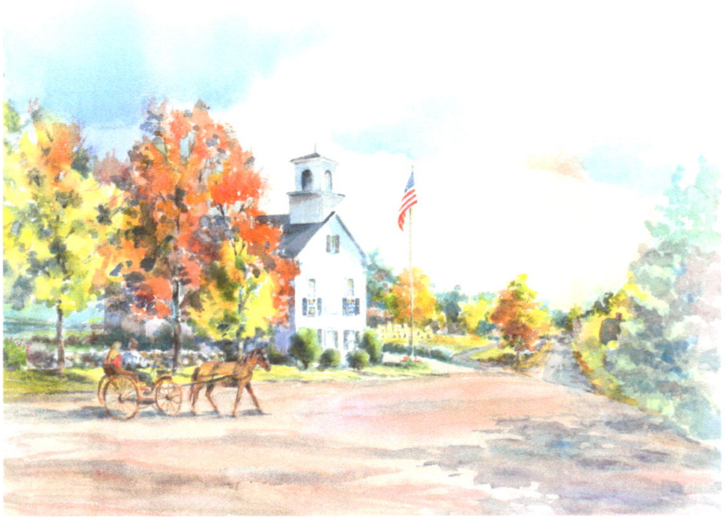

Rye Town Hall

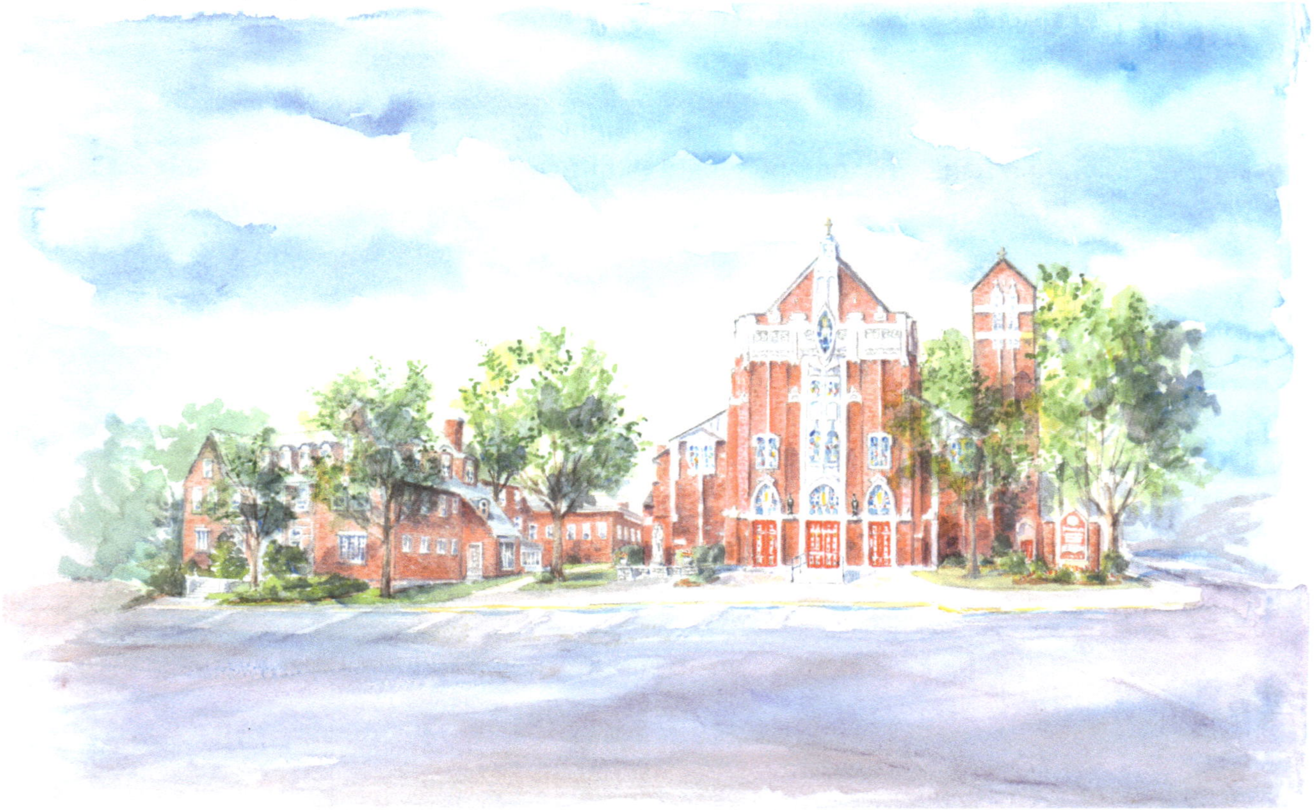

Immaculate Conception Church in Portsmouth

Water Views

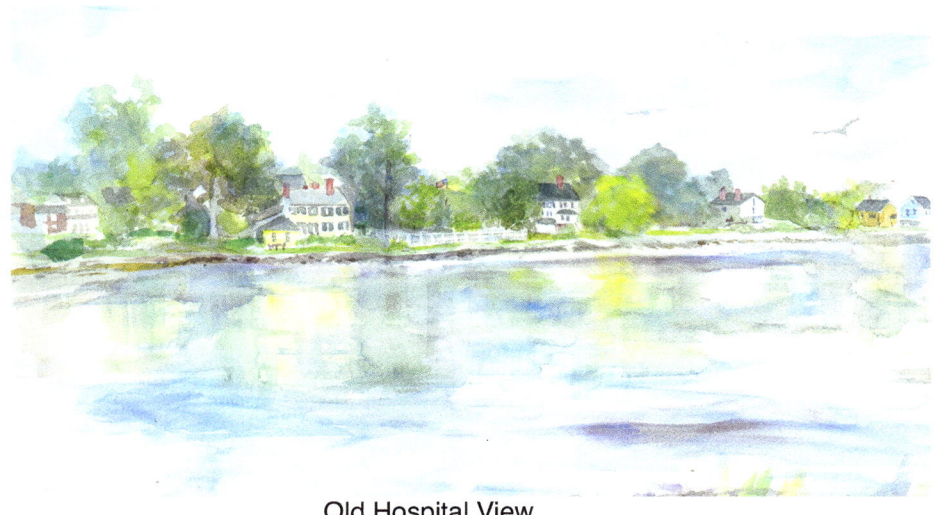

Old Hospital View

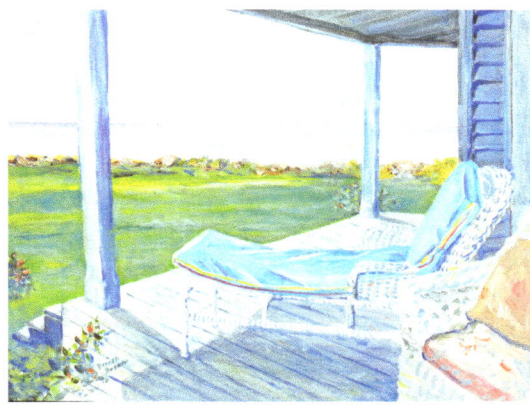

Meig's Back Porch

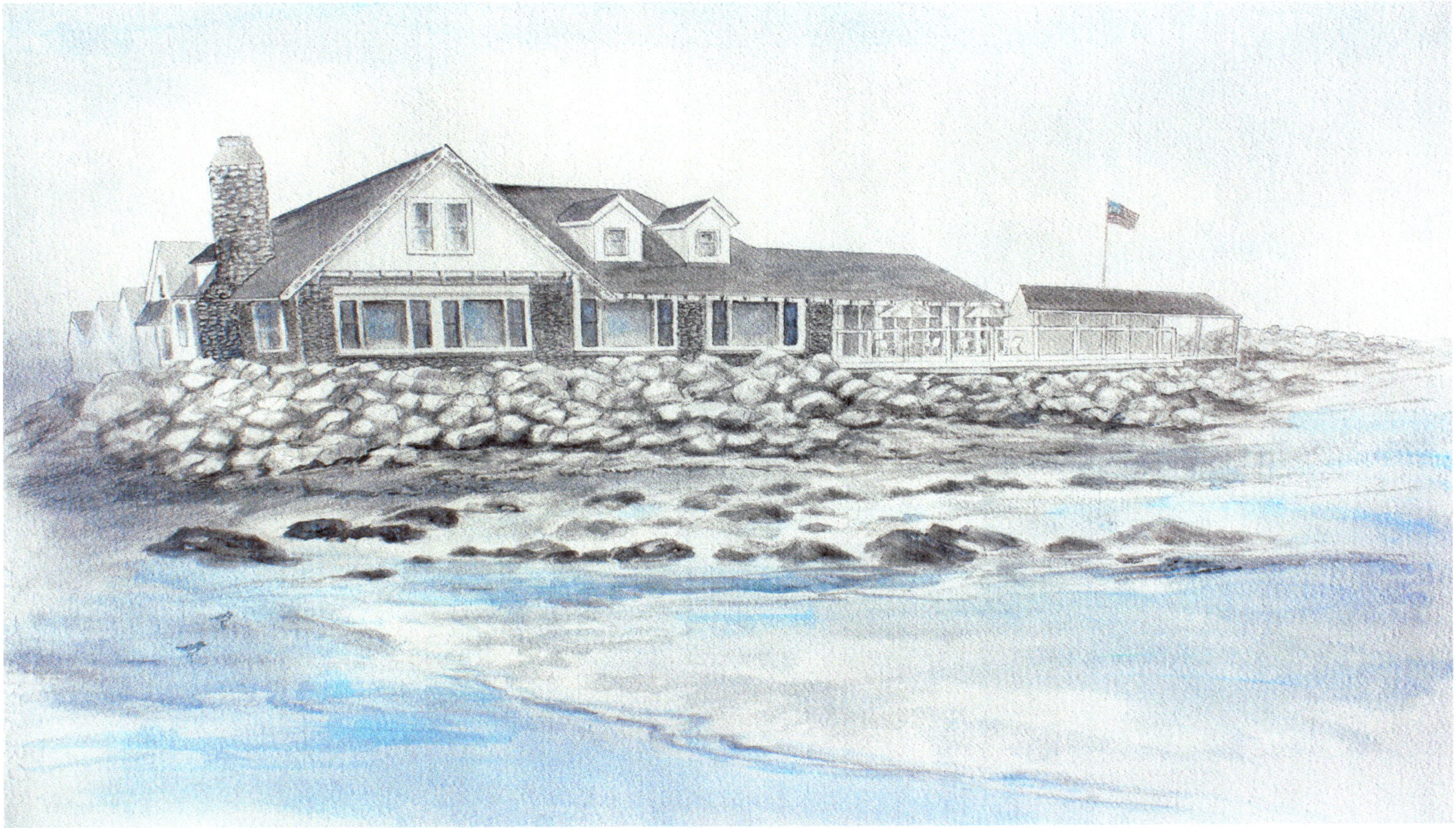

Rye Beach Club

37

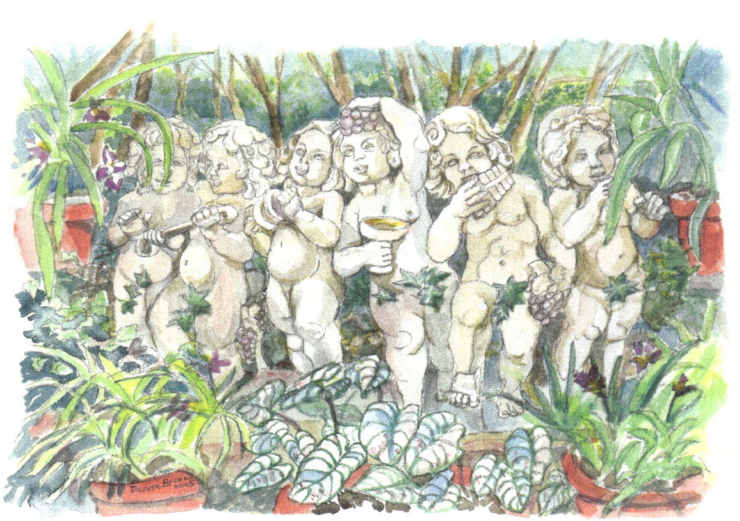

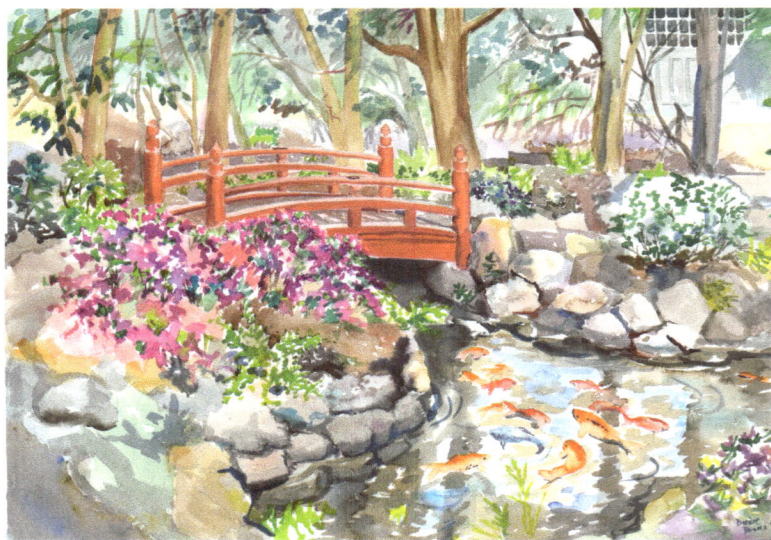

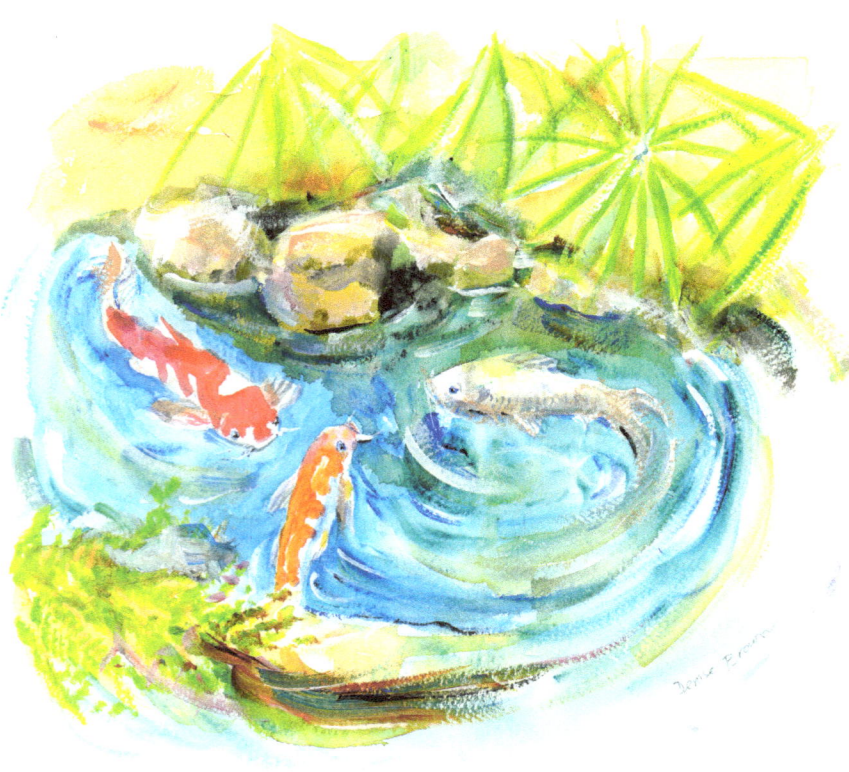

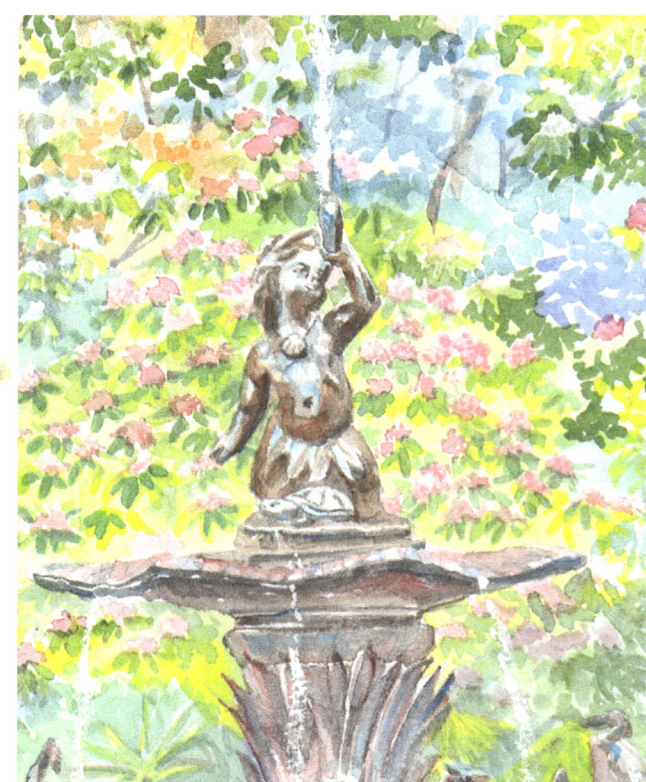

Fuller Gardens,
North Hampton

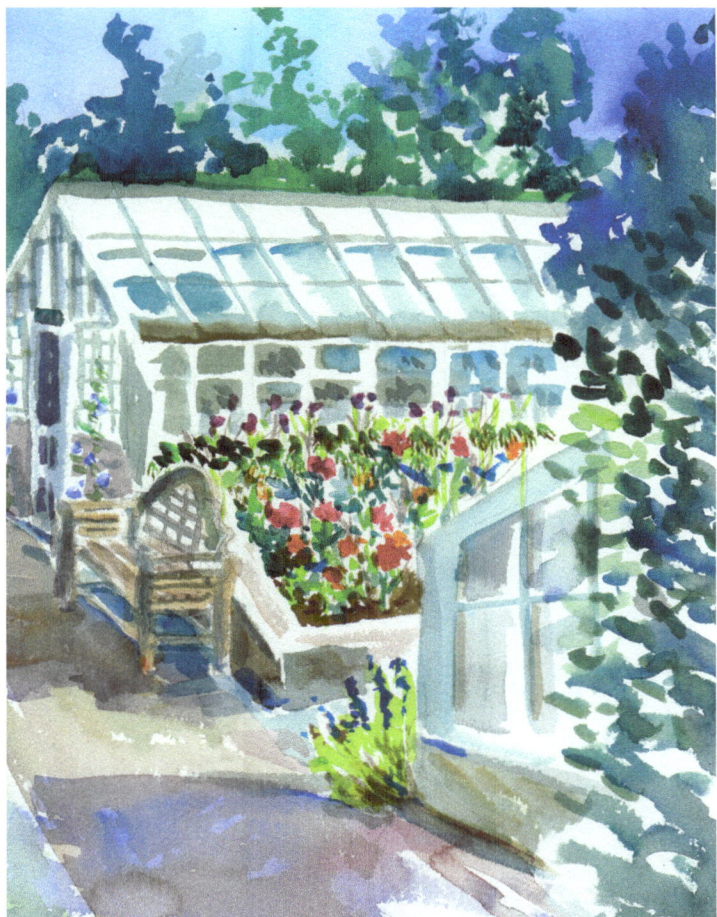

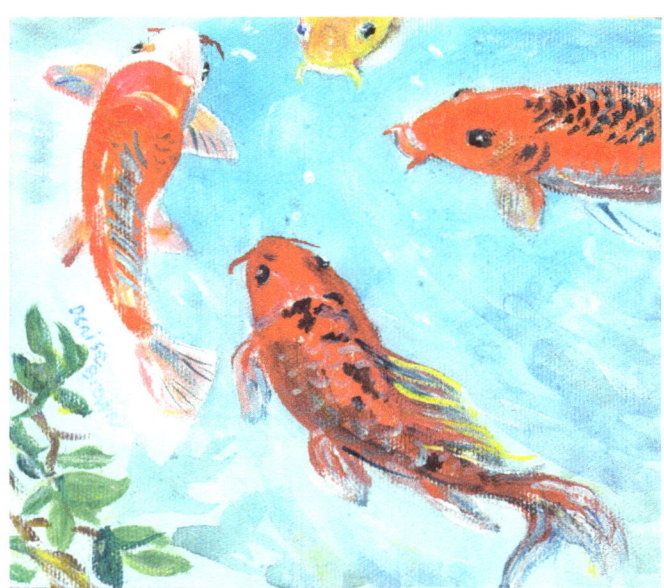

Koi at Fuller Gardens

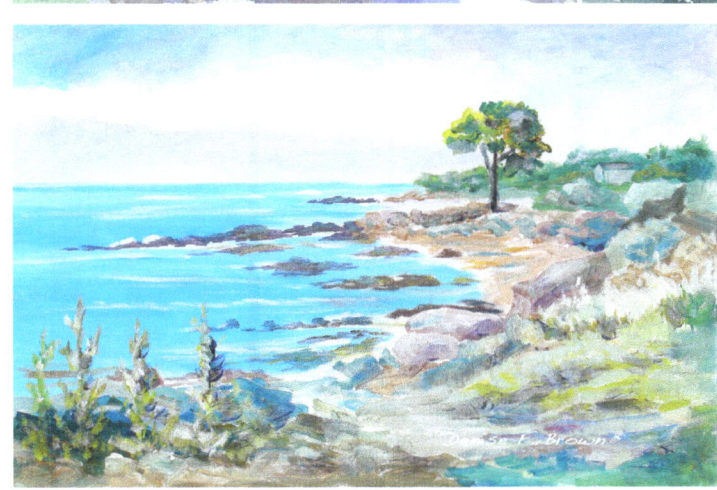

New Castle Commons

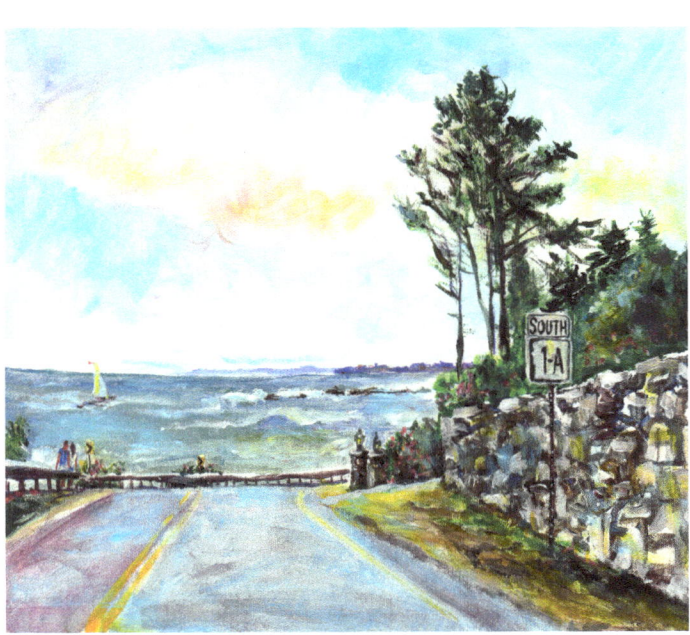

Route 1A Curve, North Hampton

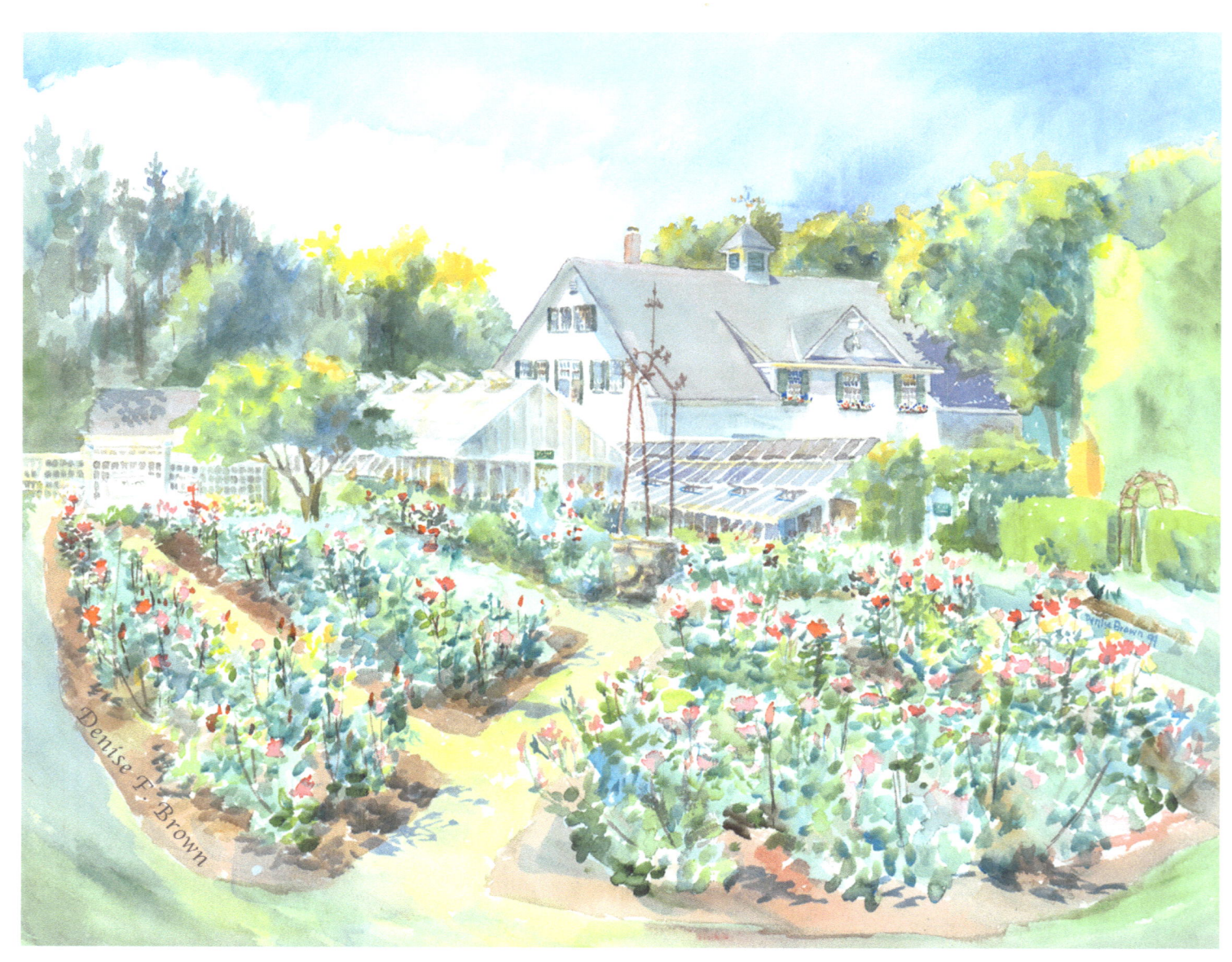

Fuller Gardens

Tip #9:
Practice, practice, and more practice...

It starts with a few doodles and scratches, a few tips and classes, some more art lessons, and a lifetime of observation to learn how to draw and learn how to paint.

Art is something that becomes part of your existence and a quest to paint that masterpiece. Yes, some people are "born with" a natural gift, but most artists learn as they go, and with each painting that they work on.

It is something for young and old, rich and not so rich.

The excitement of painting and its rewards last forever.

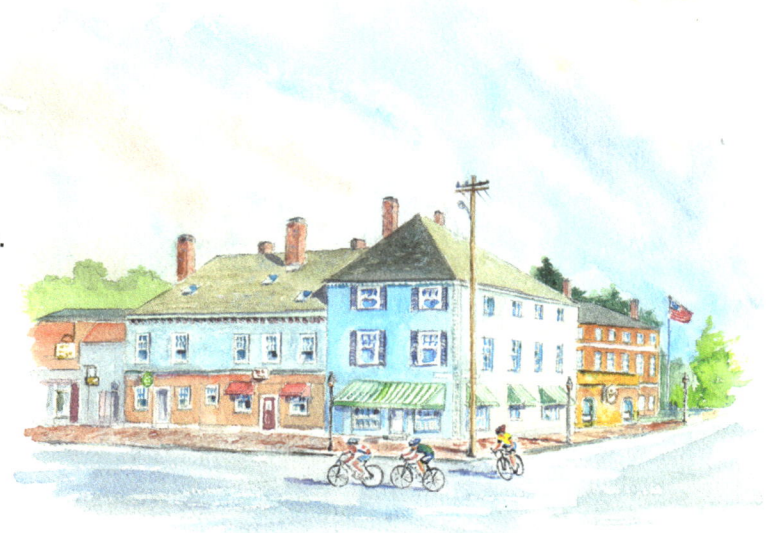

Marple Real Estate Corner

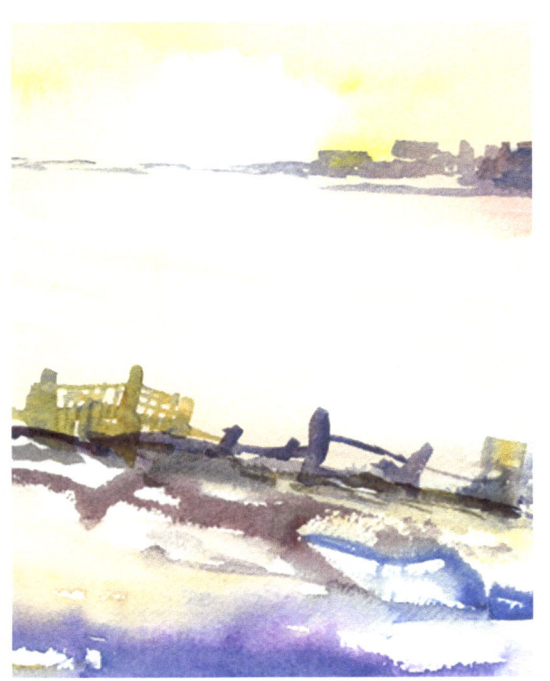

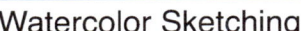

Watercolor Sketching

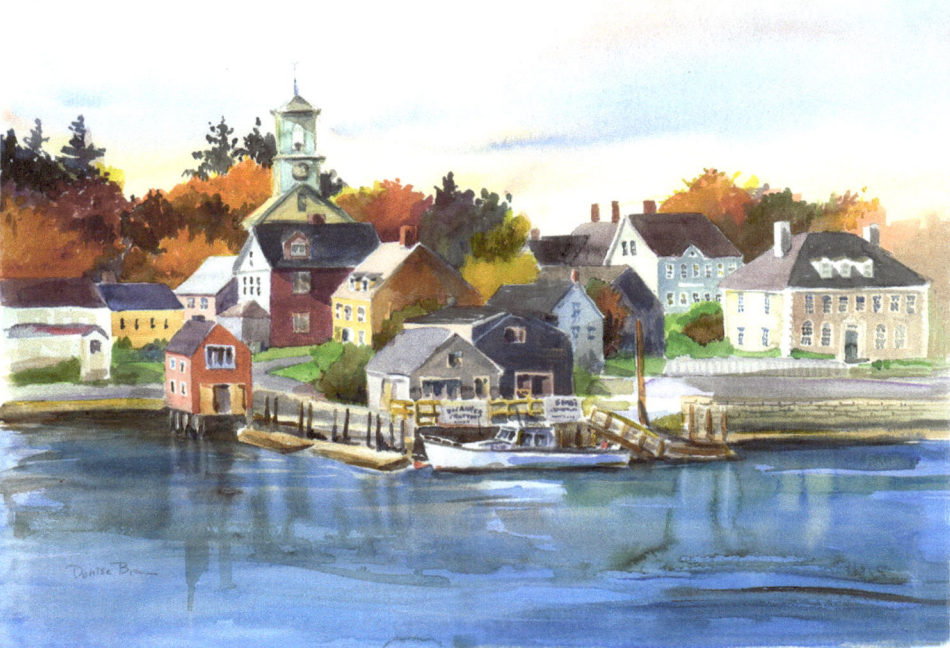

Portsmouth Waterfront

Portsmouth

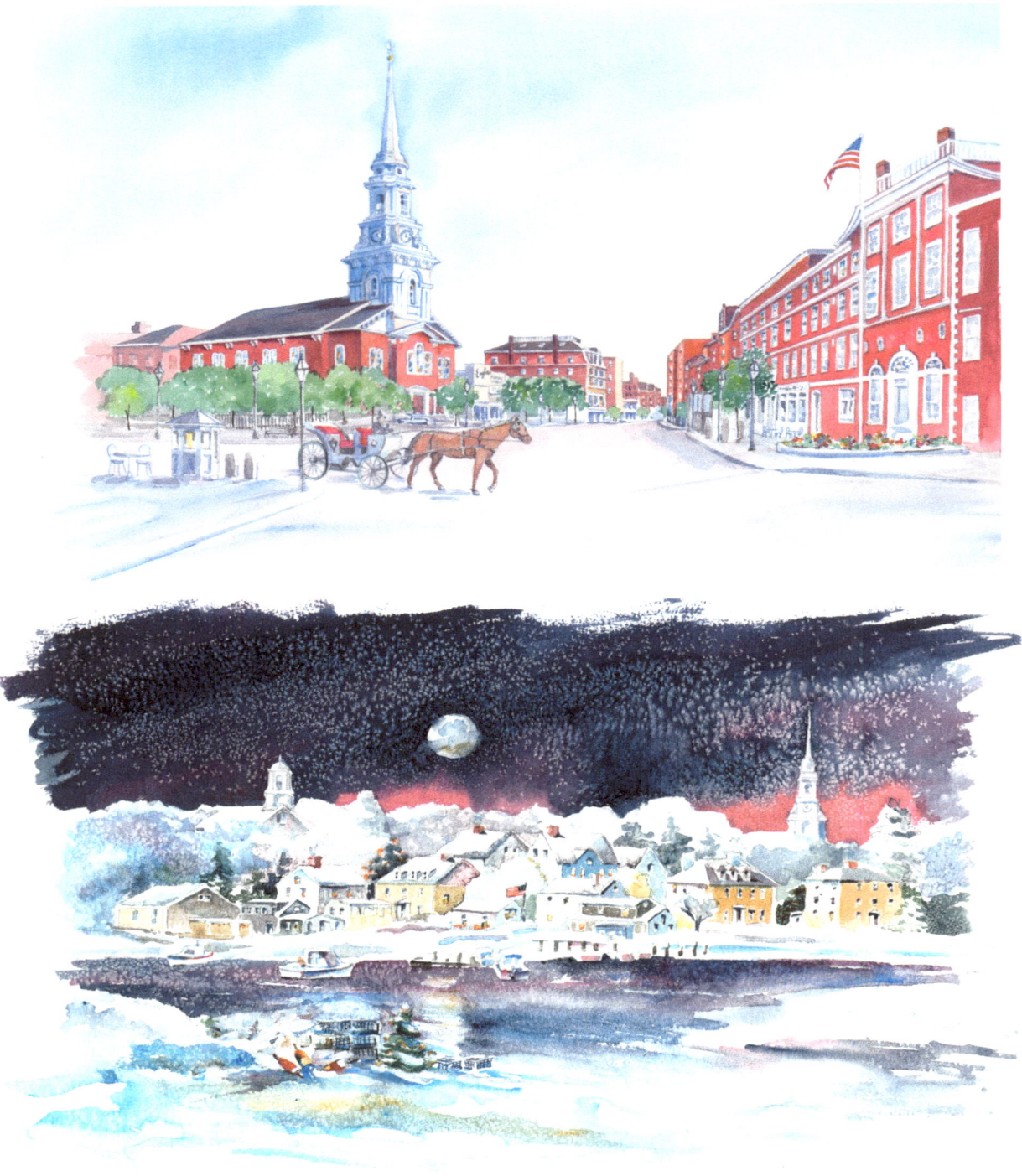

Portsmouth

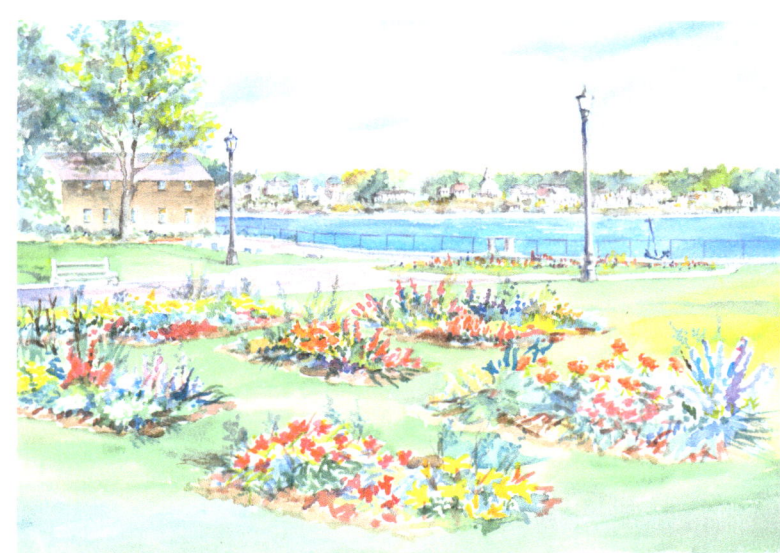

Prescott Park Gardens

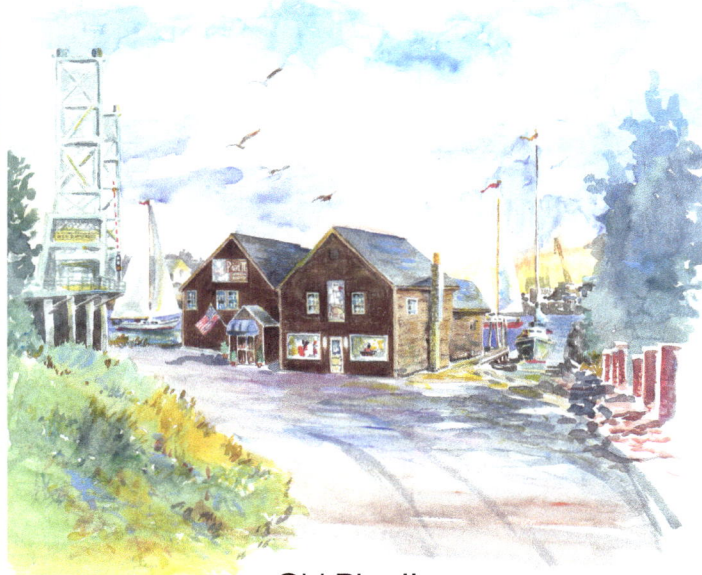

Old Pier II

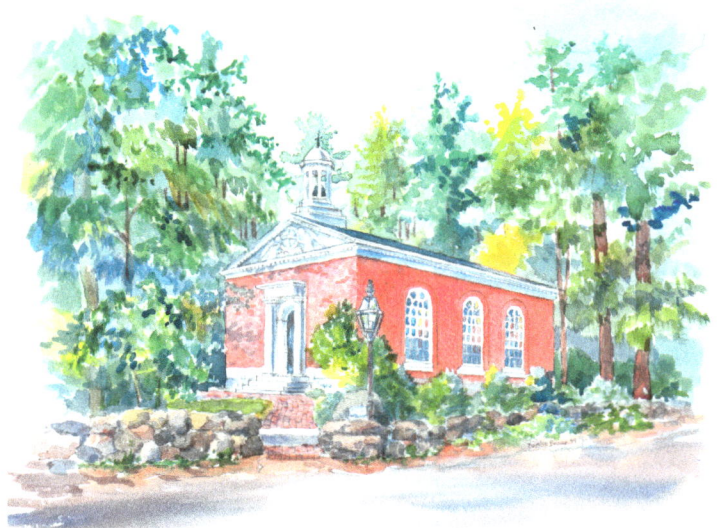

Little Harbor Chapel

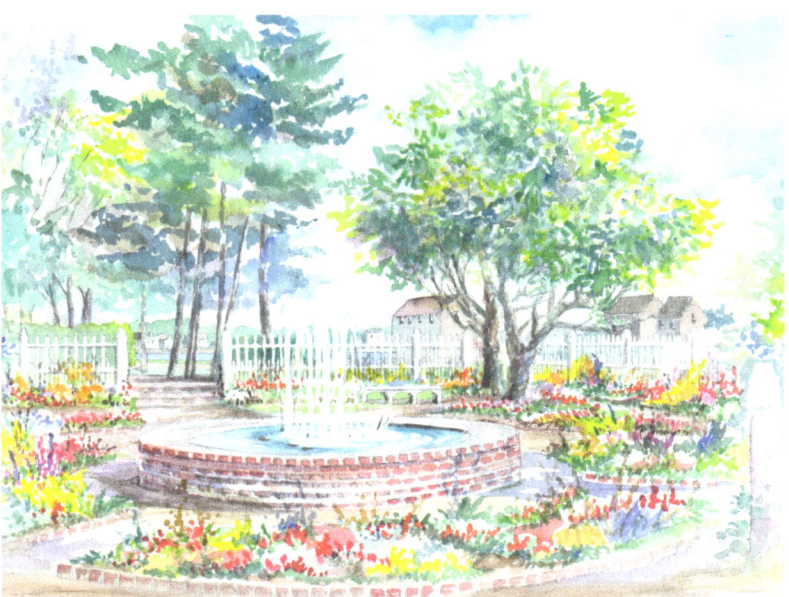

Prescott Park Fountain

Portsmouth

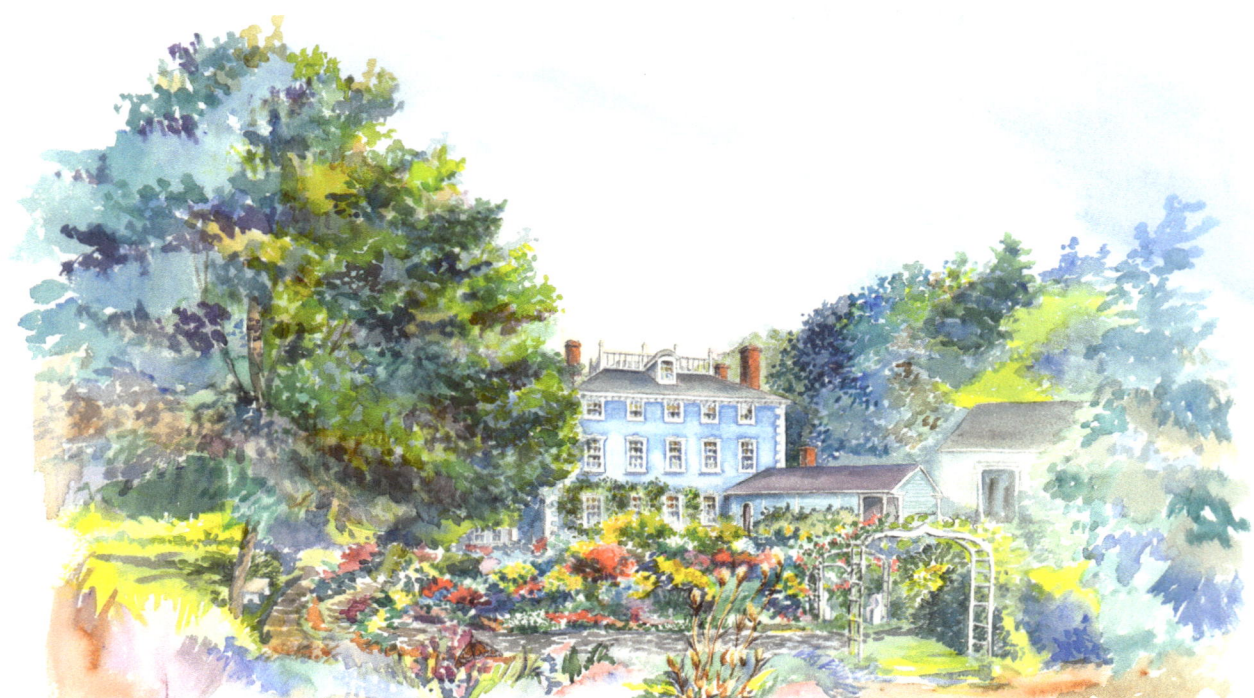

Moffatt-Ladd House and Garden

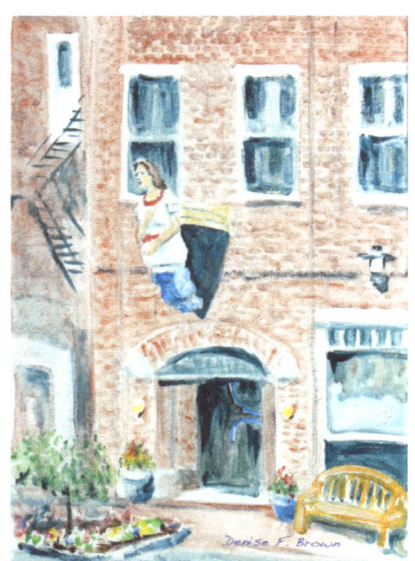

Bowsprit on Bow Street

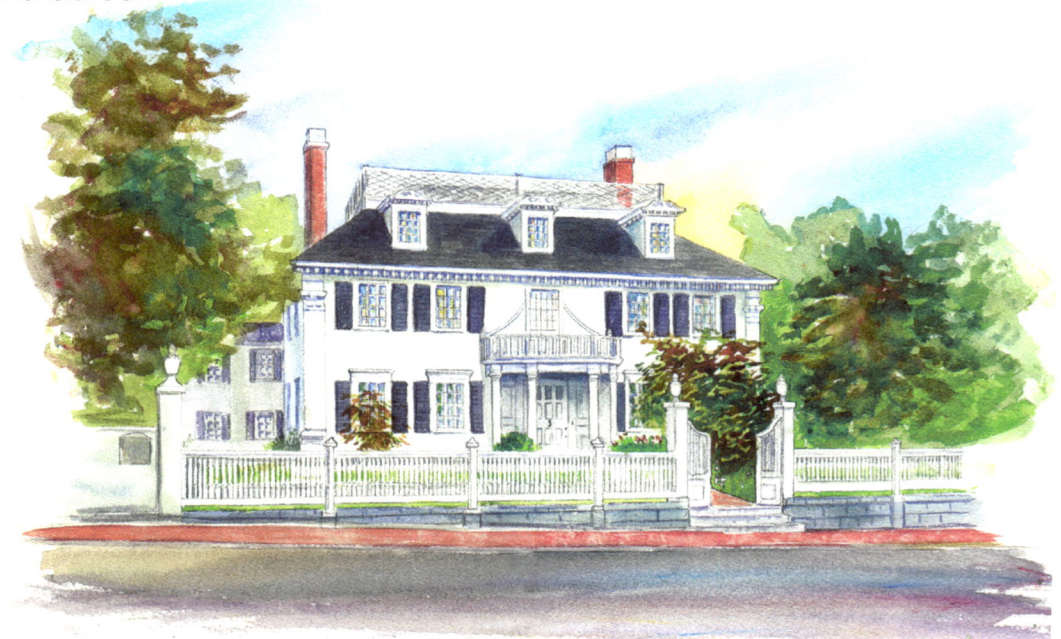

Governor John Langdon House

Portsmouth

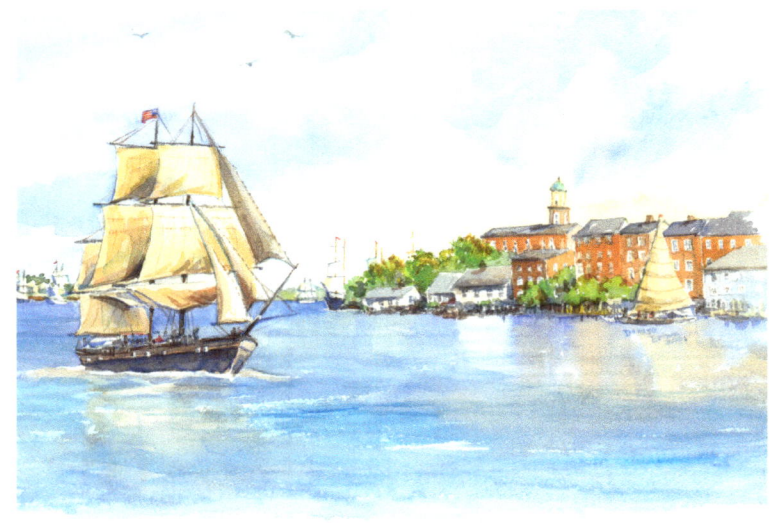

The Ranger Ship

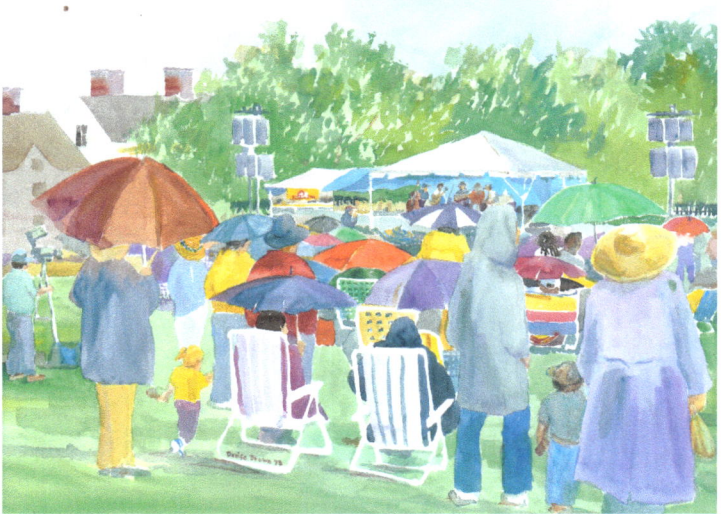

Rainy Jazz Fest at Strawbery Banke

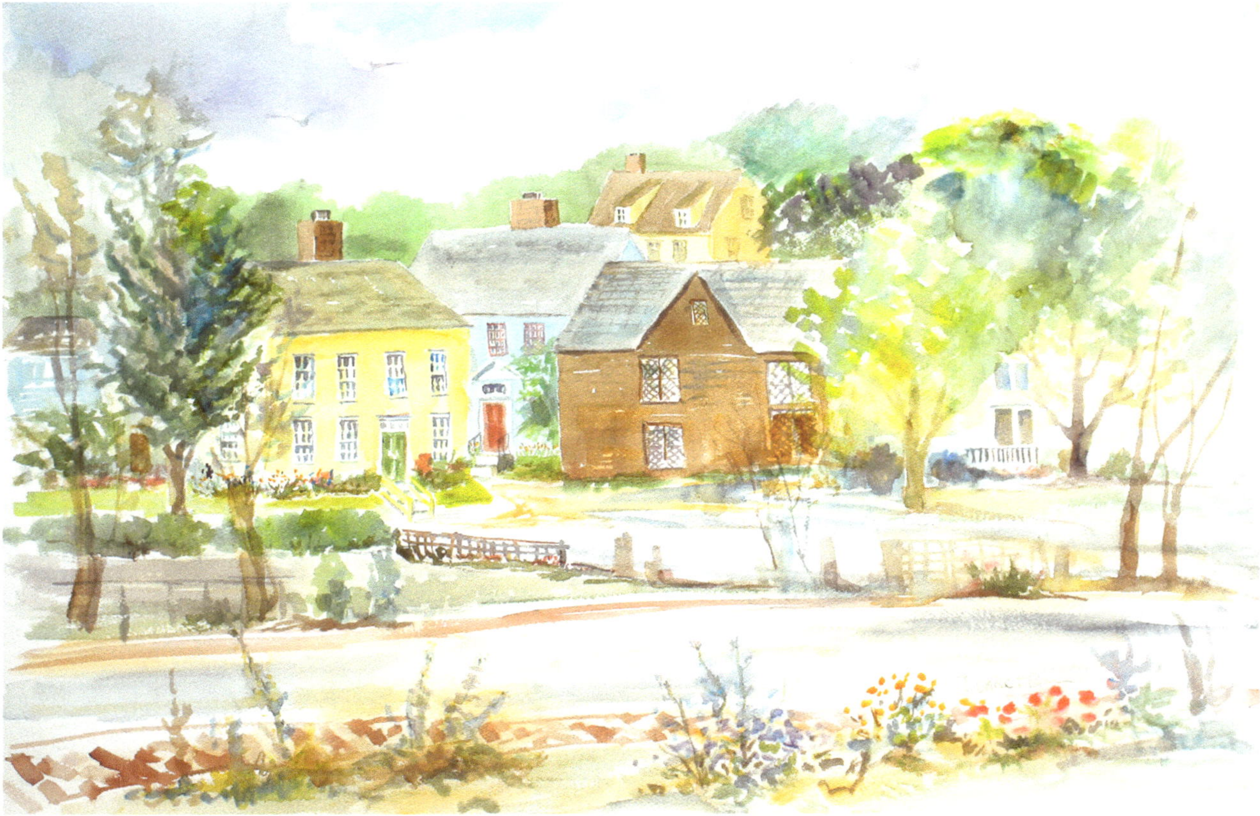

Strawbery Banke, Portsmouth

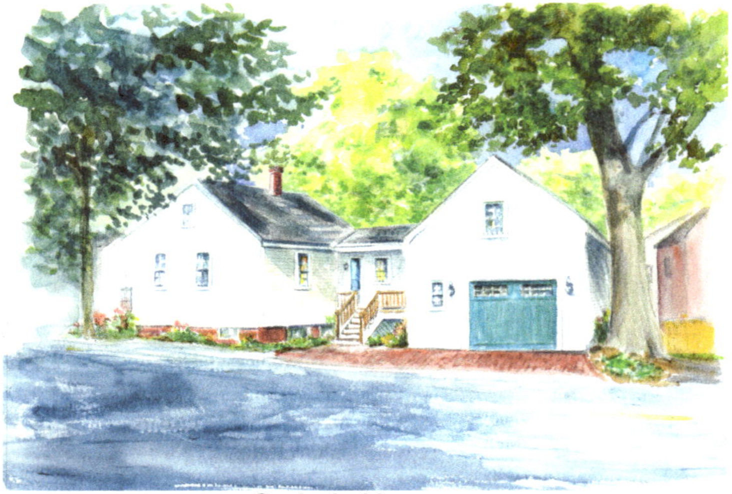

Portsmouth

Cathy's House

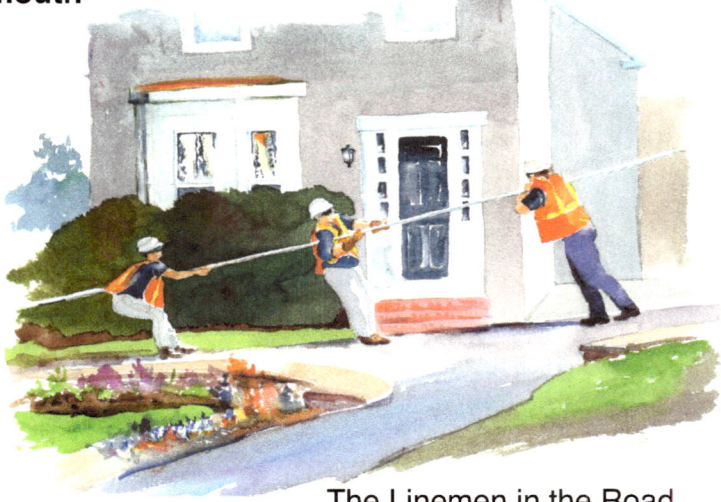

The Linemen in the Road

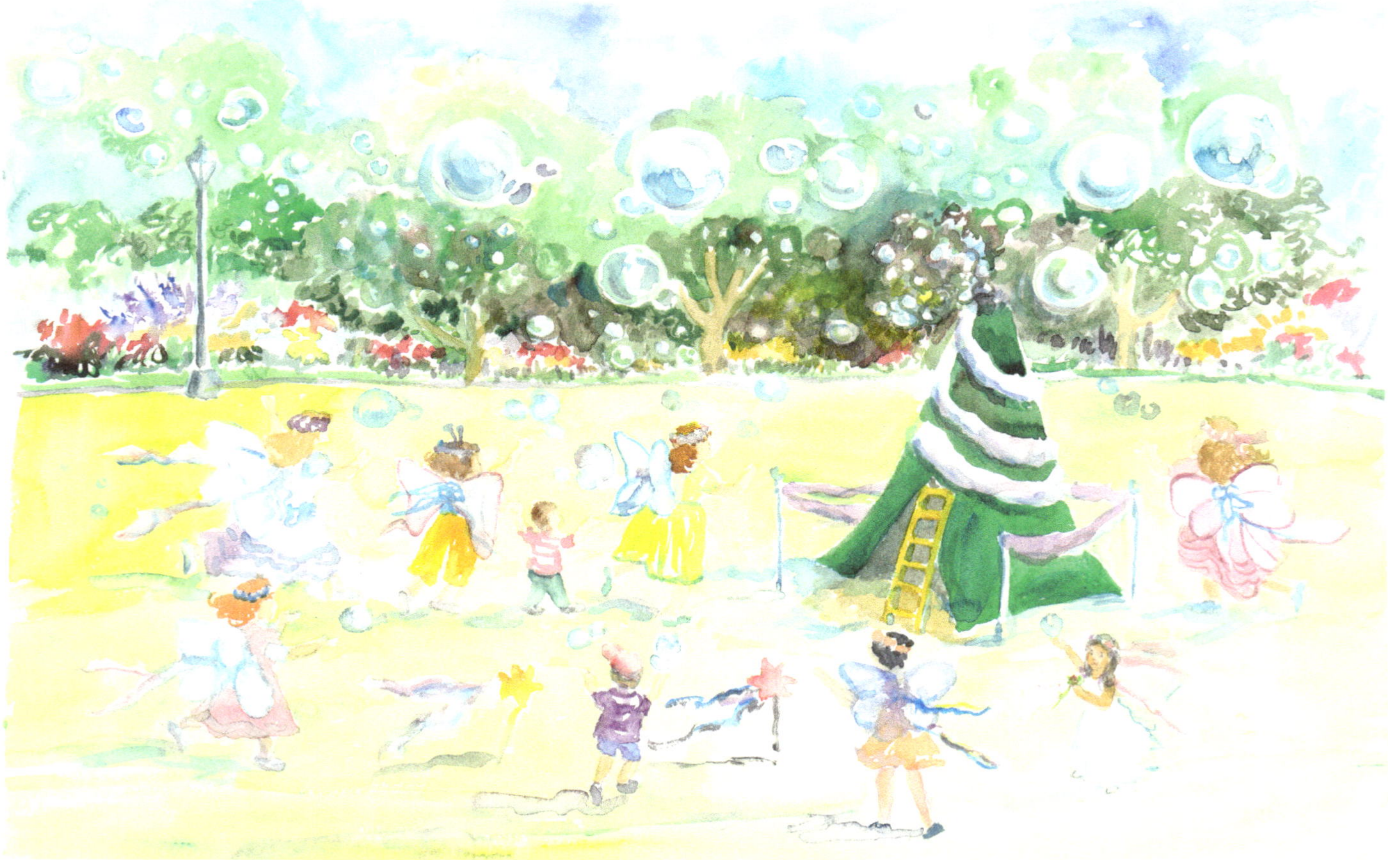

Fairy Garden Tour, Portsmouth

North Hampton, New Hampshire

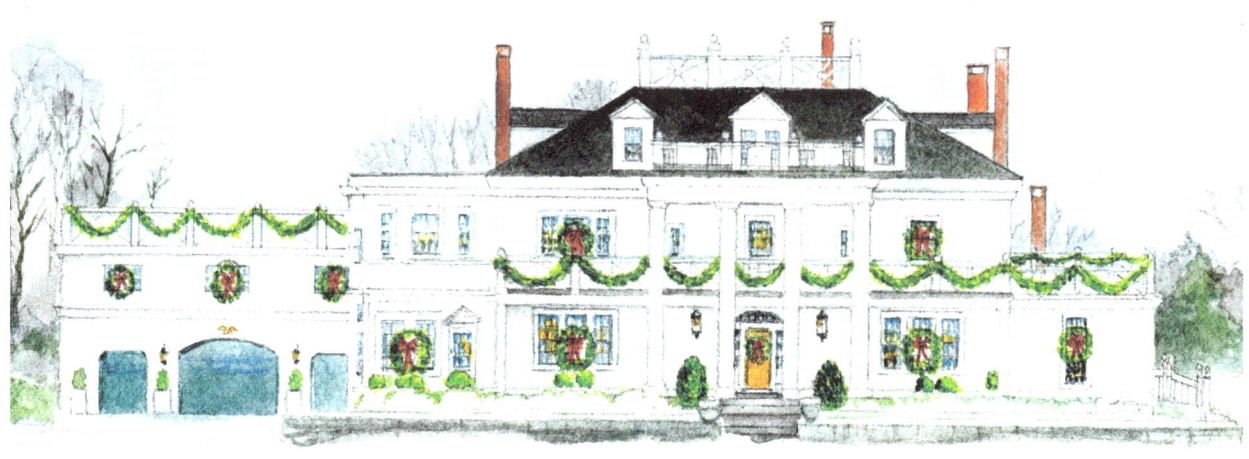

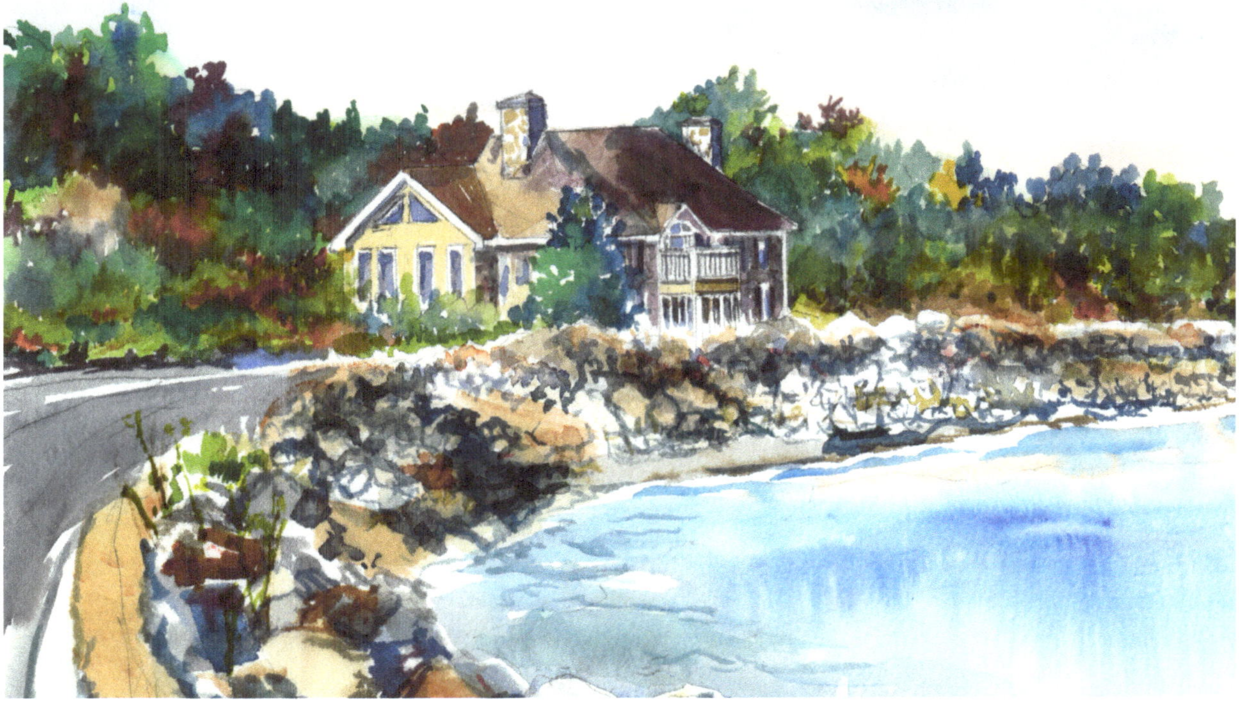

No Rules...
Tip #10:
Rules in art are meant to be broken.

Don't worry about all the "how to draw or paint" instructions. You might discover something brilliant that no one has tried before. Experiment with compositions, colors and shapes. Try different media.

I enjoy using water media like watercolors, acrylics, and water-based oils, and they are better for the environment, but other artists will use nothing but oils or pastels. Artists often continue to work with what is in their studio, because it is costly to start over with a new medium. It's up to you to choose what medium motivates you to keep painting and be successful.

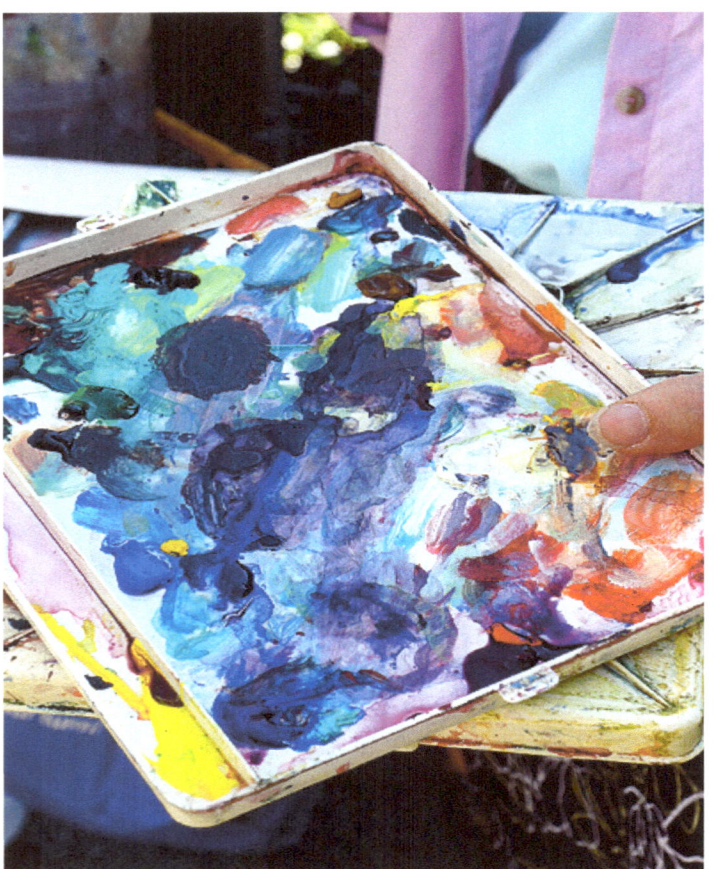

I'm a messy painter. Other artists need to have all of their colors lined up in rows in strick palettes. I find mixing paints on the palette verses on the board changes the way colors look in a painting. On the board, results often become exciting combinations and happy accidents worth keeping.

You can use many of your messy paint mixings throughout your painting to unify the colors. Add a bit of each color to the sky or the shadows, or in the trees, and see what colors work together for pleasing effects.

Remember, a sky is rarely just a blue sky. A tree is rarely just a green tree. A rock is rarely just a gray rock. Study your subjects and you will begin to see colors that non artists don't see. Sometimes someone who looks at your painting will ask you, "How did you see that color." I usually say, "Well, it's just there."

Maritime Icons

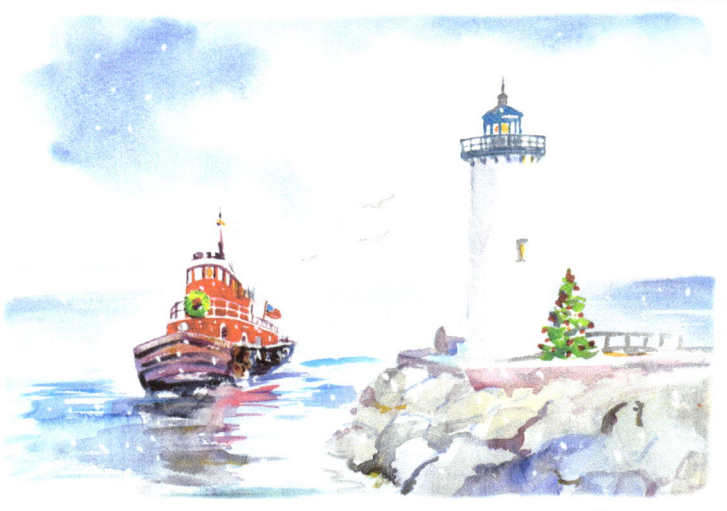

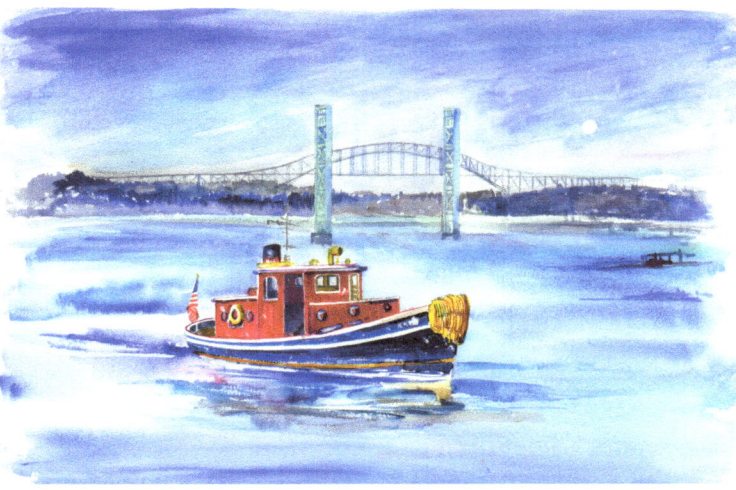

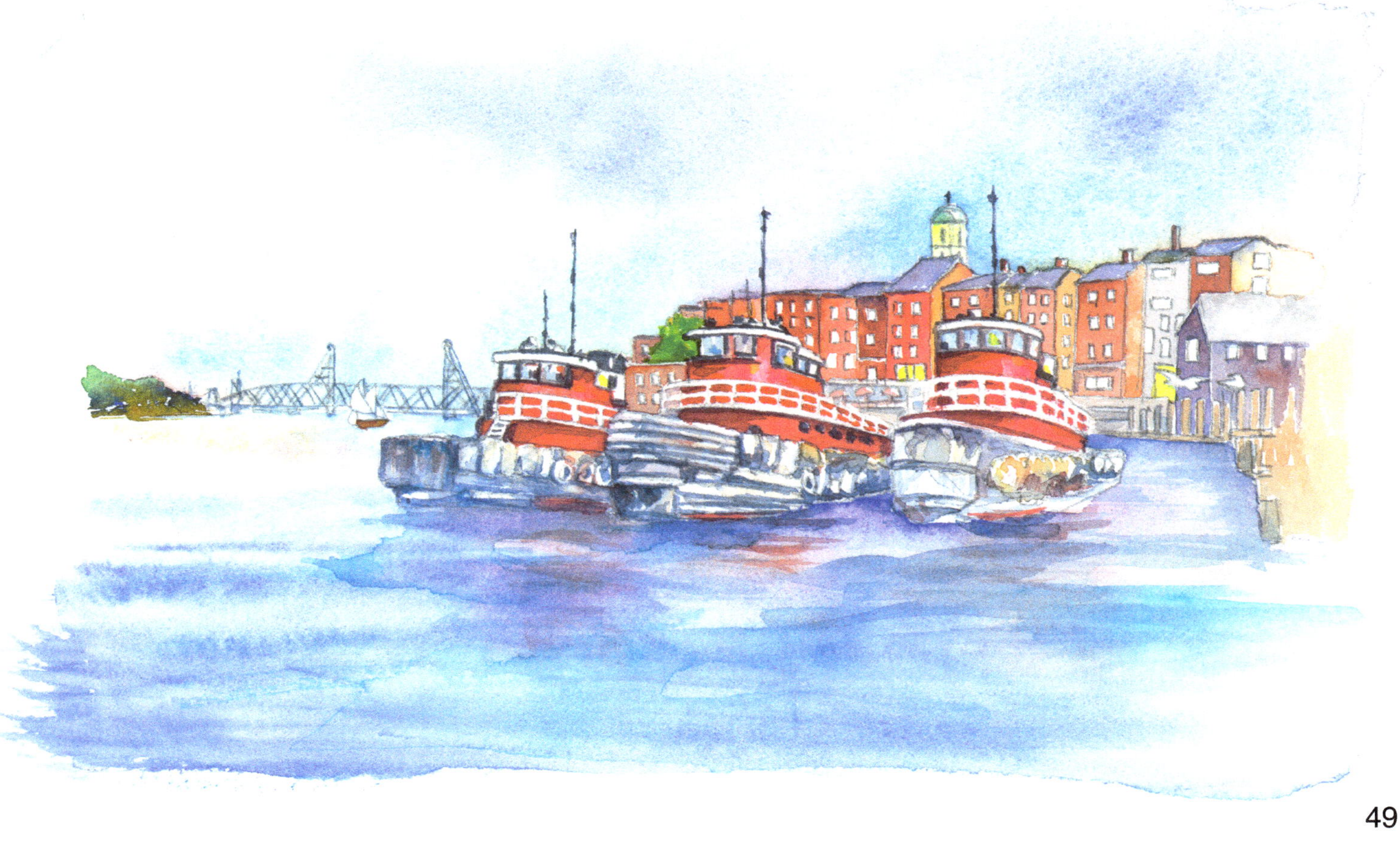

Local Lighthouse Icons

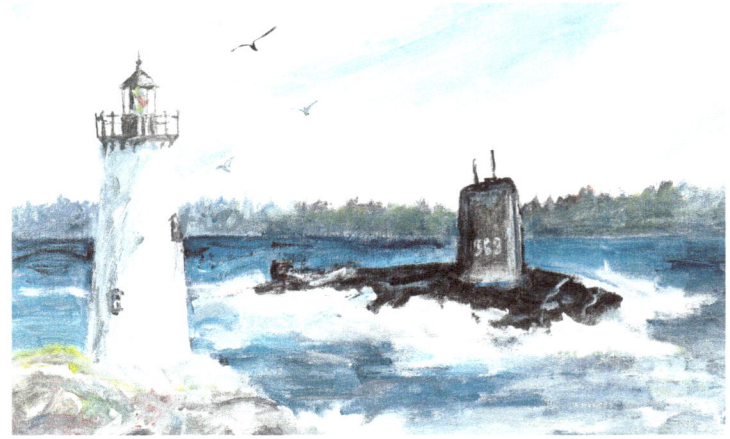

U.S.S Albacore Submarine

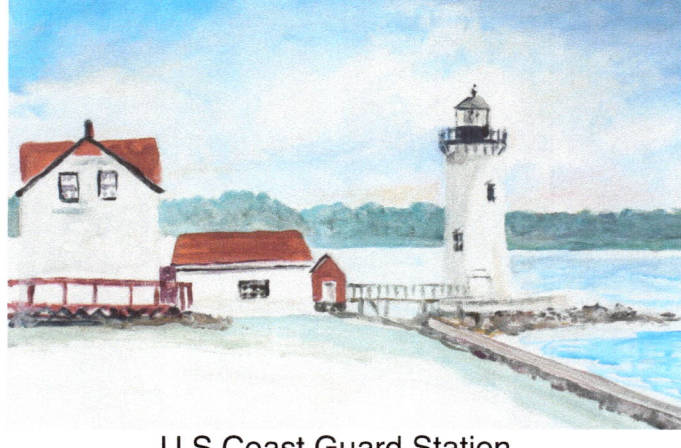

U.S.Coast Guard Station

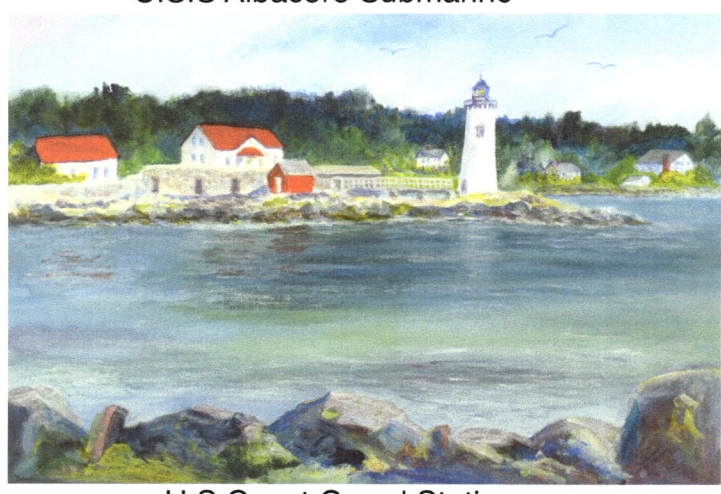

U.S.Coast Guard Station

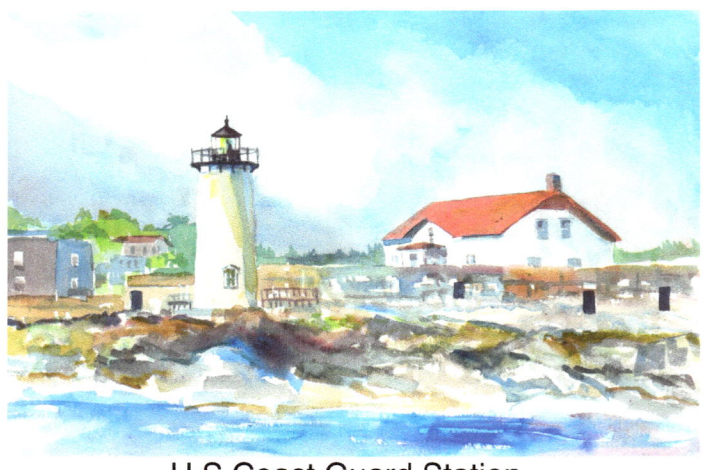

U.S.Coast Guard Station

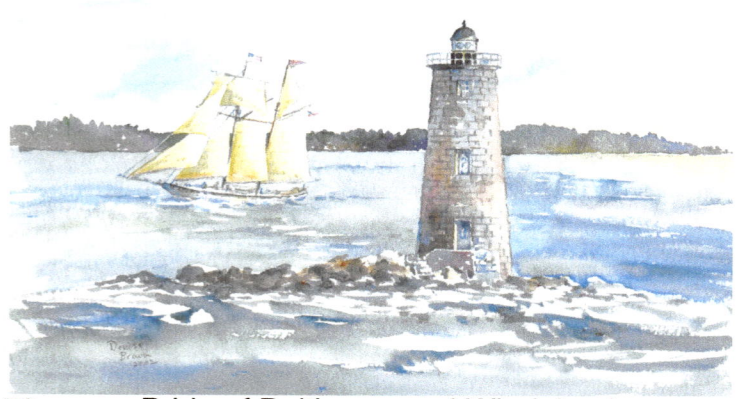

Pride of Baltimore and Whaleback

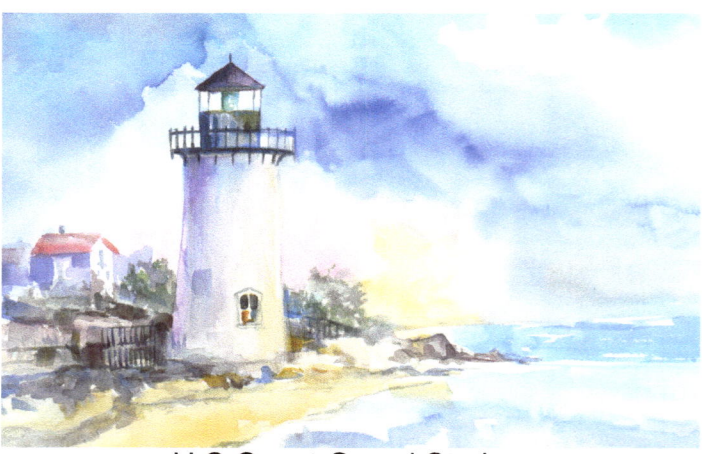

U.S.Coast Guard Station

Tugboats and the Memorial Bridge Paintings for Holiday Cards

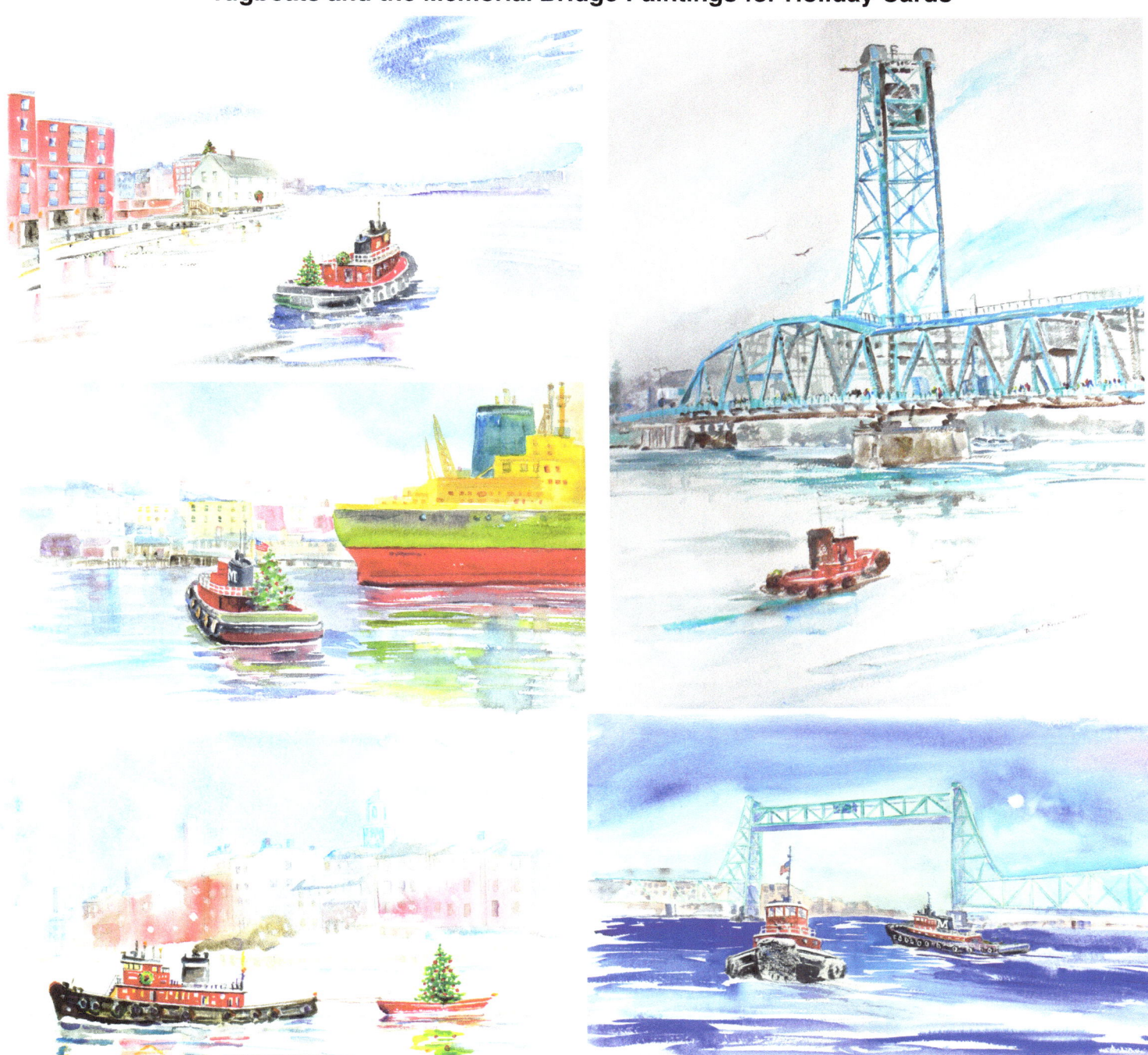

York Harbor, Maine

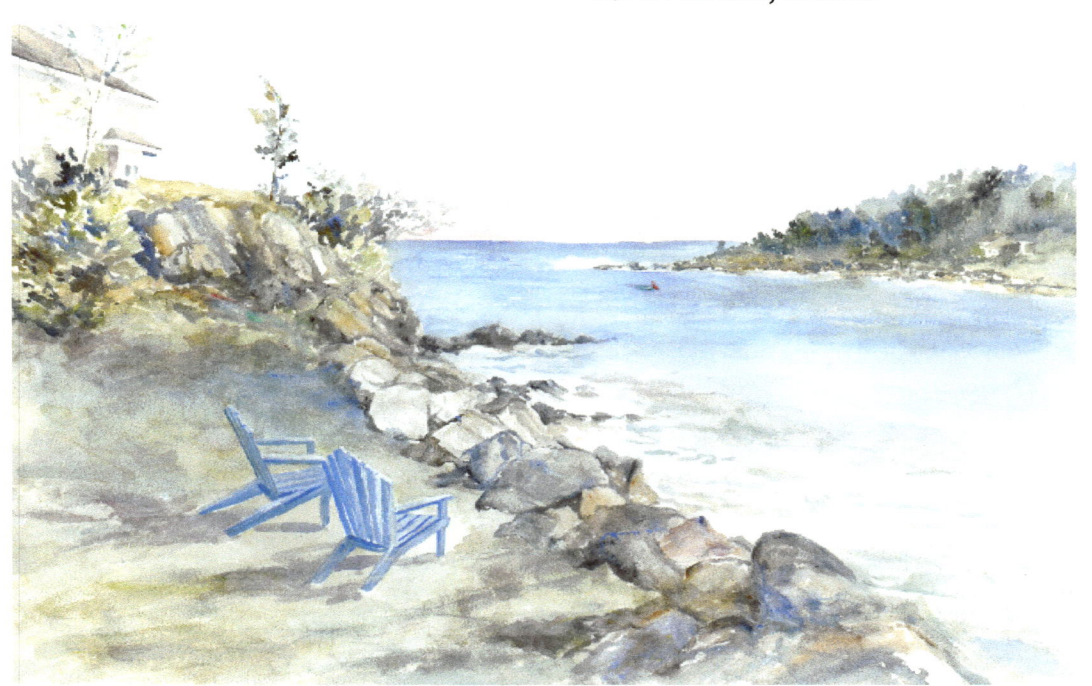

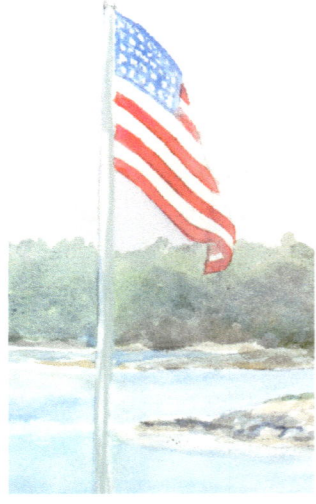

Stage Neck Inn

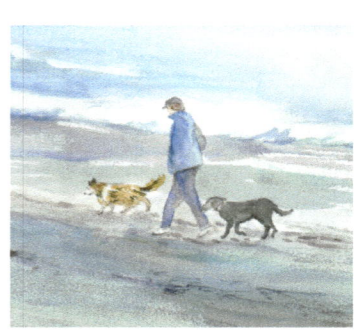

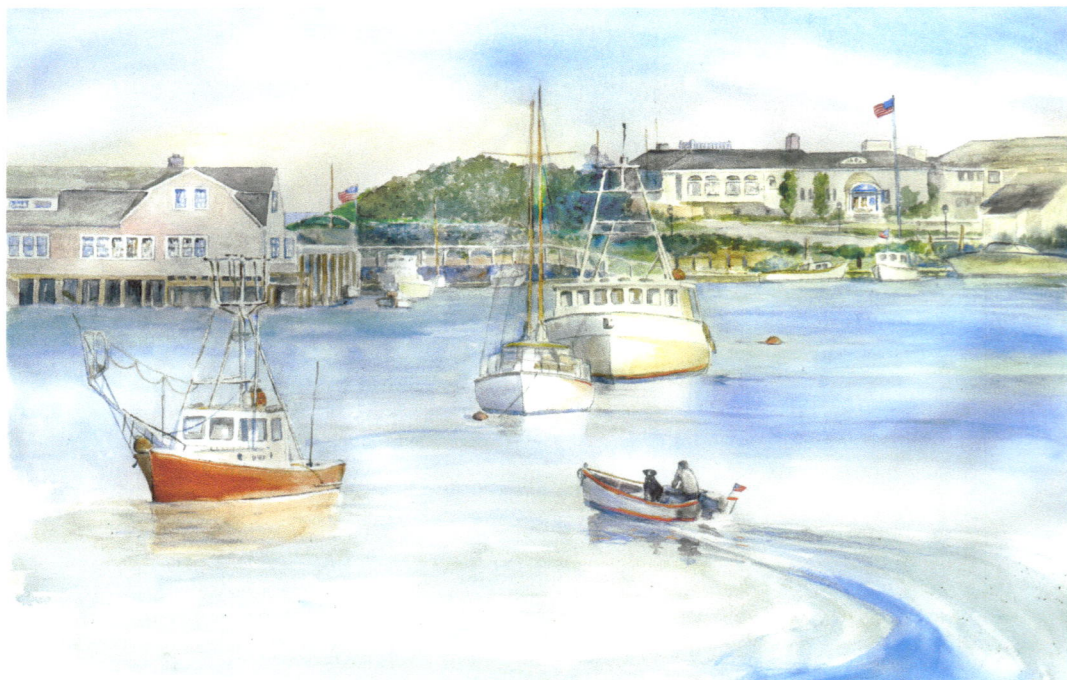

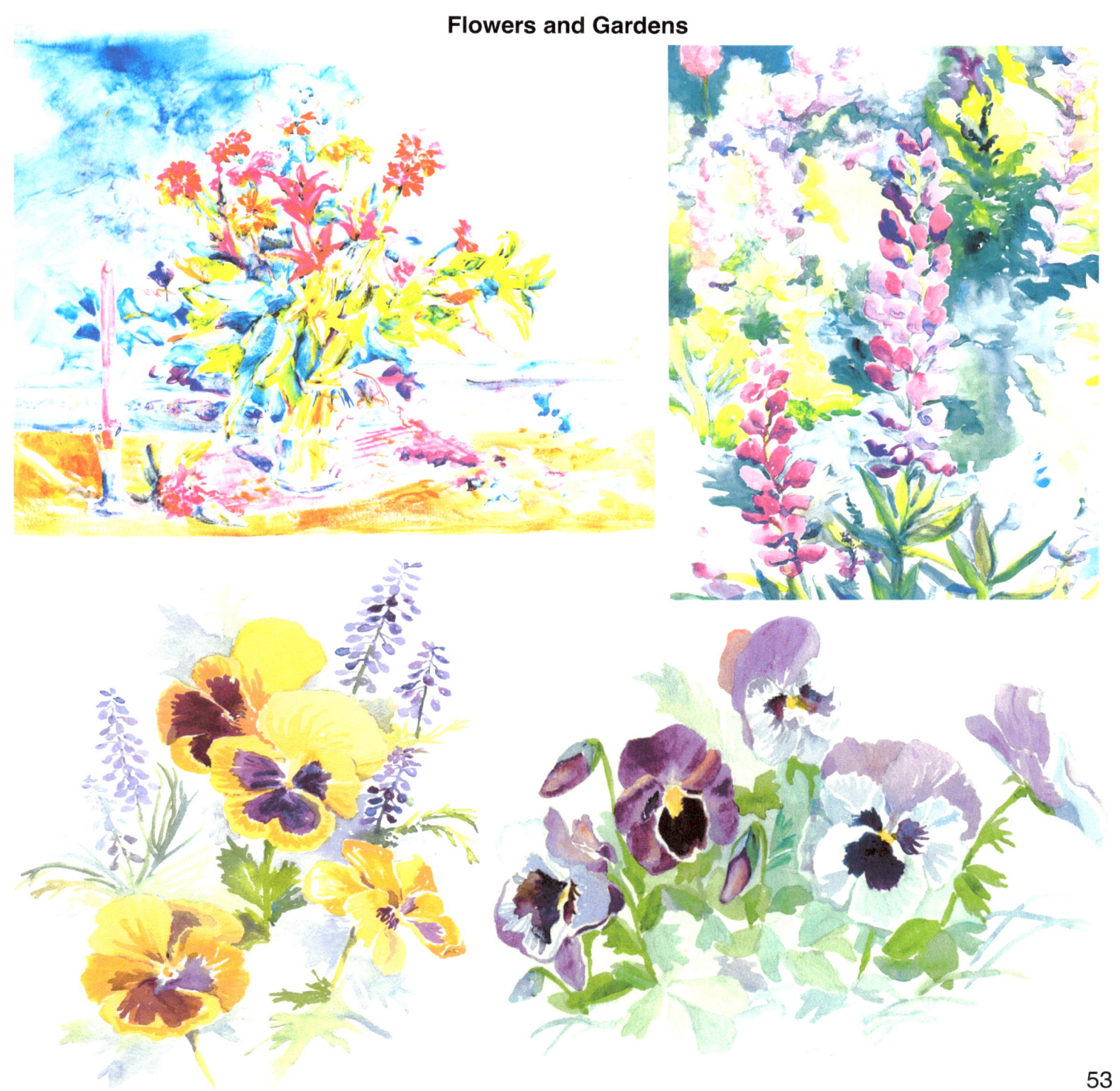

Flowers and Gardens

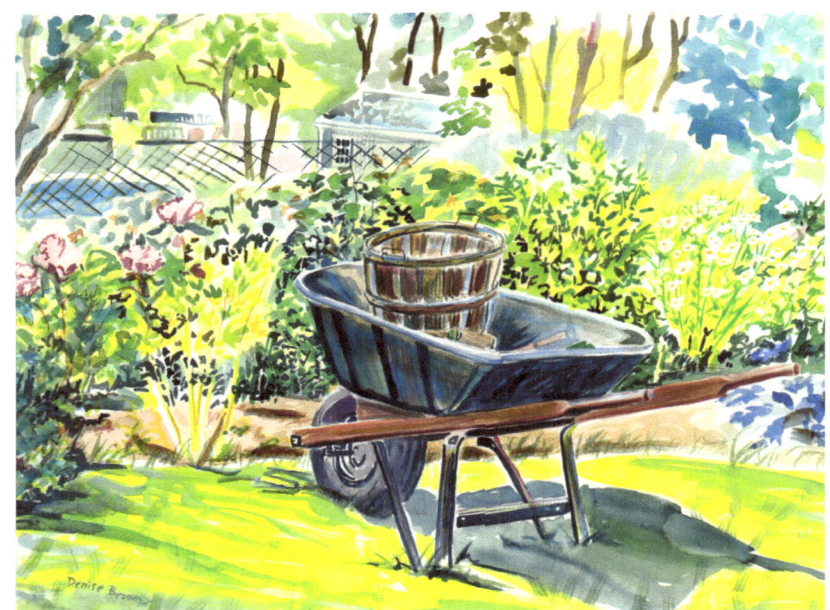

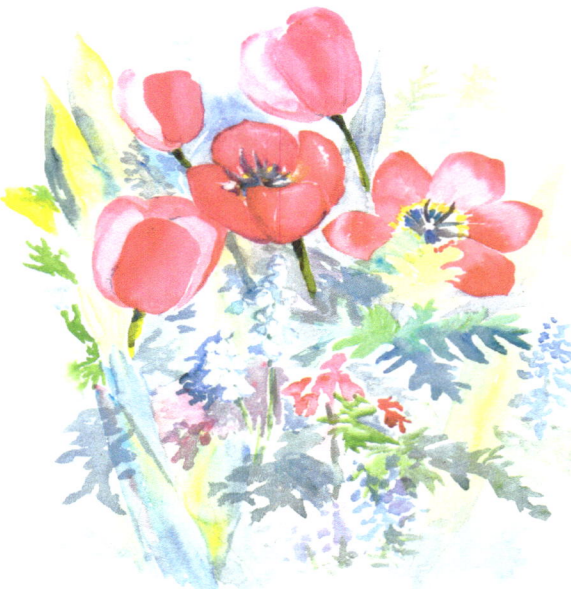

My Wheelbarrow

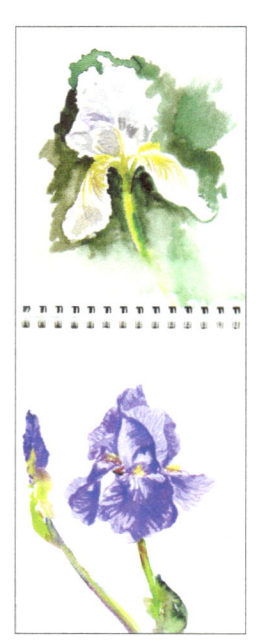

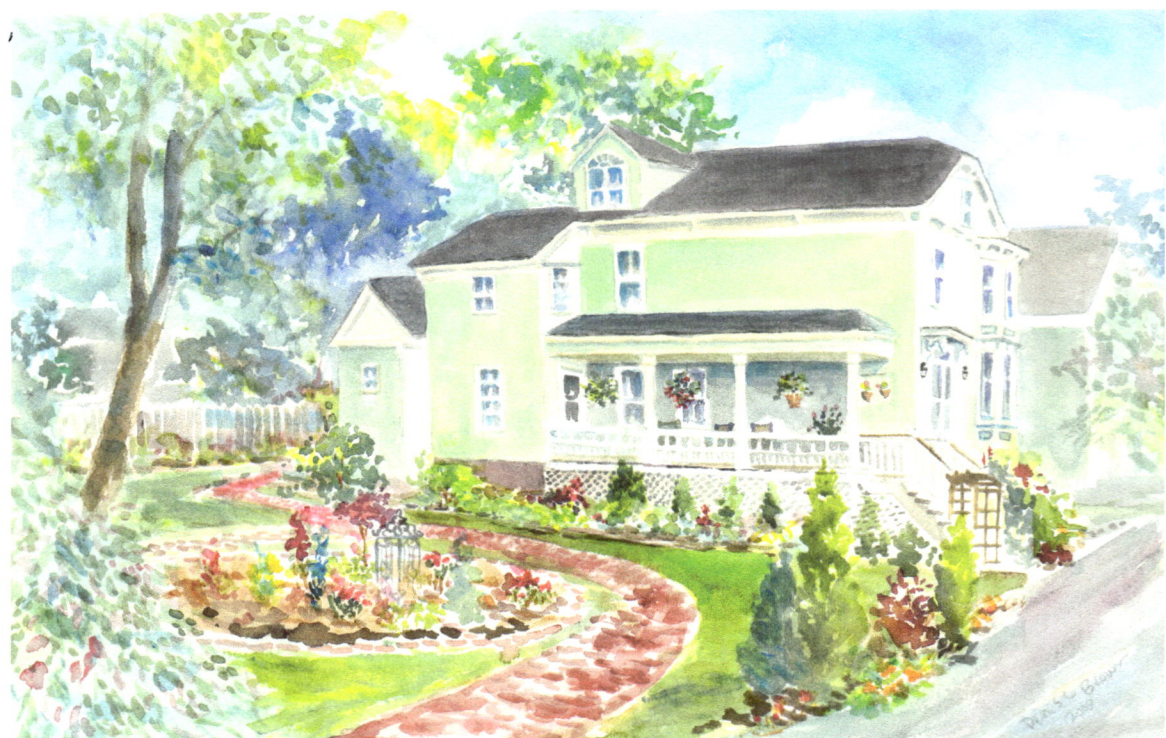

Rachel & Jeffrey's First Garden Tour

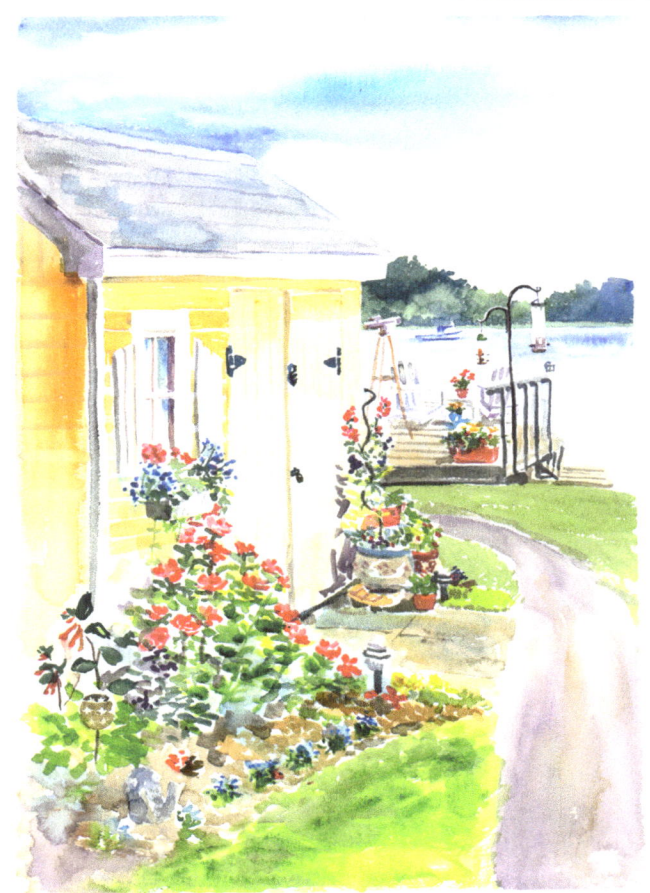

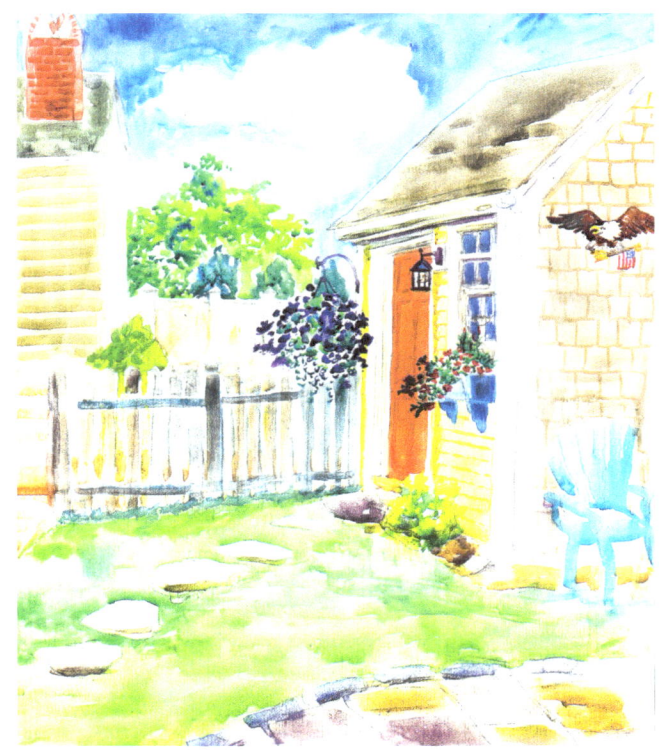

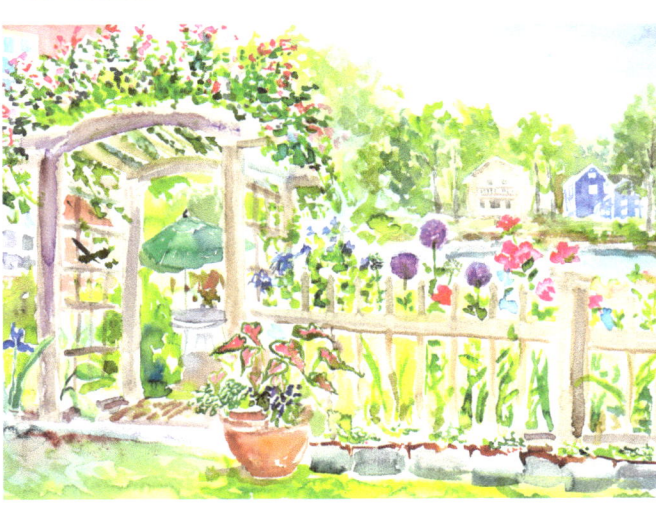

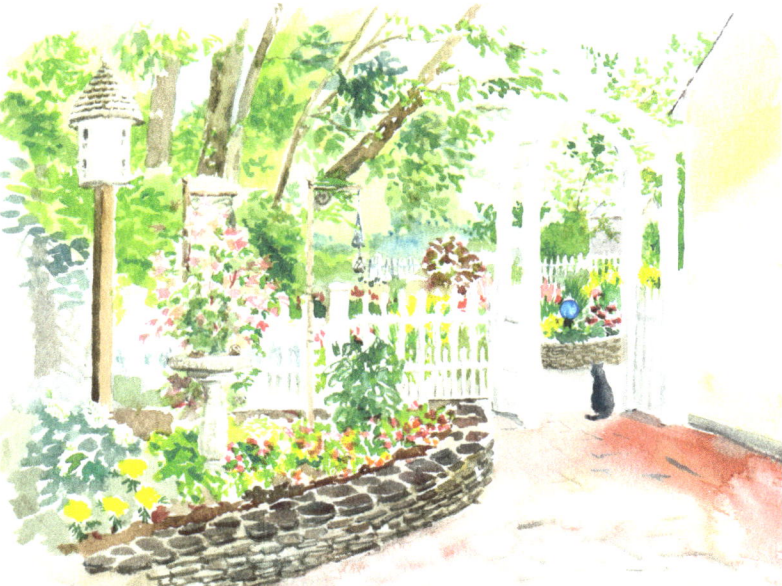

Piscataqua River

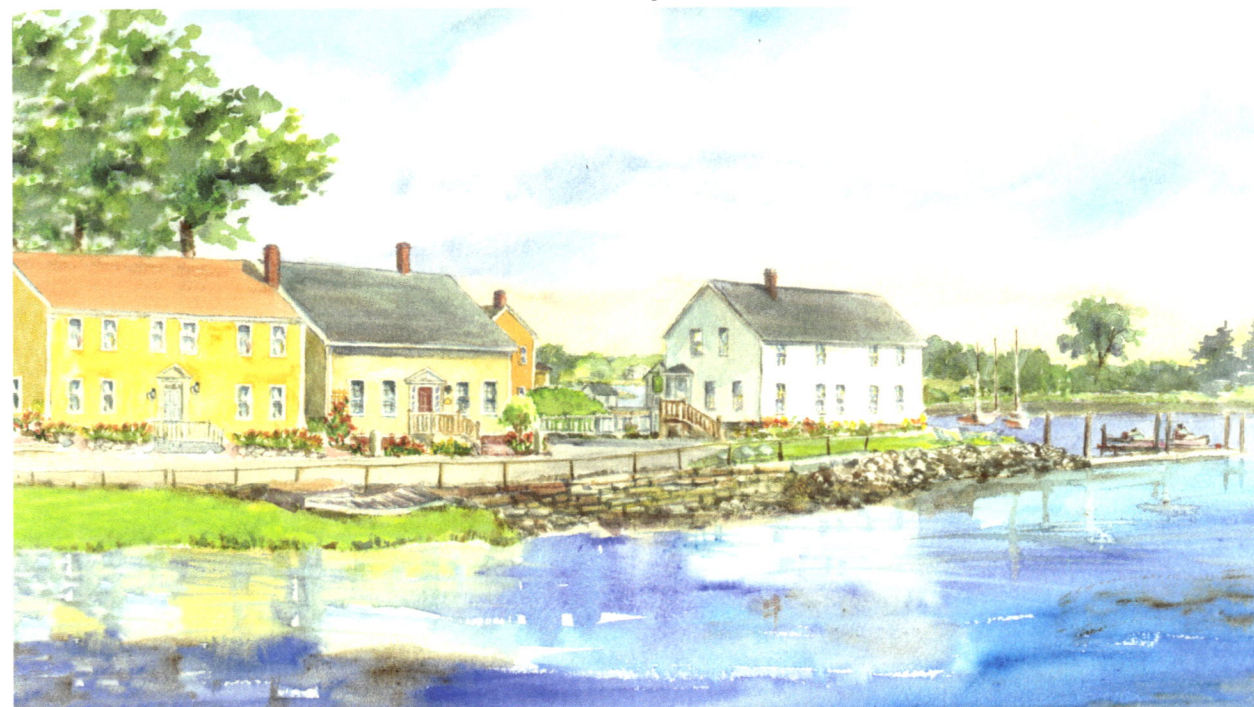

Stuart and Ryan's little house

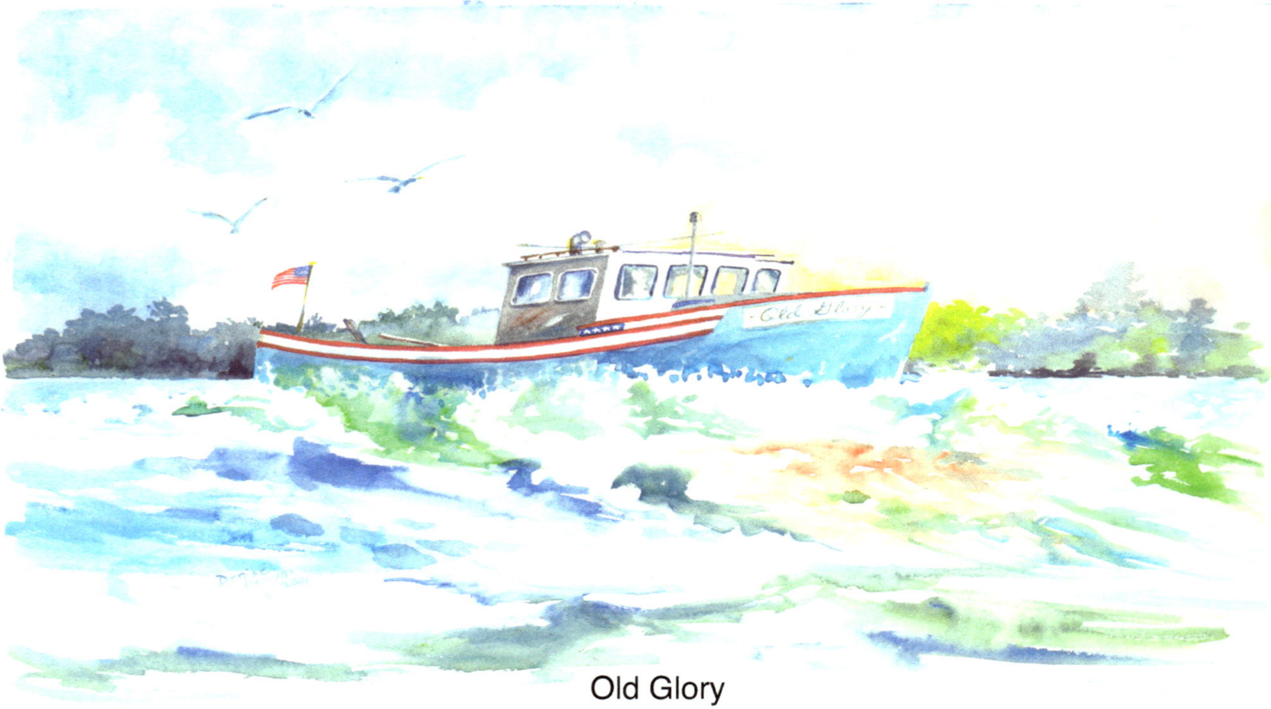

Old Glory

Wentworth-Coolidge Mansion, Portsmouth

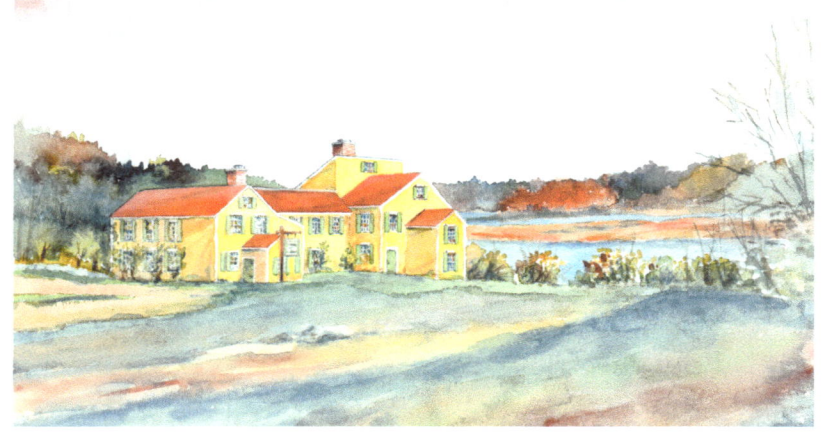

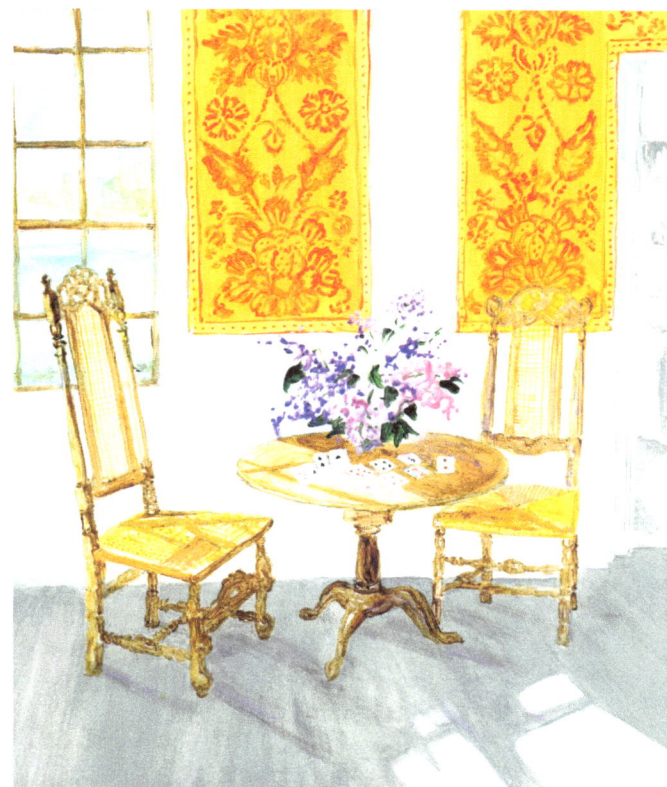

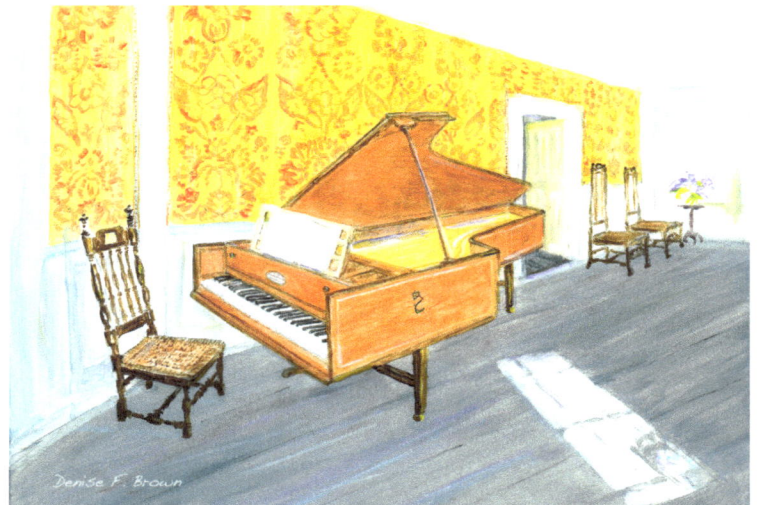

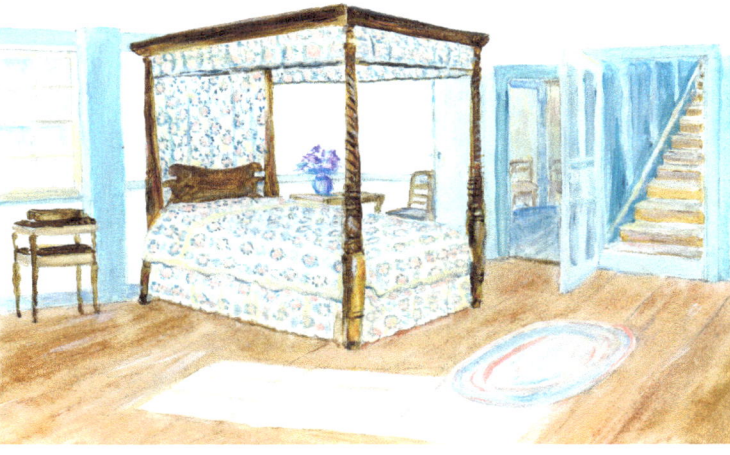

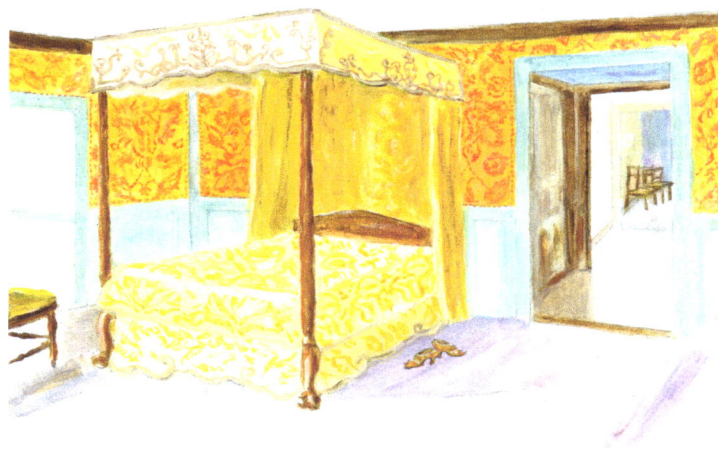

Four Seasons

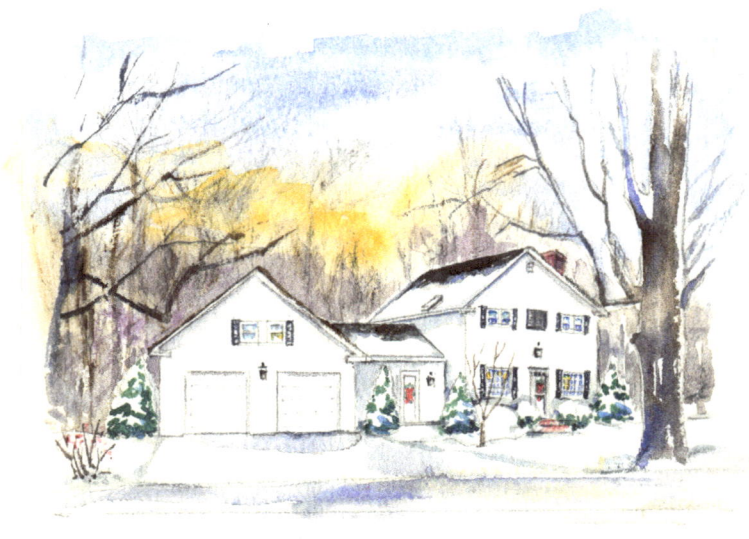

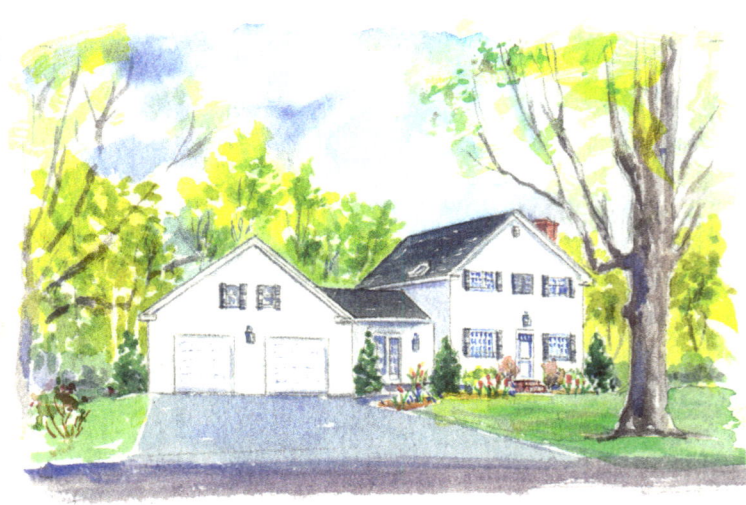

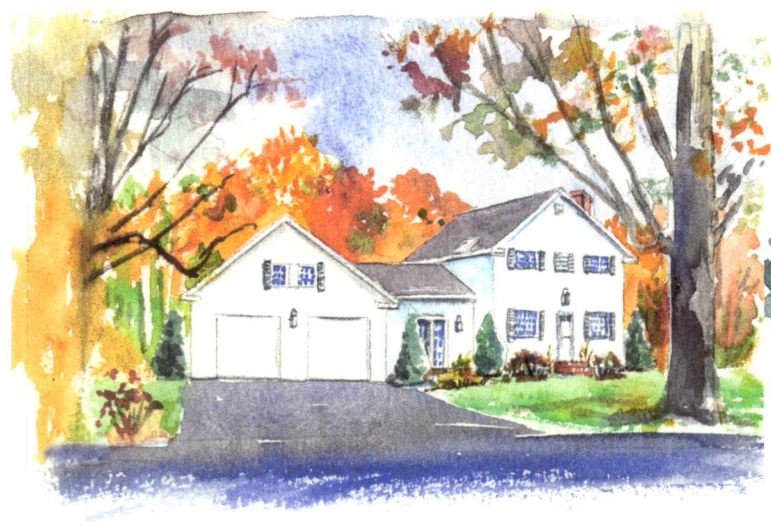

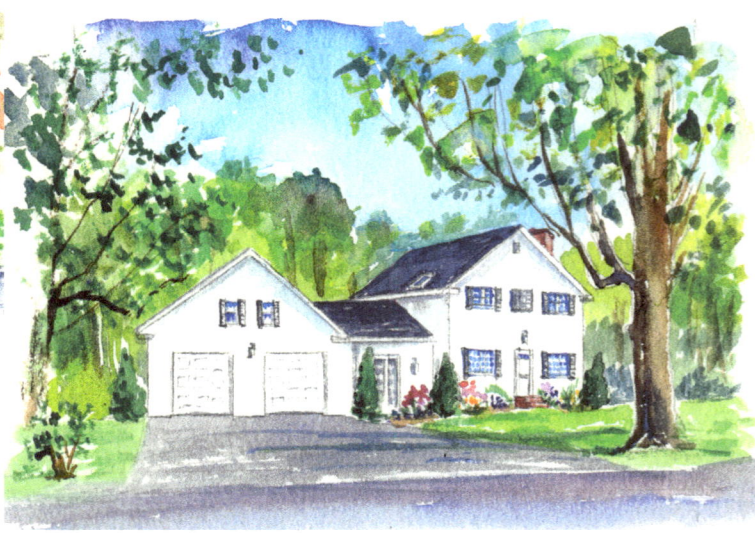

Find Your Style...

Tip #11:

Paint what you like to paint and enjoy it.

Learn as much as you can about whatever subject you like to paint. You might need to study anatomy or architecture or the texture of an animal's fur.

Practice mixing different color combinations and test new papers and brands of paint. Find what works for you. Don't worry about how another artist works or paints. Paint your subject as well as you can, in the style that you choose.

Study, but try not to just copy someone else's work. Your own style will develop with time.

Look for subjects and colors that inspire you. Better artwork will result when you paint for yourself.

If you put your heart and soul into your work, you will find your muse.

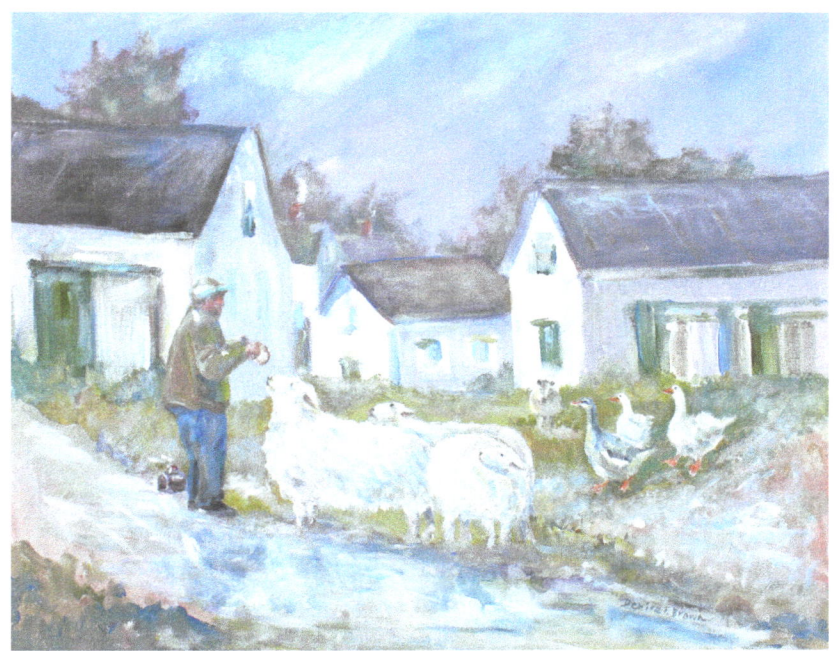

Ruth Griffin's Sheep, Portsmouth

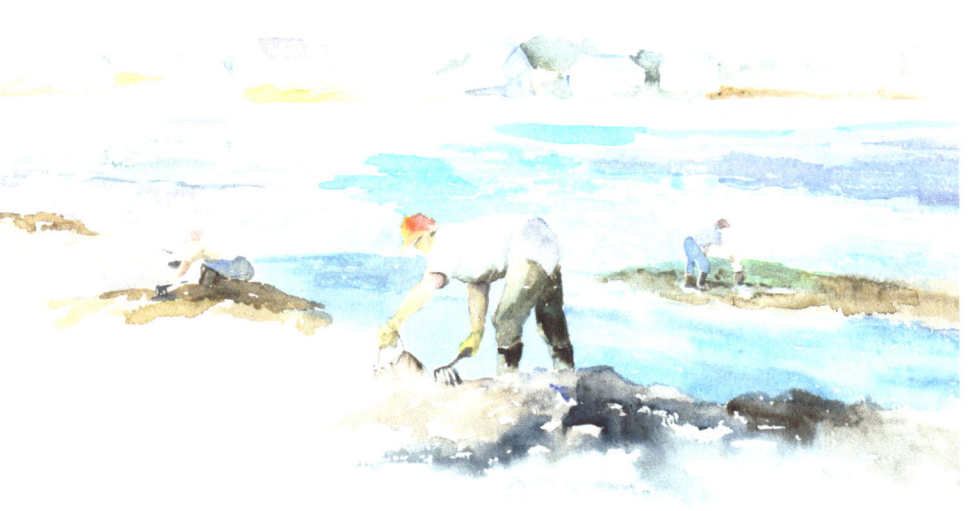

Hampton Falls Clam Diggers

Favorite New England Views

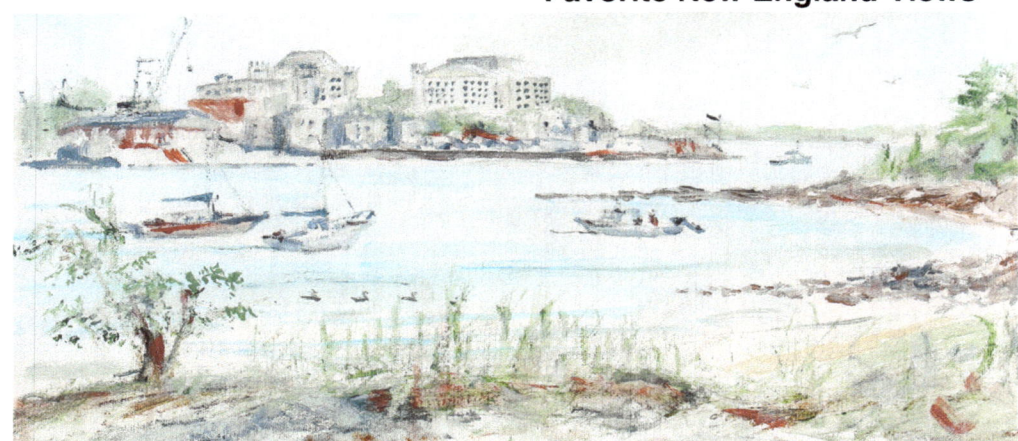

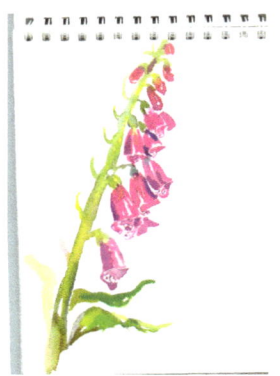

The Castle on
Piscataqua River

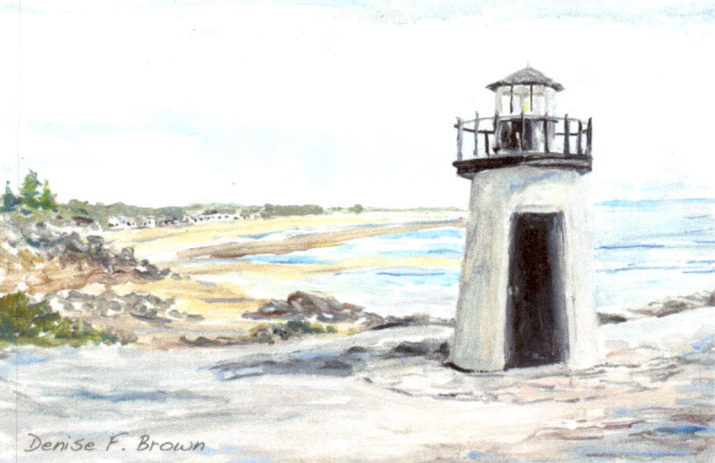

Lighthouse on Marginal Way, Ogunquit, Maine

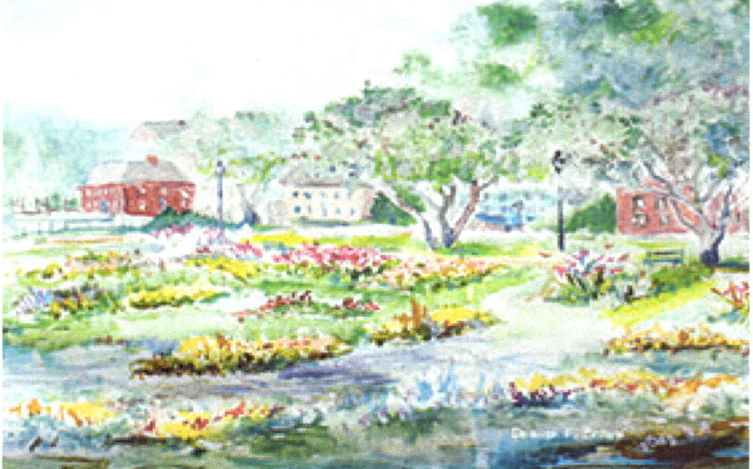

Prescott Park and Strawbery Banke

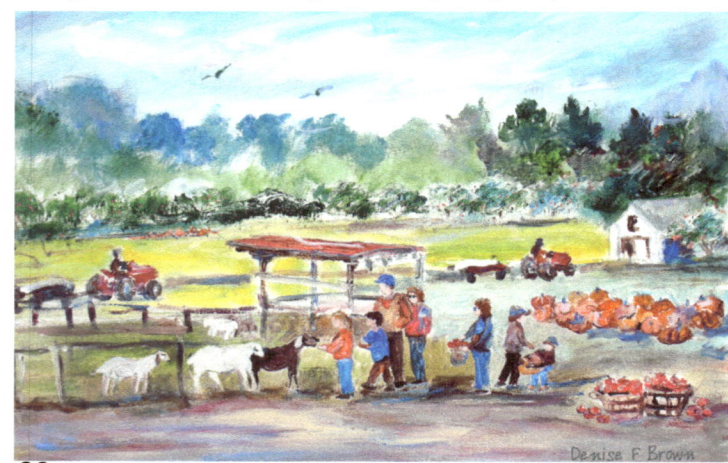

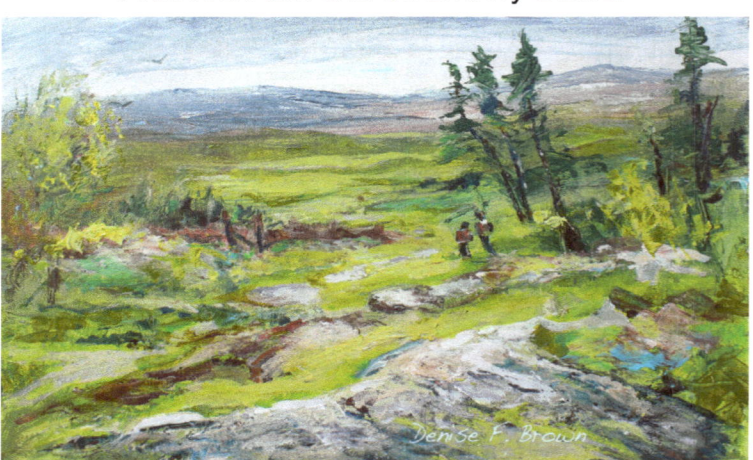

Applecrest Farm

Mount Agamenticus

Favorite Places

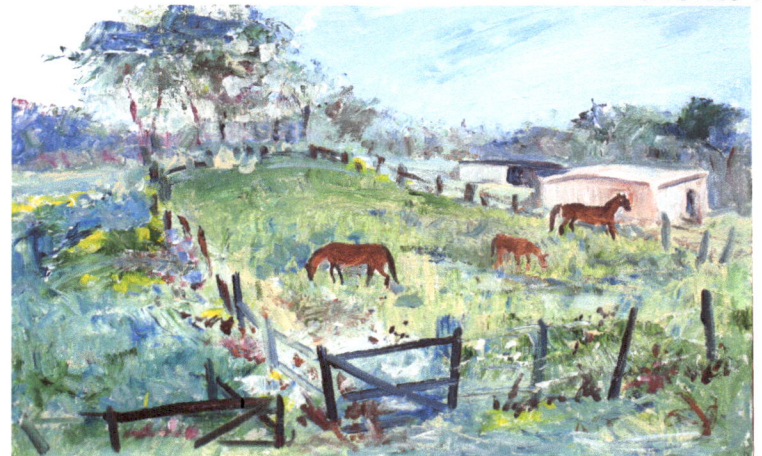

DeMeritt Orchard Pasture, Lee

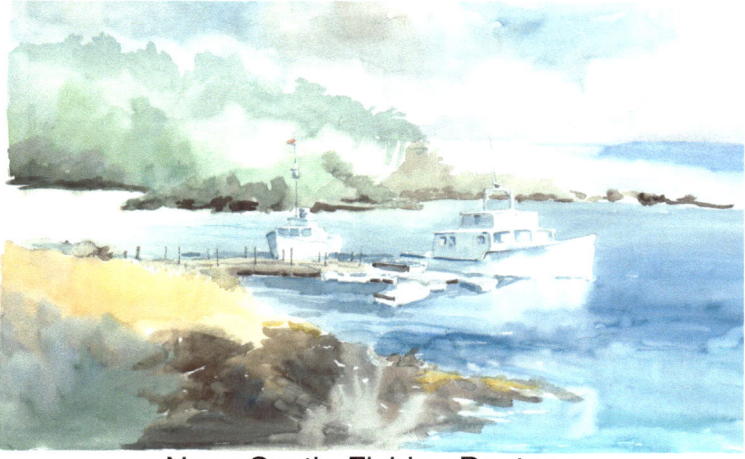

Nova Scotia Fishing Boats

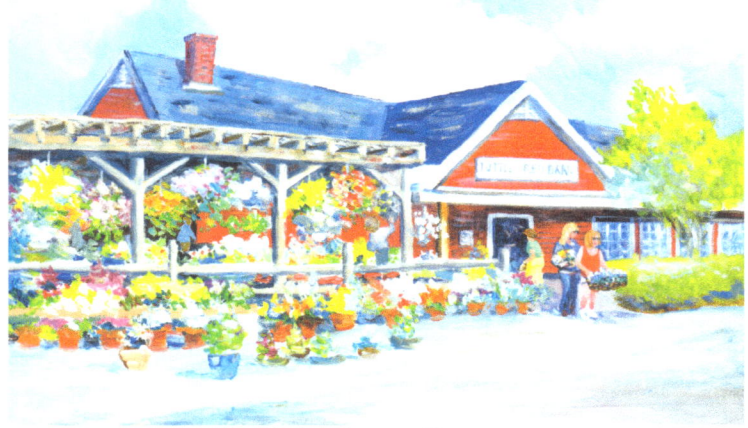

Tuttle's Farm, Dover

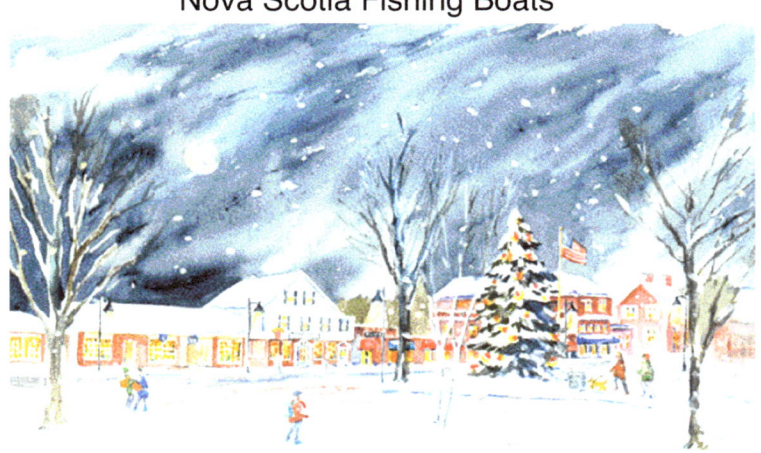

Durham

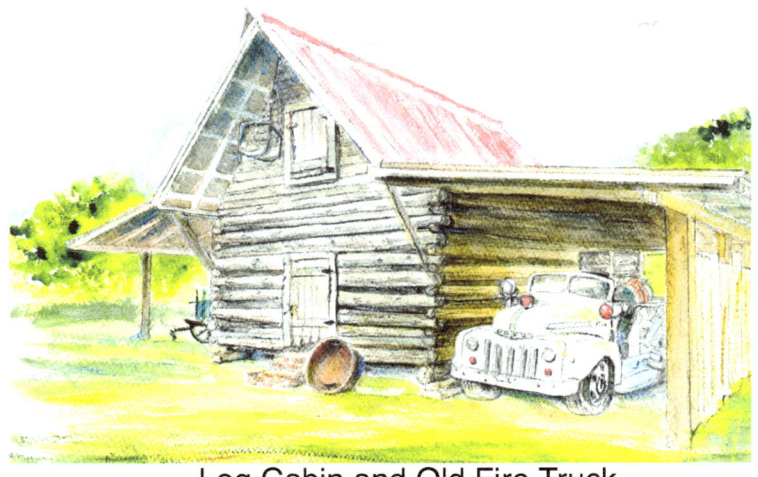

Log Cabin and Old Fire Truck

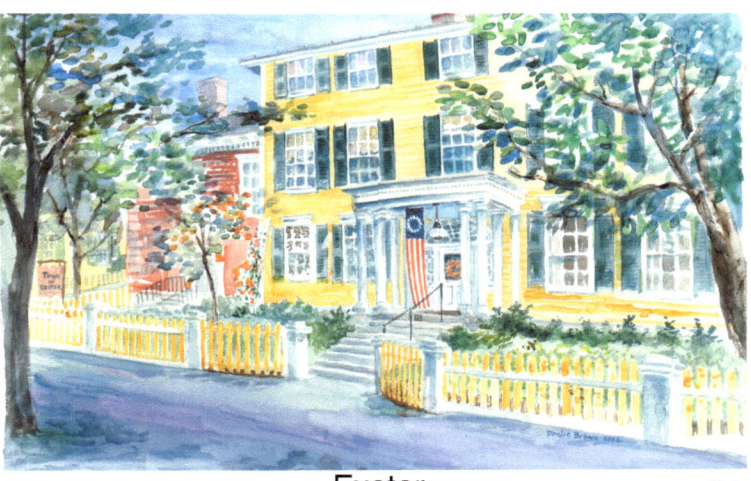

Exeter

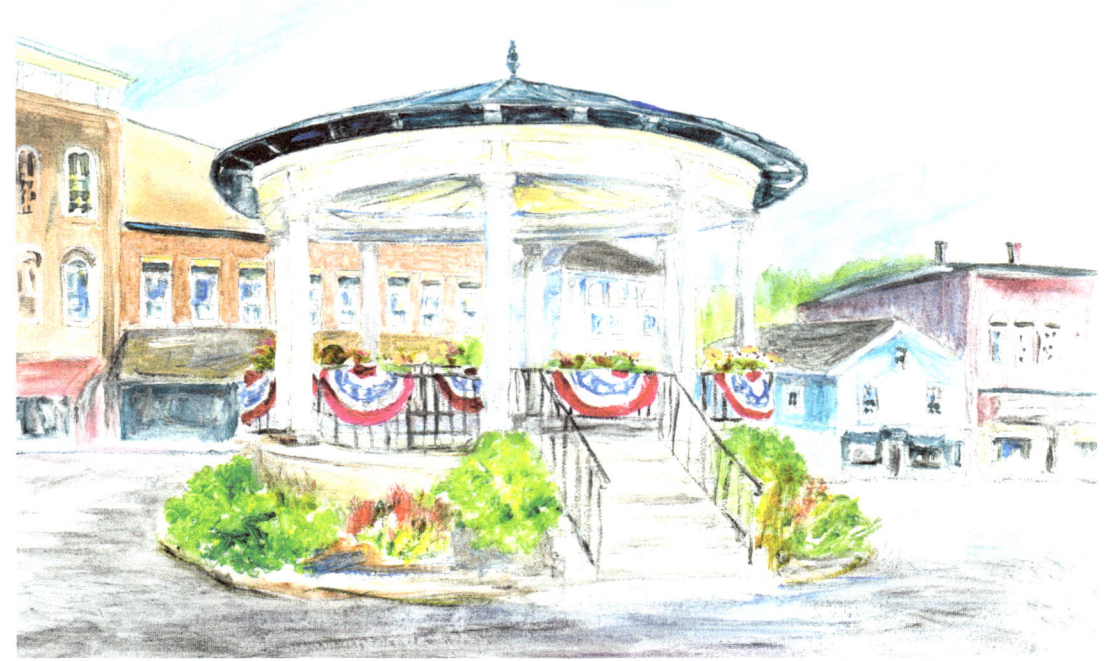

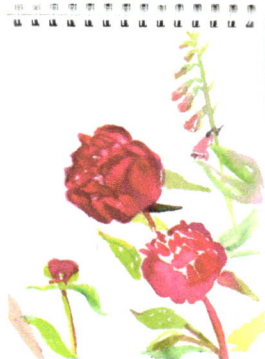

Flower Sketch

Ambrose Swasey Bandstand, Exeter

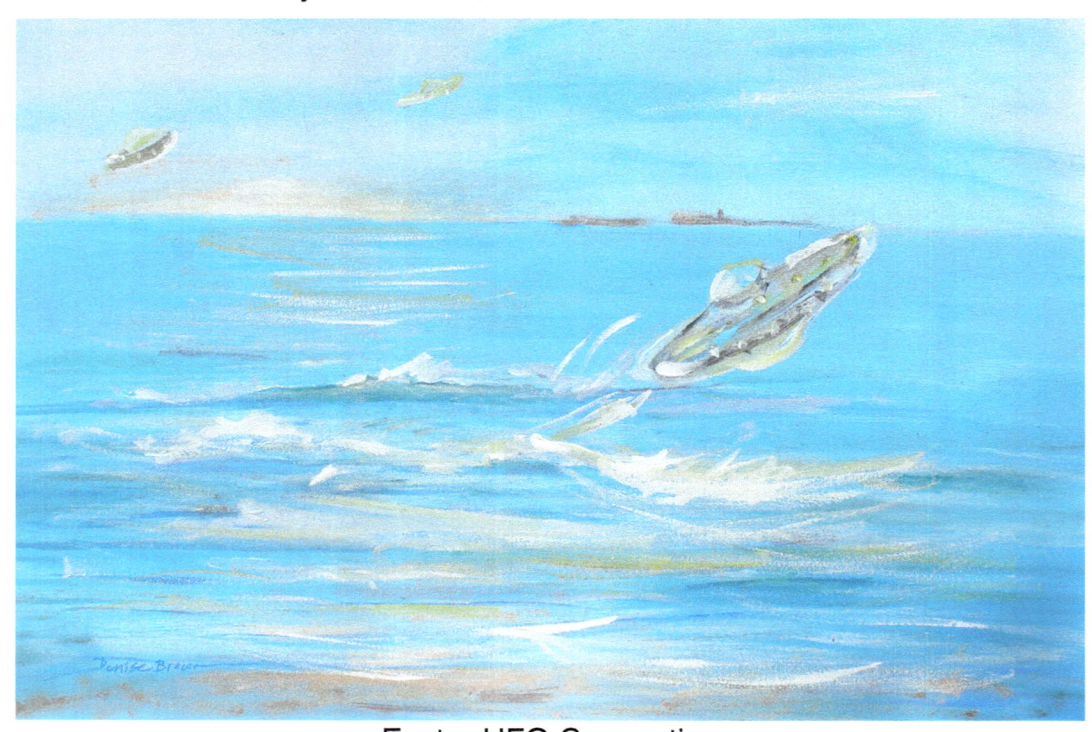

Exeter UFO Convention

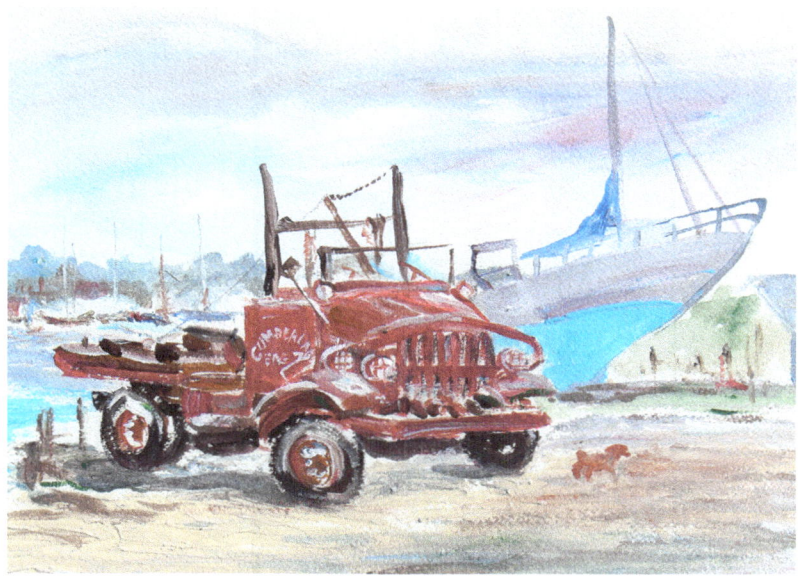

Old Fire Truck at Marina, Essex, Massachusetts

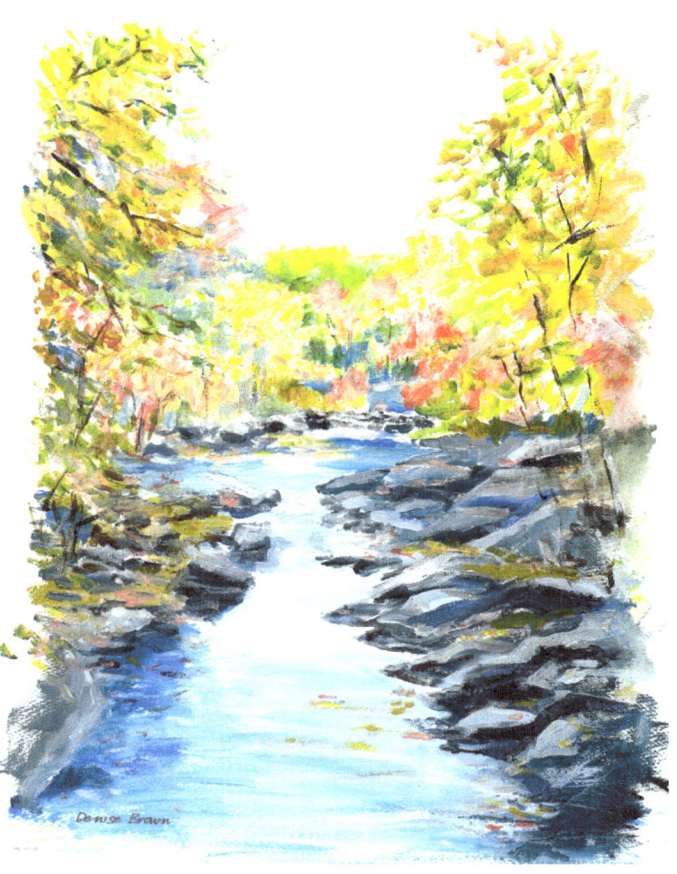

Packer's Falls, Newmarket

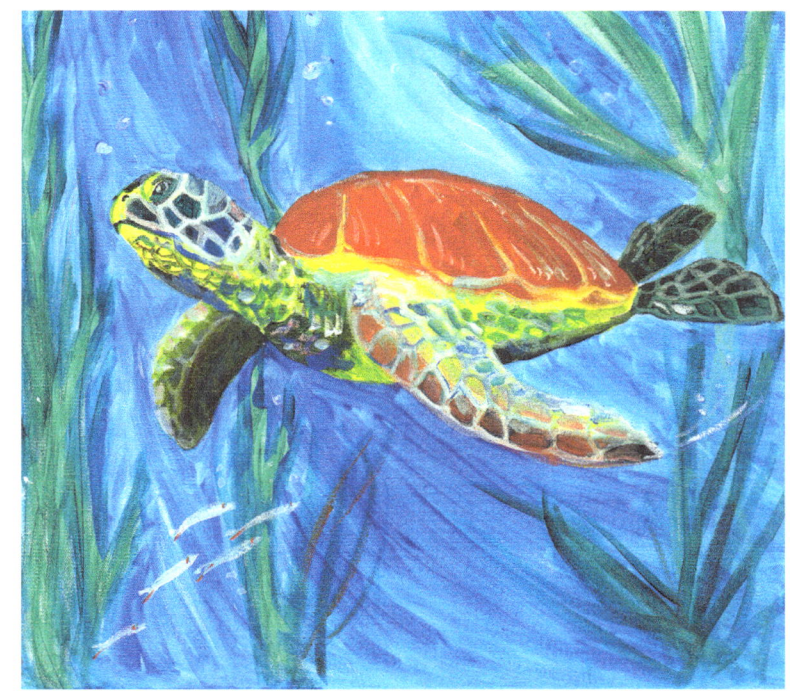

Sea Turtle

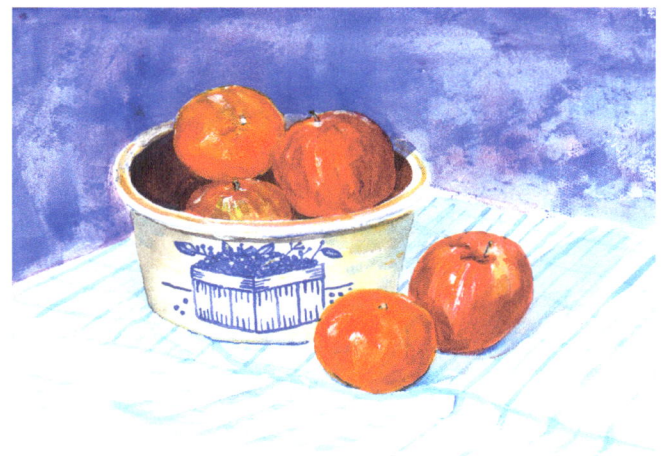

Salmon Falls Blueberry Pottery

Art and Business...

Tip #12:
Commissioned work and
art requests push you
to tell a story.

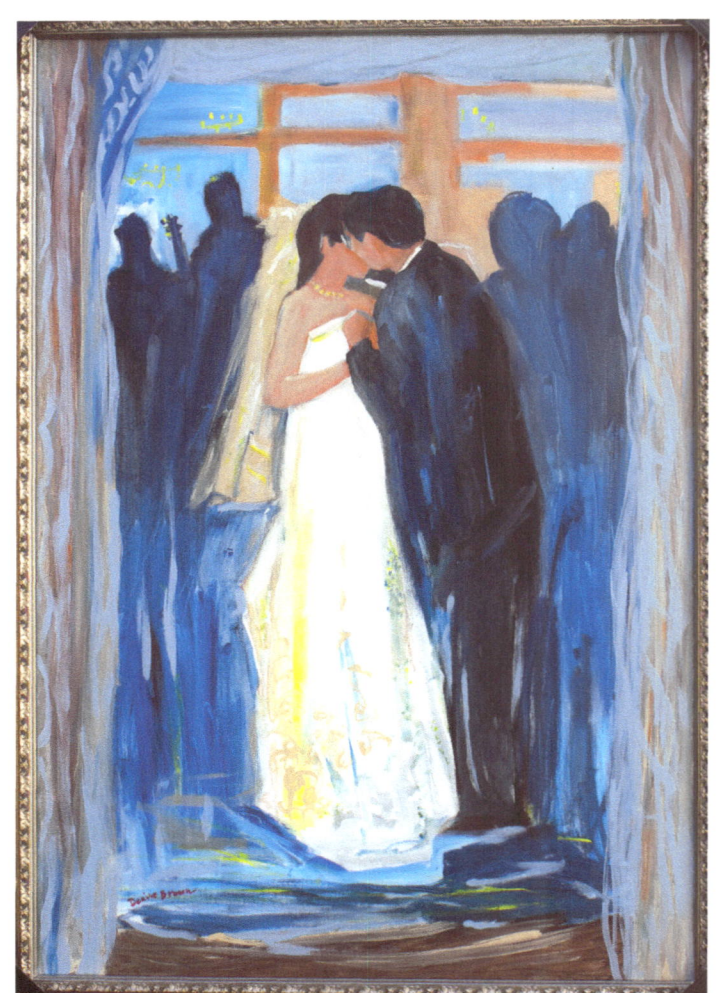

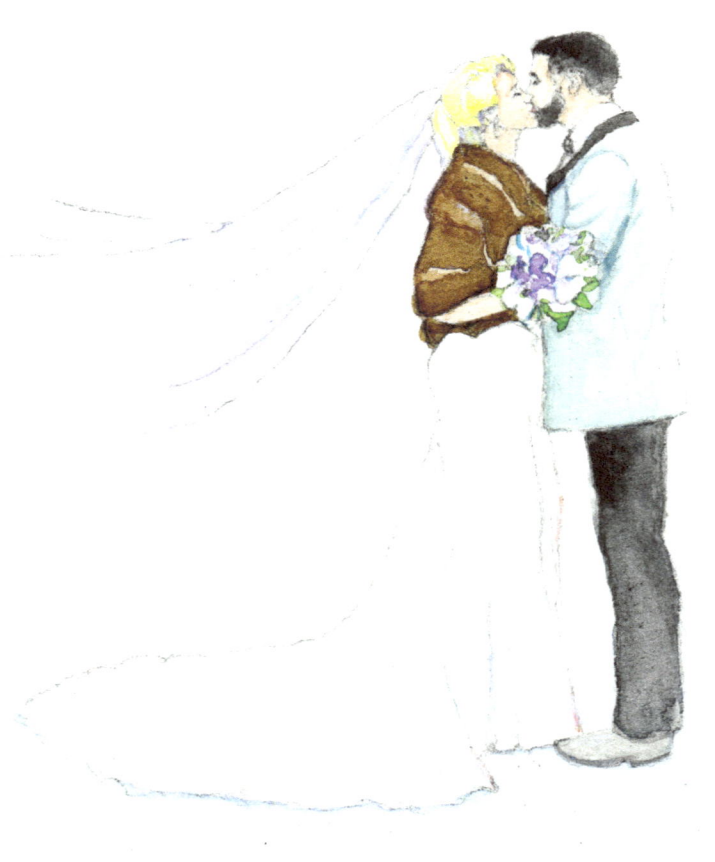

Wedding Gifts

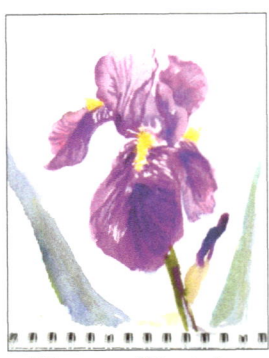

Flower Sketch

Tip #13:

Be brave and enter art shows and contests.
Contests are a challenge and can be costly, so pick and choose for the best notoriety and award benefits.

My best award was from The National Trail of Painted Ponies Contest in Scottsdale, Arizona. I was one of the top ten winners with my painted pony artwork, "Abenaki, the Indian Pony". It was an honor to be invited to the awards ceremony in Scottsdale and meet the other artists.

First, they shipped each artist a blank, white, two-foot high horse sculpture and gave us a month to paint it and ship it back to Arizona. It took me 400 hours to prep and paint my pony named Abenaki.

After the award ceremony, the winning ponies were exhibited across the country for a year. My pony sold for $60,000 at a fundraiser auction that 100% went to benefit non-profit organizations. The Trail of Painted Ponies company has donated over $1,000,000 dollars to causes including wild horses, Native American groups, women's groups and more. Since then, I have painted a dozen other smaller ponies, two of which were mass produced and sold to collectors around the world.

Painted Ponies by Denise Brown

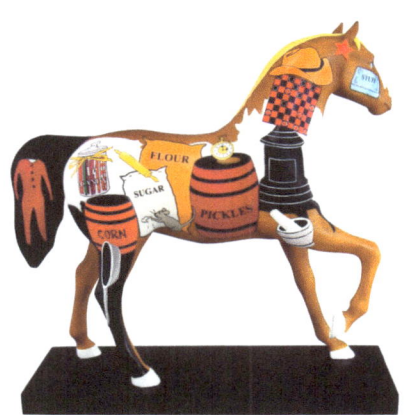 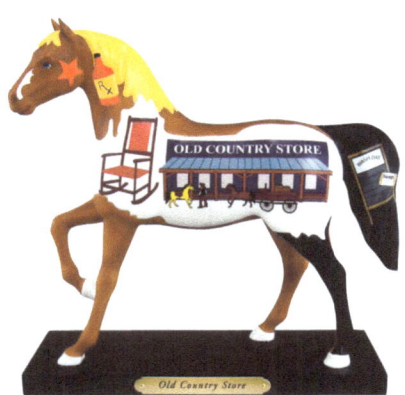 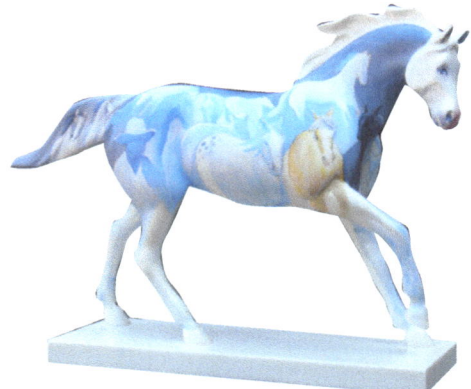

Old Country Store Pony   Ghost Pony

The Trail of Painted Ponies by Denise Brown

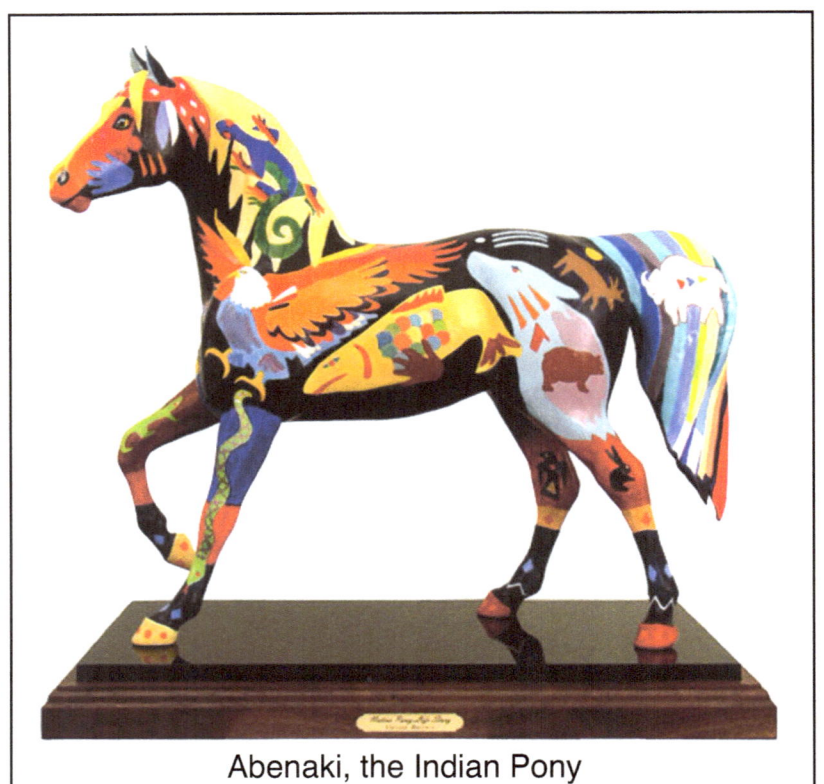

Abenaki, the Indian Pony

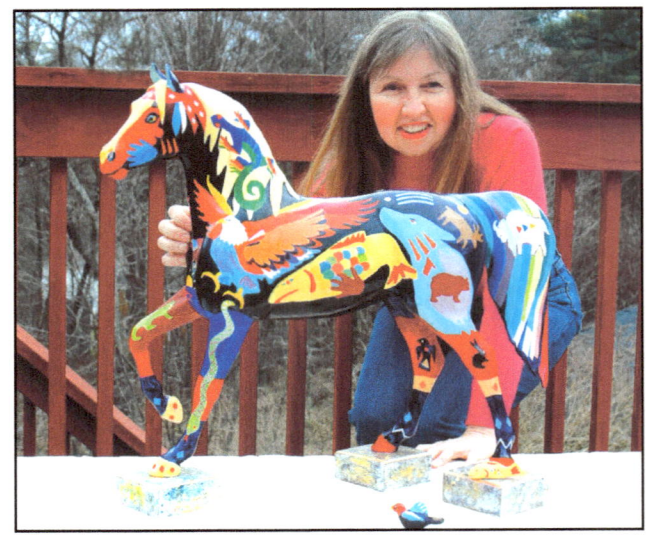

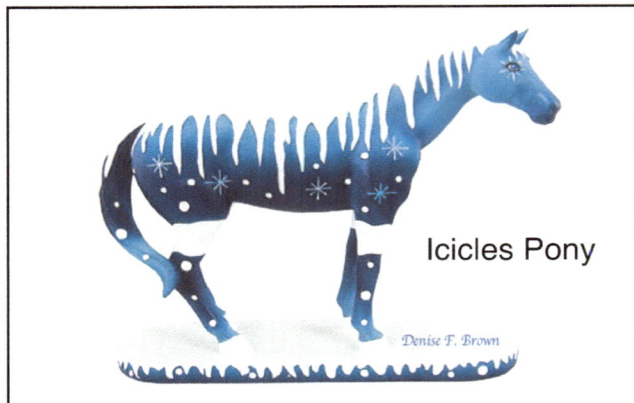

Icicles Pony

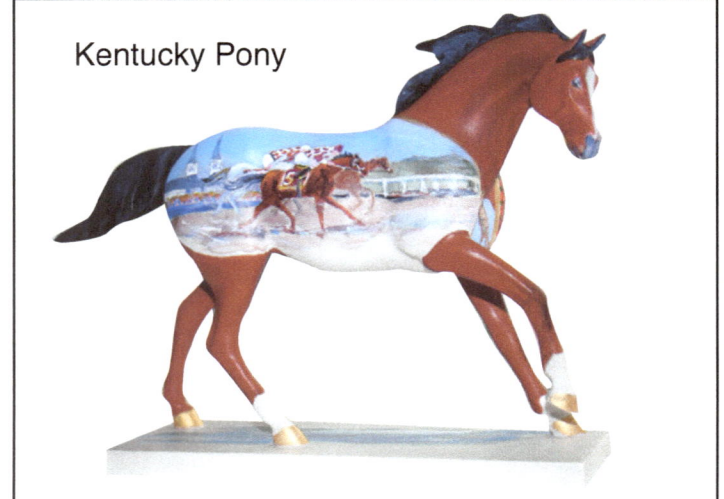

Kentucky Pony

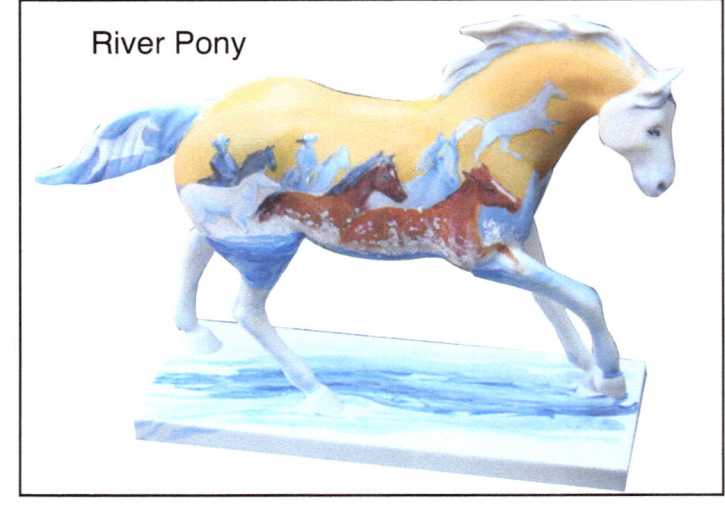

River Pony

Tip #14:

There are endless opportunities to use your art and design skills.

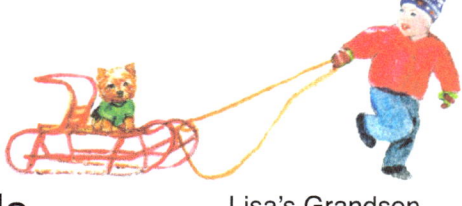

Lisa's Grandson

My clients range from small, local non-profits, historical societies, interior designers, authors, retail stores, national and international companies. Some jobs include creating packaging, trade show marketing, museum displays, signs, brochures, t-shirts, logos, books, holiday cards, and more.

Painting commissioned work, including pet portraits, house portraits, landscapes, seascapes, and architectural drawings is another challenging part of my business.

People love a painting of their beloved pet or home and personalized custom holiday cards.

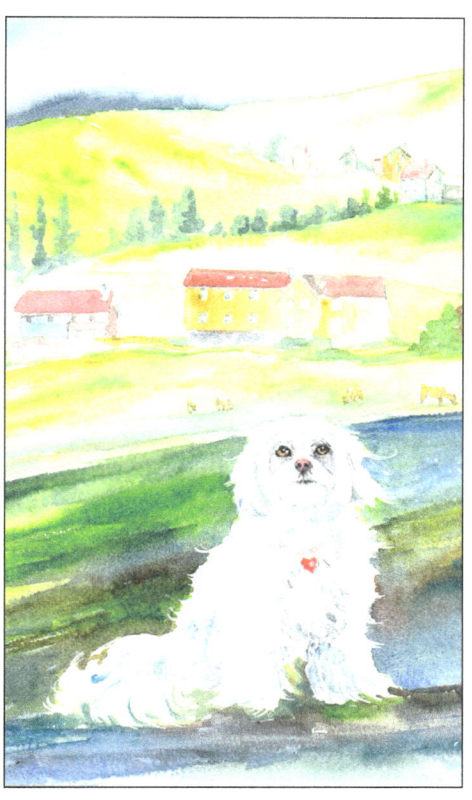

Portrait for
"Angel Come Home"
Book by Stuart Wisong

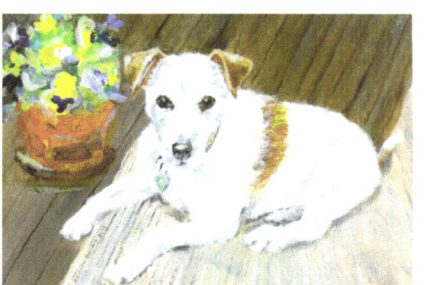

Shari's Belle

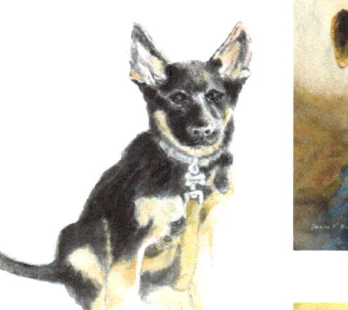

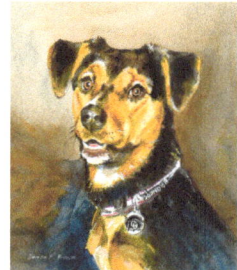

Bear

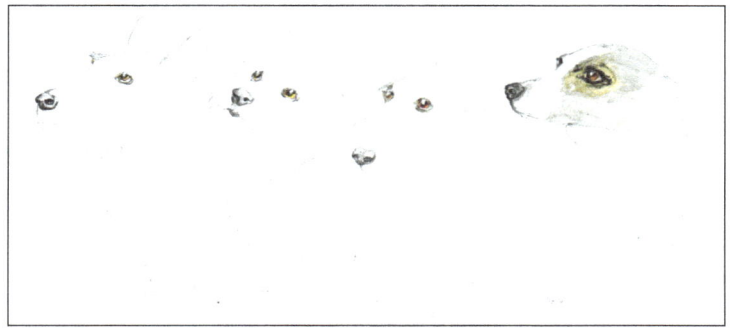

Cathy's Pups Sketch

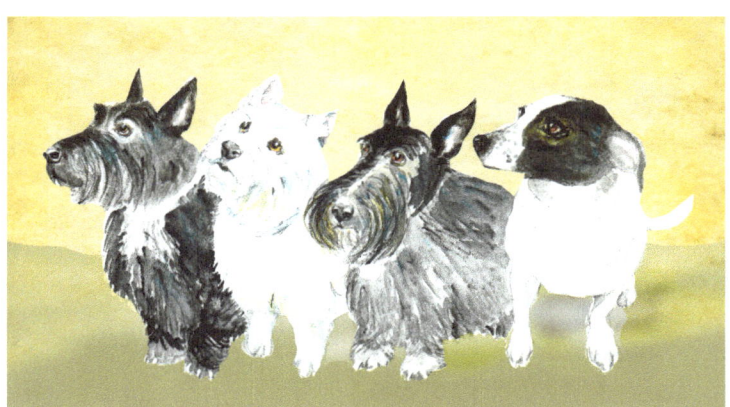

Cathy's Pups Finished Painting

Pet Portrait Commissions

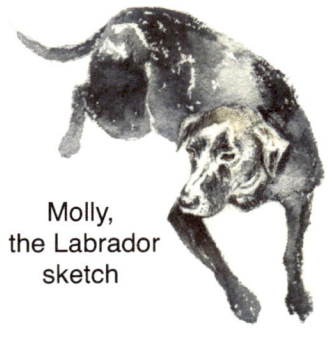

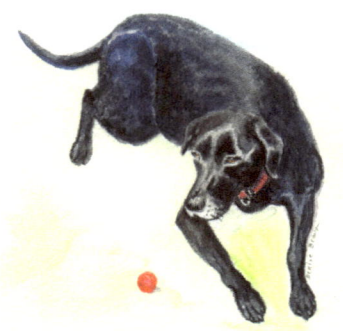

Molly,
the Labrador
sketch

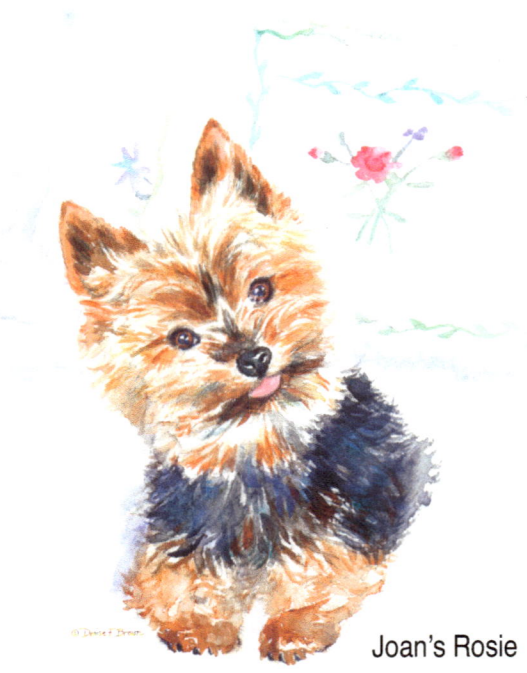

Joan's Rosie

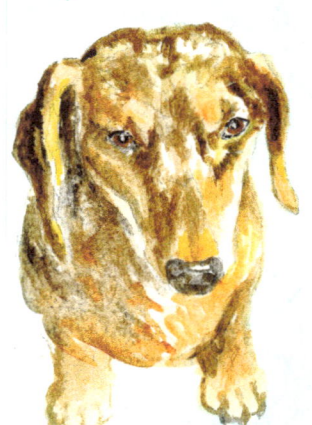

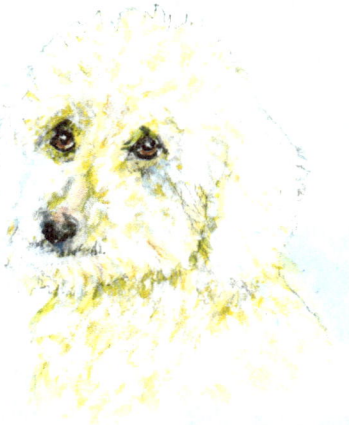

Gail's friends

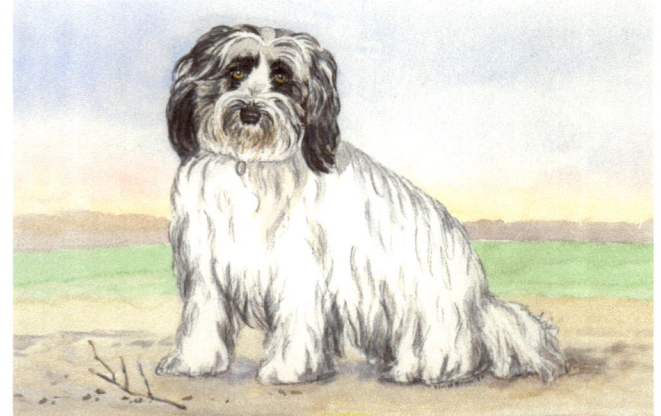
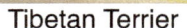

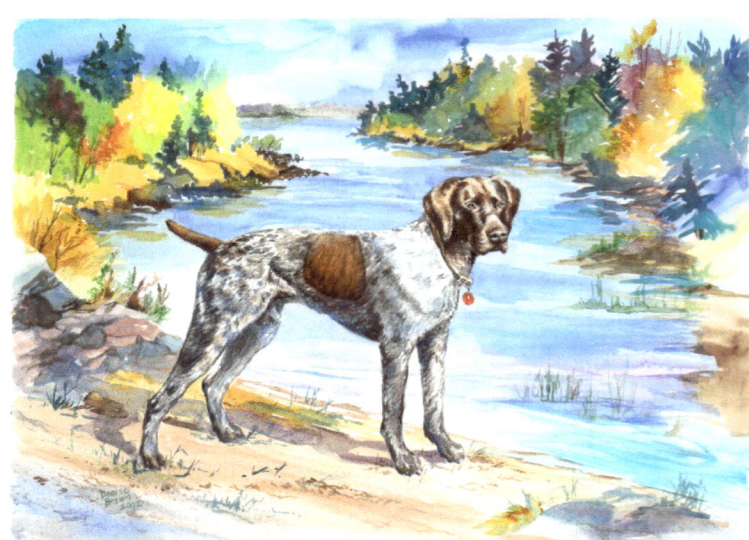

Tibetan Terrier

Peter Millette's friend

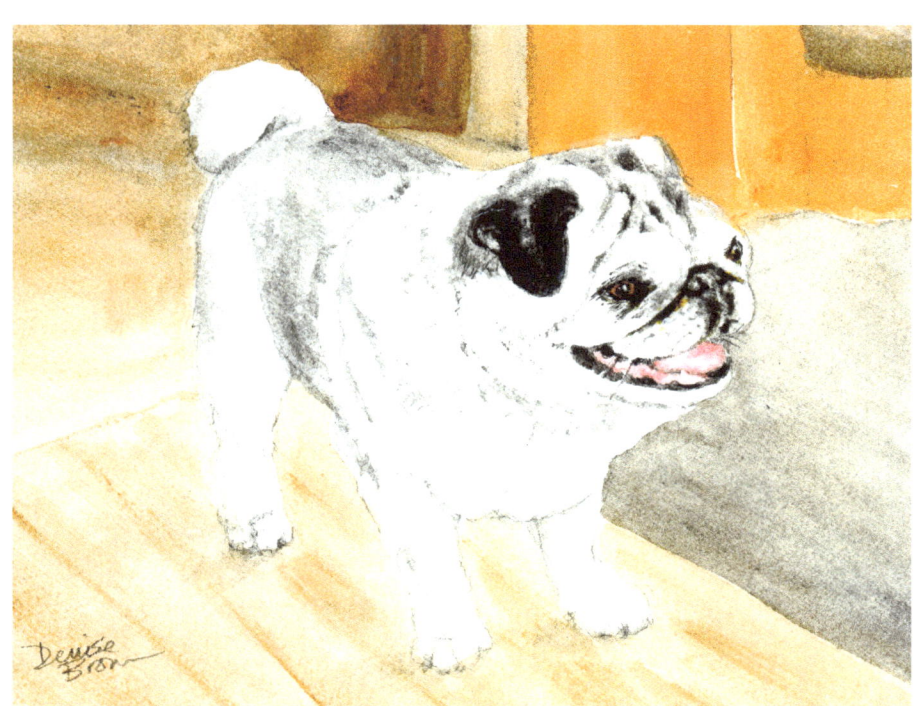

Jamie's Sir Dewey

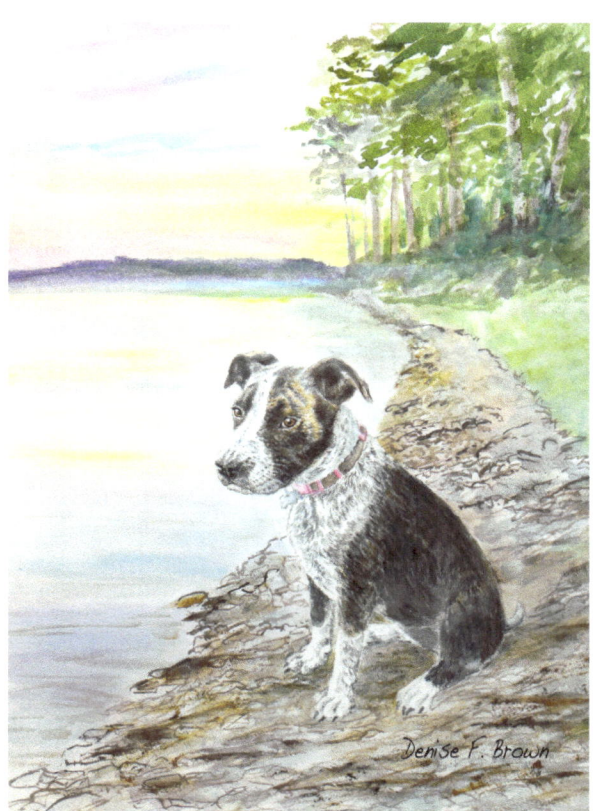

Bossee's "Boo"
Blue Healer/Old English Bull Dog

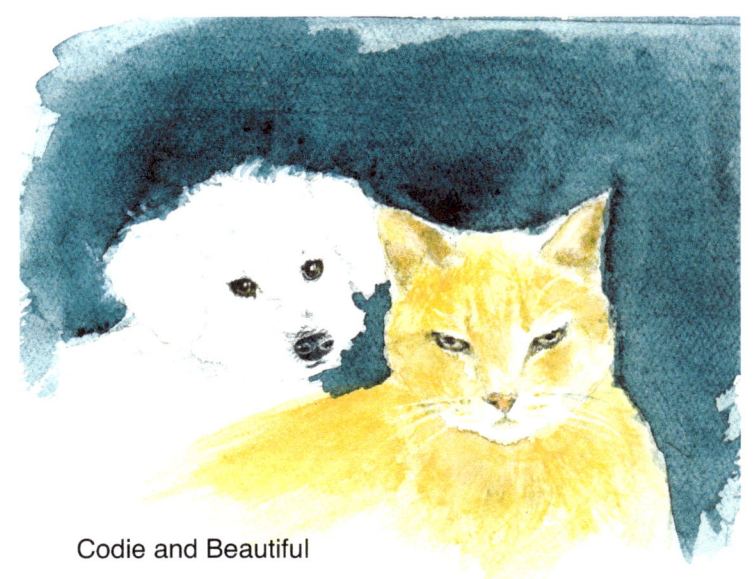

Codie and Beautiful

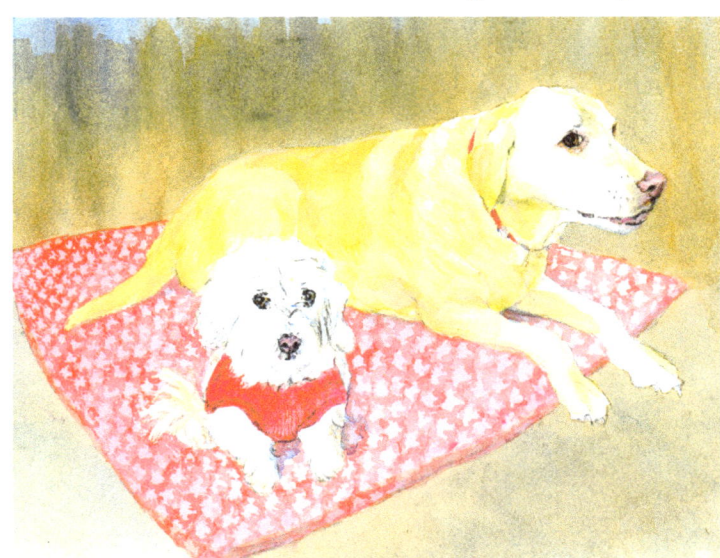

Suzie and Milo

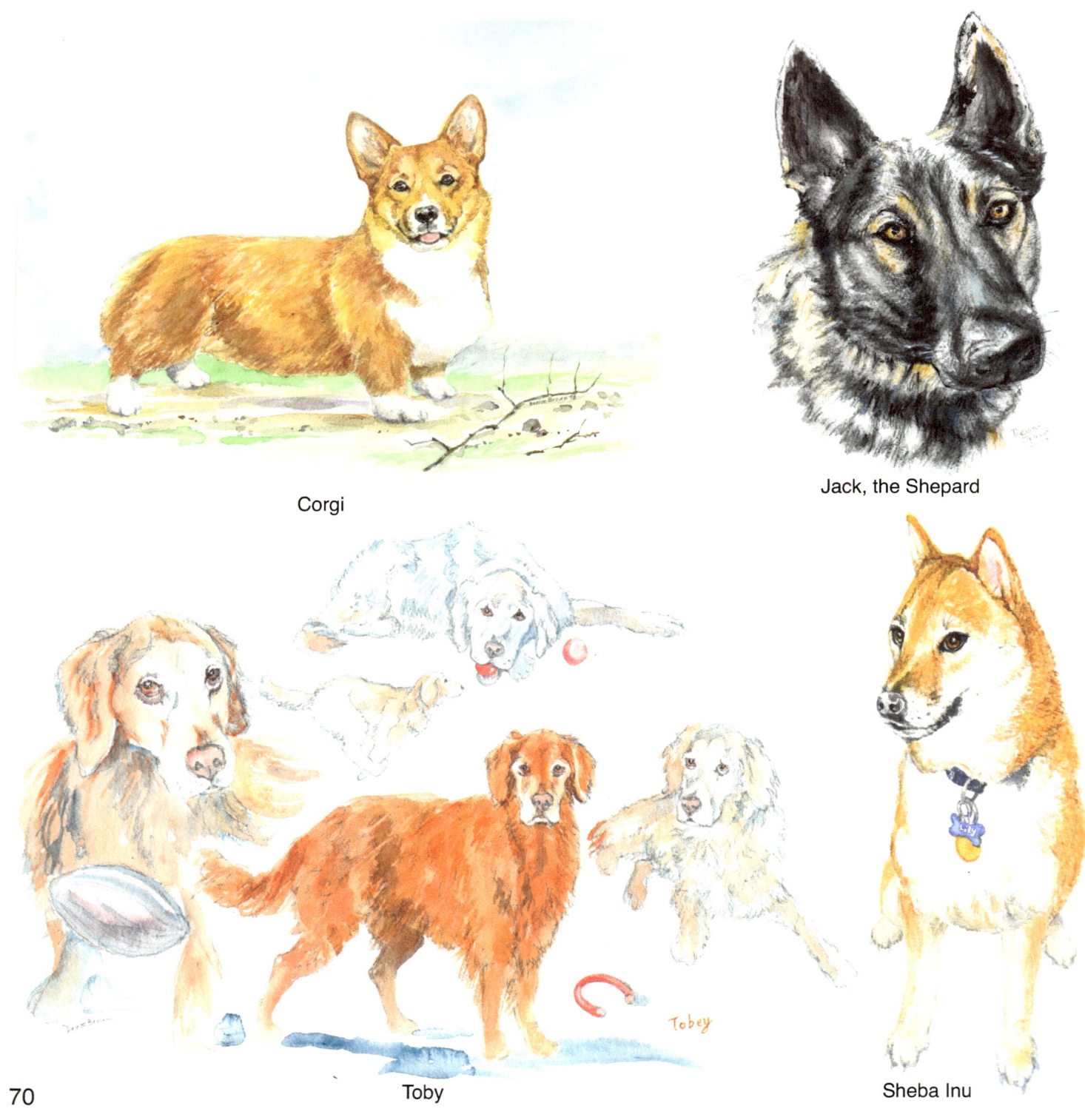

Corgi

Jack, the Shepard

Toby

Sheba Inu

70

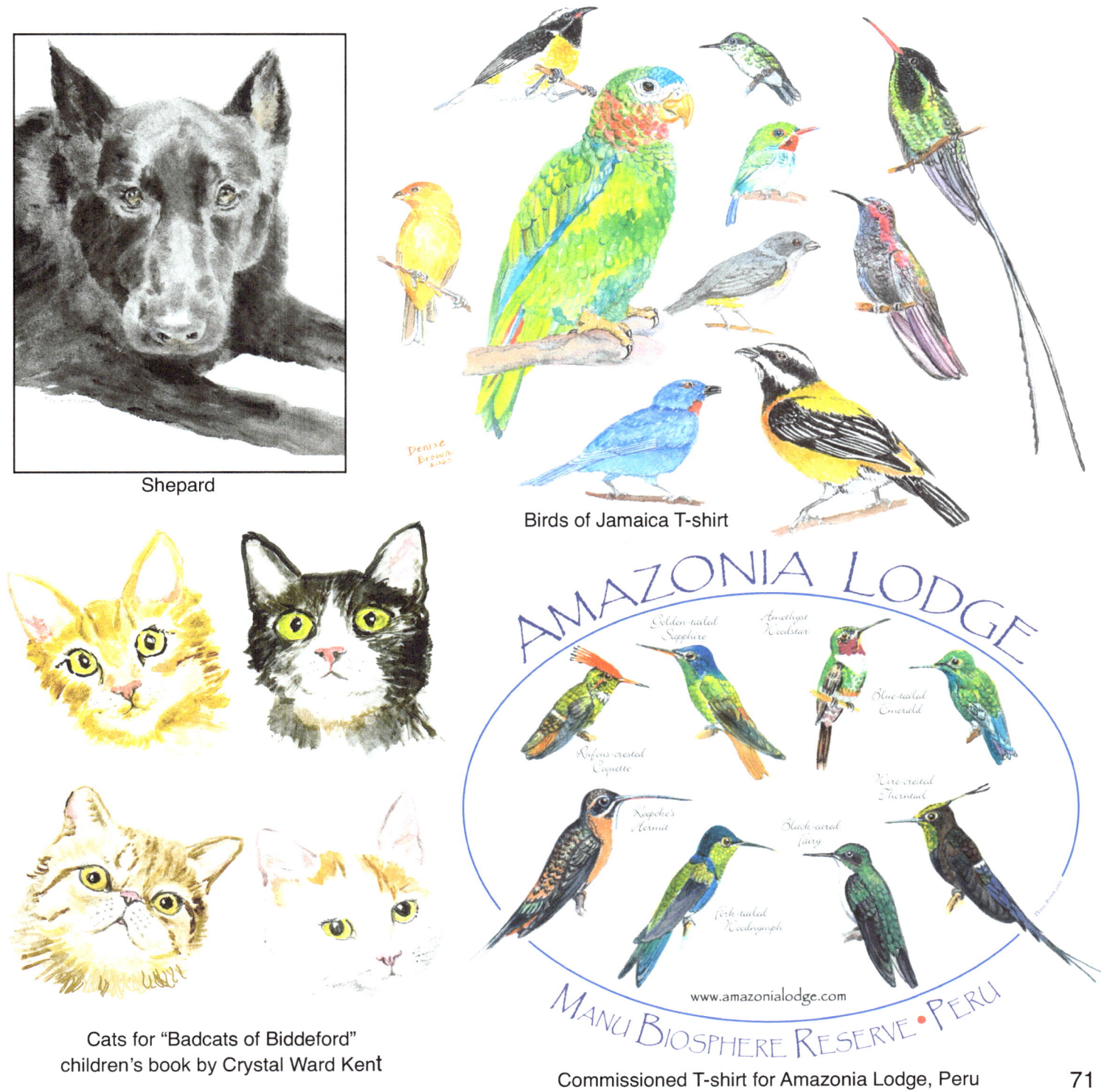

Shepard

Birds of Jamaica T-shirt

Cats for "Badcats of Biddeford"
children's book by Crystal Ward Kent

Commissioned T-shirt for Amazonia Lodge, Peru

AMAZONIA LODGE

Golden-tailed Sapphire

Amethyst Woodstar

Blue-tailed Emerald

Rufous-crested Coquette

Wire-crested Thorntail

Koepche's Hermit

Black-eared Fairy

Fork-tailed Woodnymph

www.amazonialodge.com

MANU BIOSPHERE RESERVE • PERU

71

Tip #15:

Share your work and your art tips, and motivate other artists.

People stop to talk to me and watch me work. One of my favorite things is when kids stop and ask me what I'm painting. Their eyes light up when I ask them what they like to paint. Picasso said that every child is an artist.

Always have a sketchbook and pencil with you.

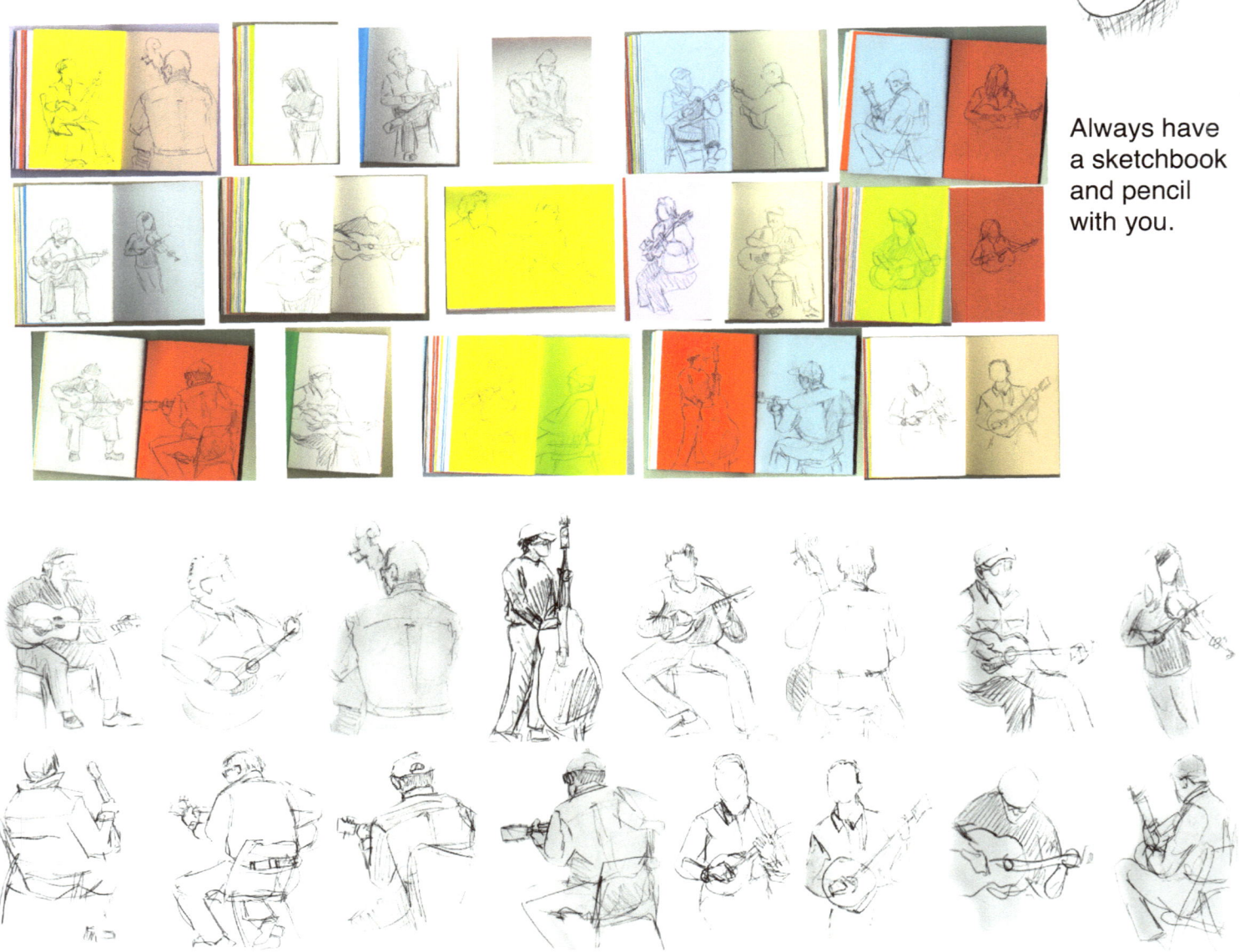

Musician sketches

Tip #16:

Authors need illustrators for magazines and books.

Clients need artists for illustrating and designing books. Getting referrals is a good way to spread the word that you're available for commission work.

Here are a few of the books that I have authored, illustrated and produced, or collaborated with other authors.

To see more, visit **www.raccoonstudios.com**

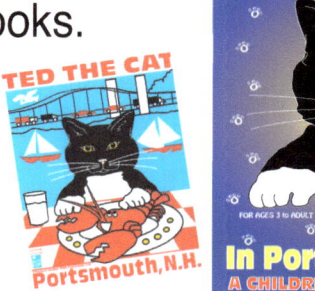

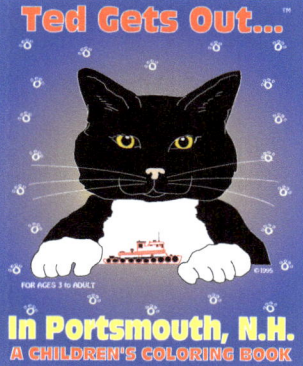

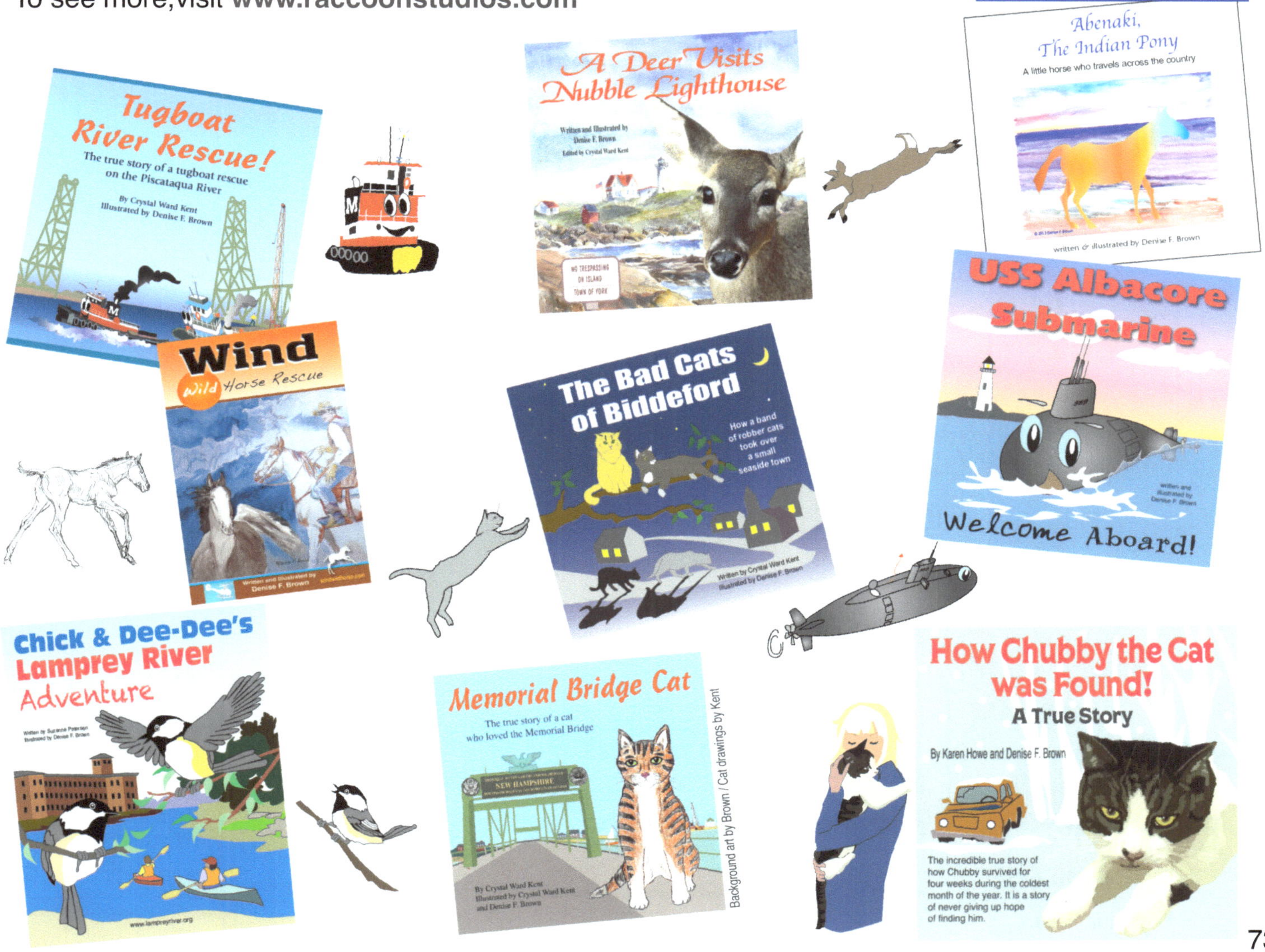

Tip #17:

You can use your artwork for business clients.

Logos, murals, illustrations, maps, labels, t-shirts, and other items need creative art and design work. Ask business clients if you can create something for them.

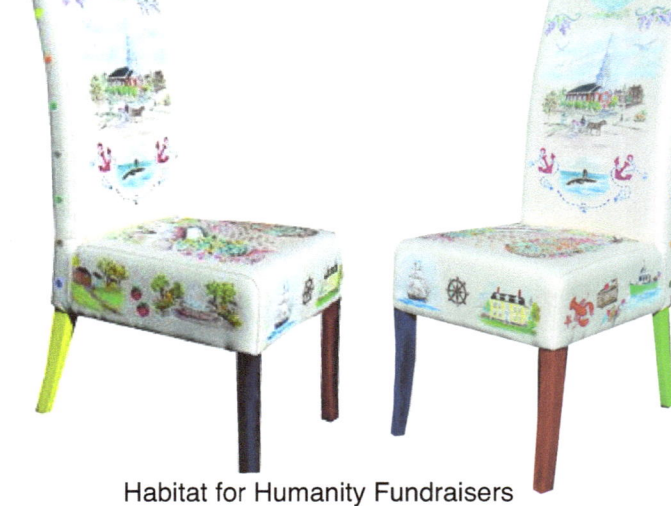

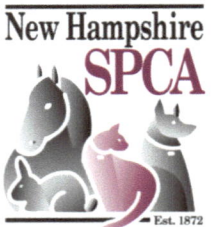

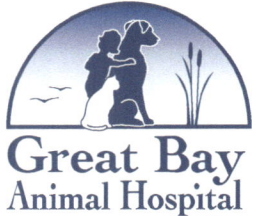

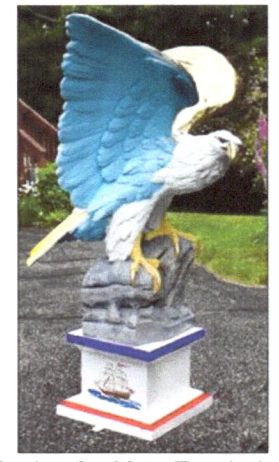

Eagles for Vets Fundraiser

Habitat for Humanity Fundraisers

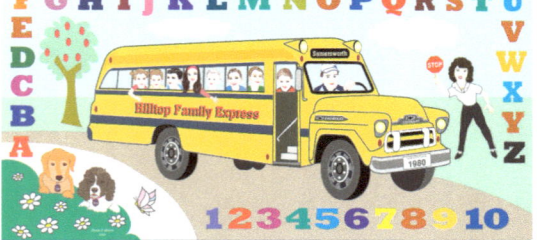

Hilltop Chevrolet Childrens' Room Mural

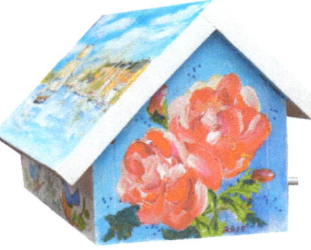

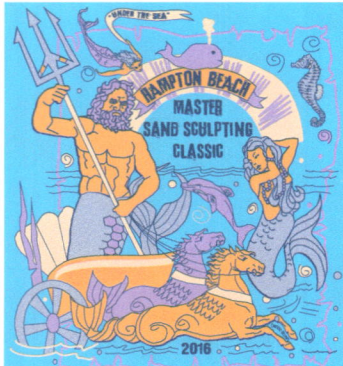

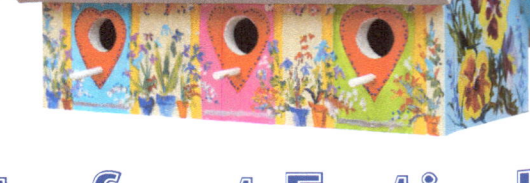

Piscataqua Waterfront Festival

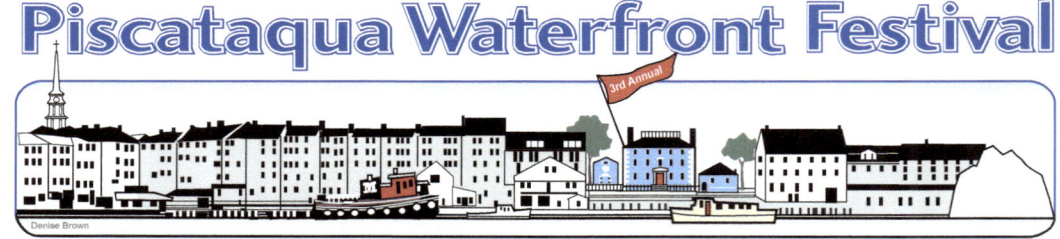

74 Hampton Beach Sand Competition T-shirt

At Moffatt-Ladd House and Garden

Life is Art...

Tip #18:

An artist's passion knows no bounds. It is a life filled with variety, surprises, hard work, perseverance and creativity. You just have to dream big and keep painting!

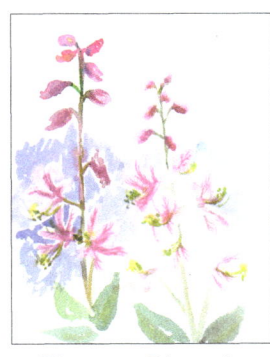

Flower Sketch

I hope you have enjoyed my work, my comments, and travels. Art is not always a highly profitable career, but it is exciting to see your artwork at an exhibit or hanging in an admirer's home... whether or not it matches their couch.

I have organized art exhibits and judged art shows....not easy tasks, but you meet new clients.

There are so many talented people in the world...from Degas to Winslow Homer to the Wyeths, and every artist before and after them. I admire them all for their struggles, their hard work and accomplishments, and because they followed their dreams.

As for another dream... who knows, maybe someday you or I will be recognized as a Living Treasure artist, like my favorite artist, Professor John Hatch.

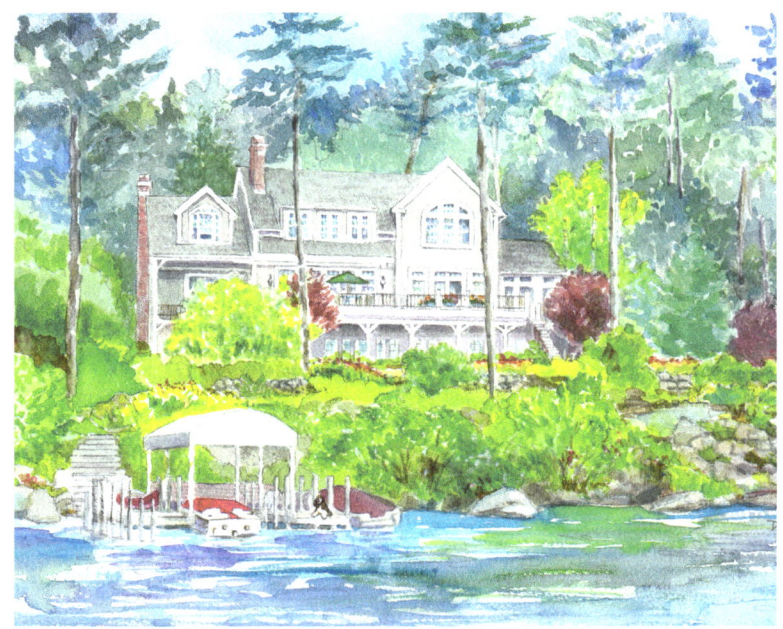

Scott's Lake House and Dock

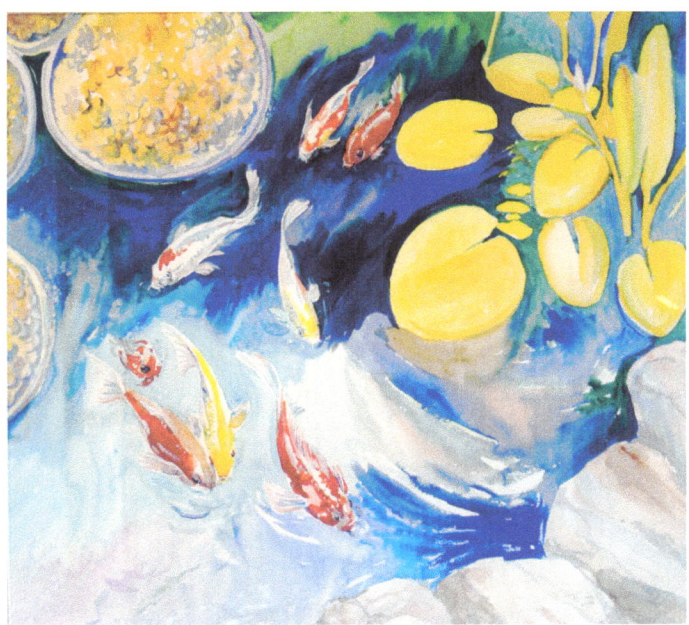

Joey's Pond

75

Tip #19:

Join art clubs and enter juried art associations and exhibits.

As a member of the New Hampshire Art Association, Seacoast Artist Association, and Plein Air groups, I connect with amazingly talented artists. Artists often paint alone in their studios, so it is important to be with other creative people. Local and well-known artists like to share their knowledge at demos and classes, and you get to paint with them!

Look on-line or in art magazines for art travel workshops. Keep learning and practicing new ideas.

Willow's Pocket Garden

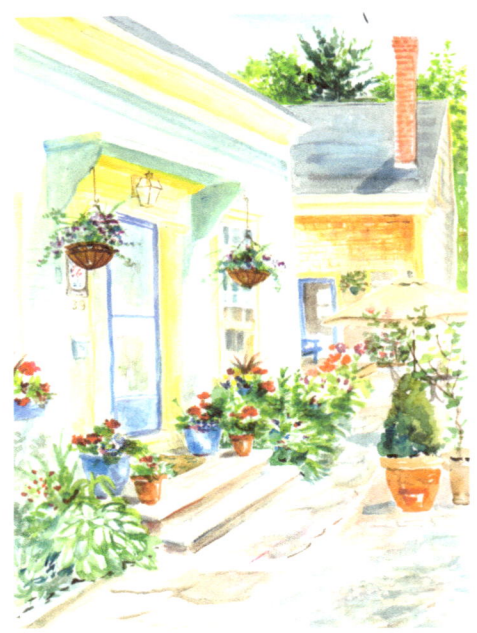

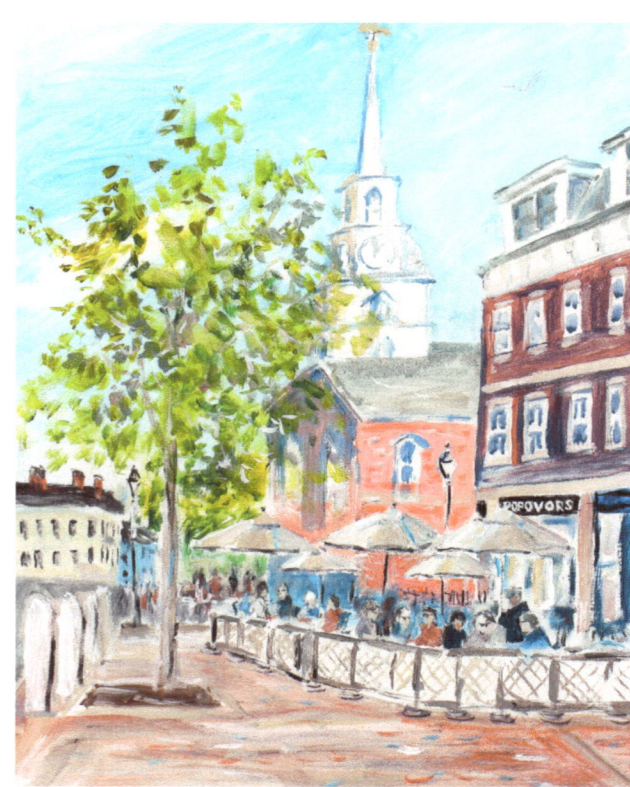

Popovers, Downtown Portsmouth

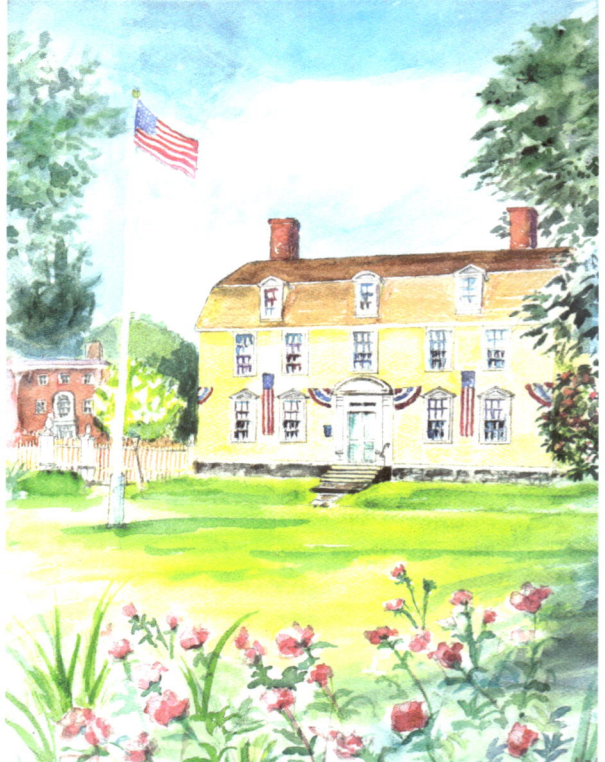

John Paul Jones House and Garden

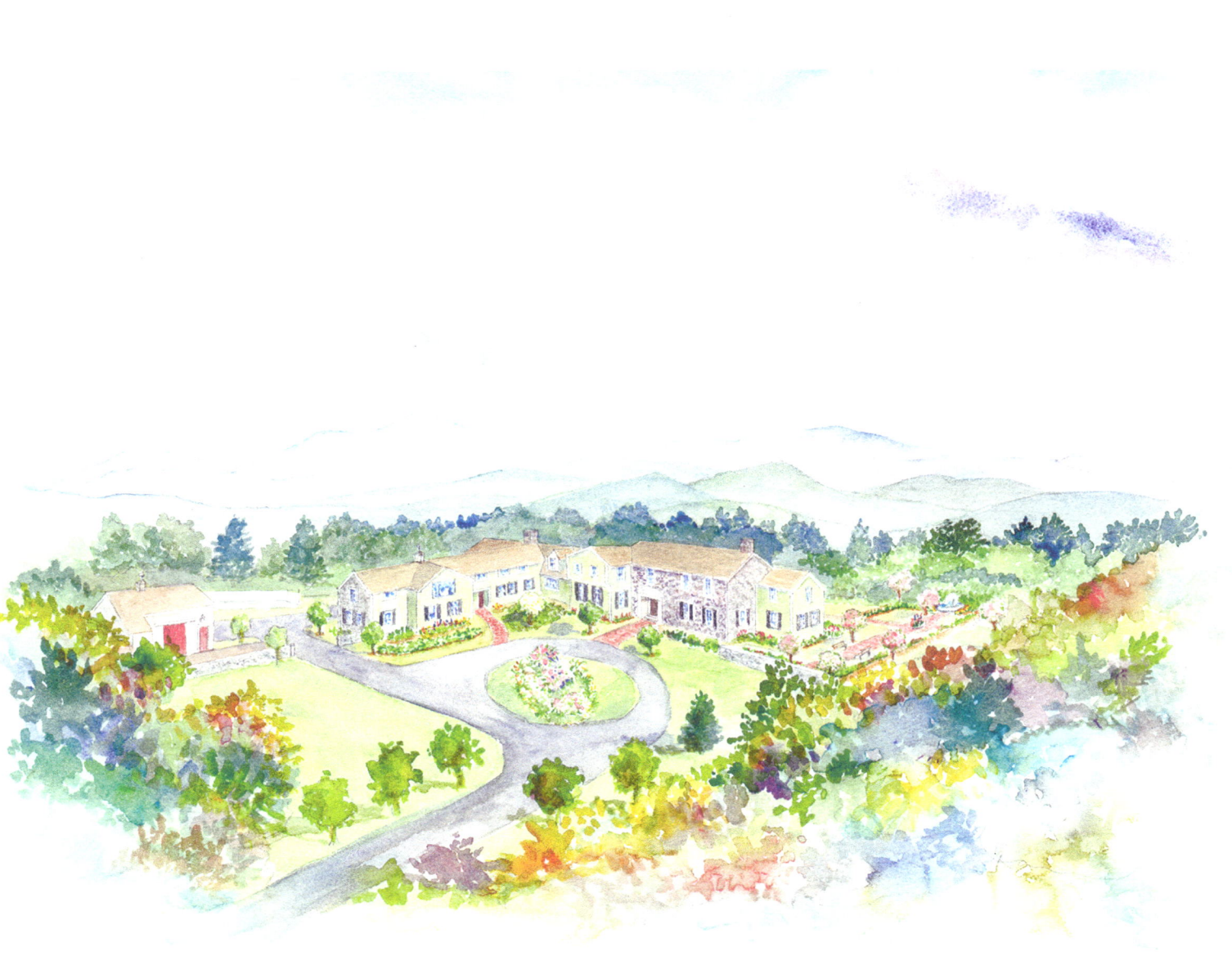

Commissioned painting for a gift to New Hampshire Governor John Lynch

"1600's"

In its early days, Great Island, home of Royal Governors, was the center of social and political intrigue. Its prison was full, its taverns overflowed with rum, and its roads were full of mariners, government officials, and British Society.

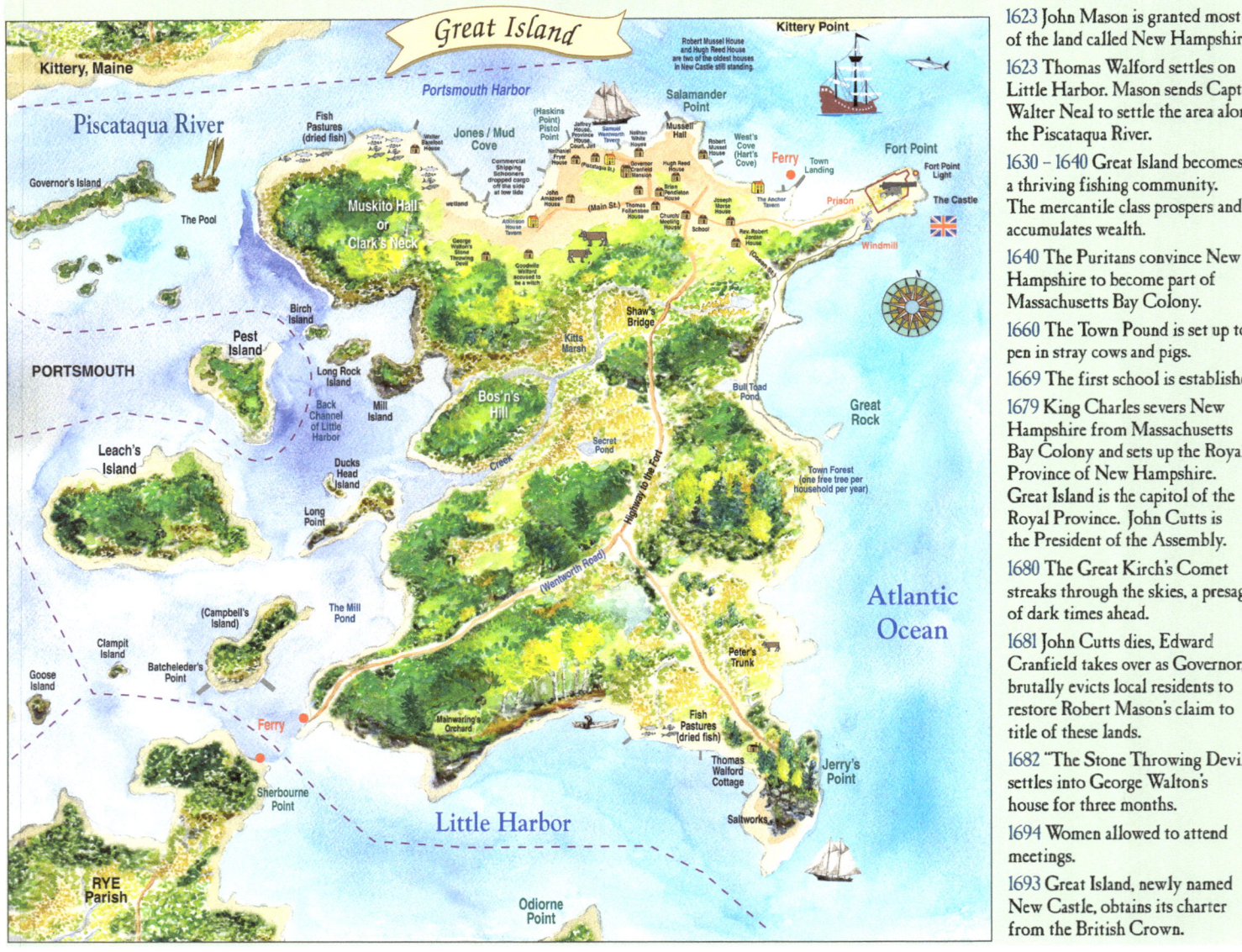

1623 John Mason is granted most of the land called New Hampshire.

1623 Thomas Walford settles on Little Harbor. Mason sends Captain Walter Neal to settle the area along the Piscataqua River.

1630 – 1640 Great Island becomes a thriving fishing community. The mercantile class prospers and accumulates wealth.

1640 The Puritans convince New Hampshire to become part of Massachusetts Bay Colony.

1660 The Town Pound is set up to pen in stray cows and pigs.

1669 The first school is established.

1679 King Charles severs New Hampshire from Massachusetts Bay Colony and sets up the Royal Province of New Hampshire. Great Island is the capitol of the Royal Province. John Cutts is the President of the Assembly.

1680 The Great Kirch's Comet streaks through the skies, a presage of dark times ahead.

1681 John Cutts dies, Edward Cranfield takes over as Governor, brutally evicts local residents to restore Robert Mason's claim to title of these lands.

1682 "The Stone Throwing Devil" settles into George Walton's house for three months.

1694 Women allowed to attend meetings.

1693 Great Island, newly named New Castle, obtains its charter from the British Crown.

Commissioned artwork for the New Castle Historical Society Museum wall panel displays

Afterward...

Tip #20:

What to do with all of your artwork?

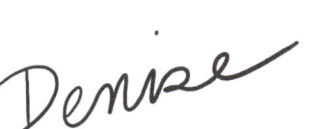

PORTSMOUTH
...Tugs at the Heart
NEW HAMPSHIRE

Over a lifetime of creating artwork, my biggest question is what to do with all of my multitude of paintings, and what will become of them?

Some paintings are too dear to my heart to sell. They are all memories of my life, but as I get older, I am now faced with a houseful of my artwork.

I often ask other artists the same question. Some of their solutions are: donate to your favorite charities for auctions; ask a museum if they would want the best pieces; cull out the ones you don't want hanging in people's homes; give them to family and friends; get a dumpster... Most artists just don't know what to do.

Maybe, there will be an art auction of your work when you pass on. So it might be a good idea to name and catalog them as you go. Then your loved ones won't have to label your paintings as just a number. And, if you become a famous artist, they might sell for a bit of money.

Perhaps I will be invited to prepare another big show someday, so contact me if you'd like to buy or order a painting for yourself or for a gift. I will check my inventory if it's for sale.

Happy painting~

Like me on Facebook! "Denise Brown"
and visit my website at www.raccoonstudios.com

Denise

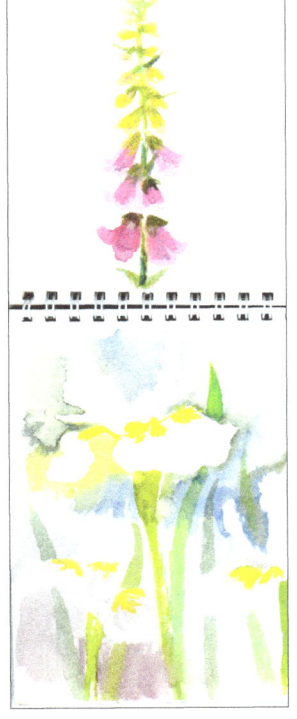

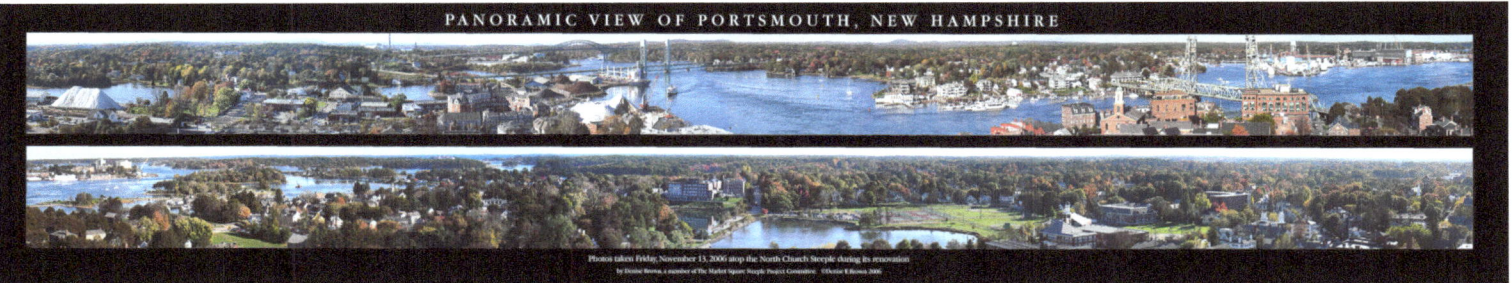

2006 Photographic Panorama of Portsmouth, NH by Denise Brown
Print is in the Portsmouth Public Library's 100 year old Time Capsule to be opened in 2106.

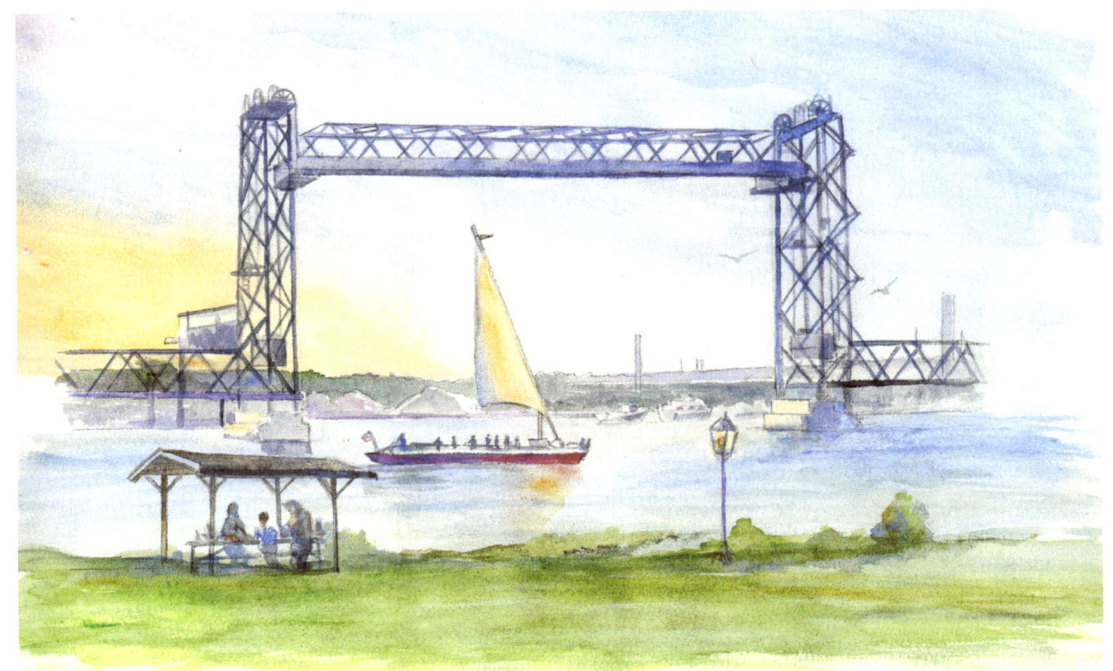

The Memorial Bridge and the Gundalow on the Piscataqua River

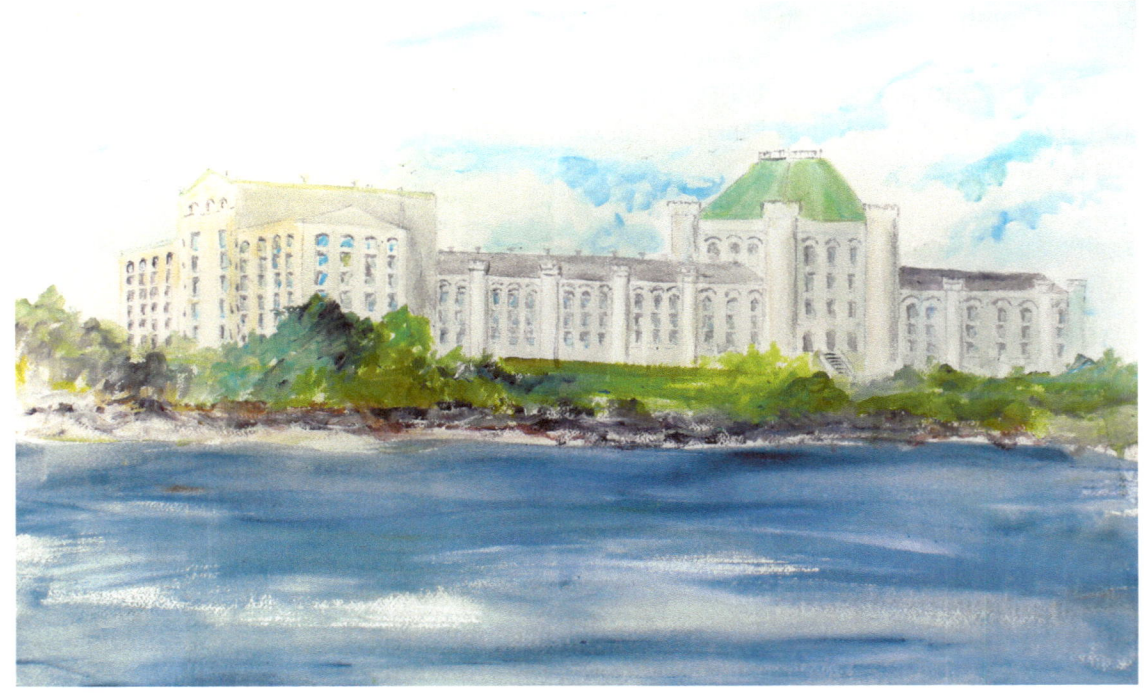

Portsmouth Naval Prison, "The Castle," on the Piscataqua River